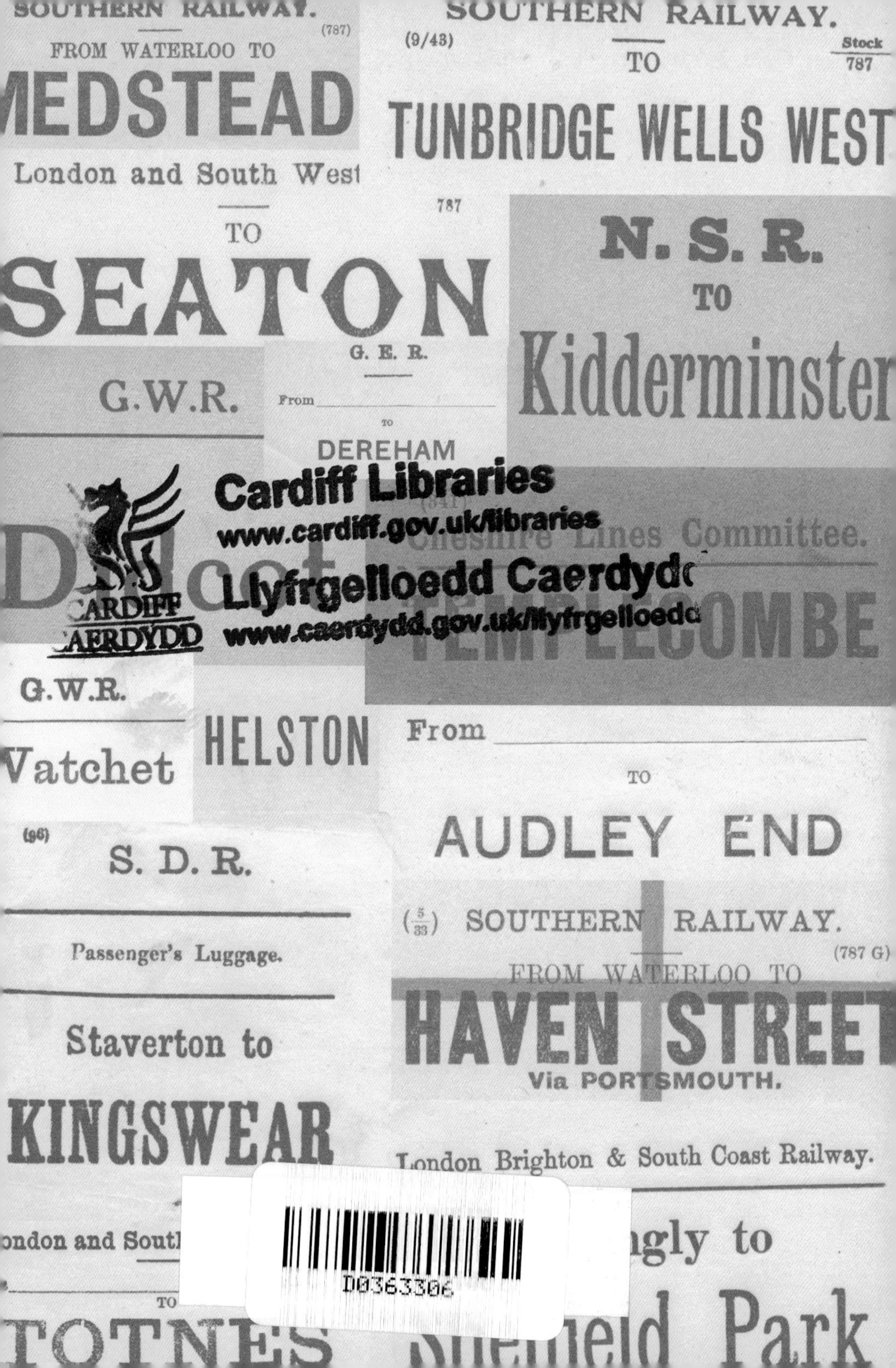

SOUTHERN RAILWAY. (787)

FROM WATERLOO TO

MEDSTEAD

London and South West

SOUTHERN RAILWAY. (9/43)

TO

TUNBRIDGE WELLS WEST

Stock 787

787

TO

SEATON

N. S. R.

TO

Kidderminster

G. E. R.

G.W.R.

From _____

TO

DEREHAM

Cheshire Lines Committee.

TEMPLECOMBE

G.W.R.

Watchet

HELSTON

From _____

TO

AUDLEY END

(96)

S. D. R.

Passenger's Luggage.

Staverton to

KINGSWEAR

($\frac{5}{33}$) SOUTHERN RAILWAY. (787 G)

FROM WATERLOO TO

HAVEN STREET

Via PORTSMOUTH.

London Brighton & South Coast Railway.

London and South

ngly to

TO

TOTNES

Sheffield Park

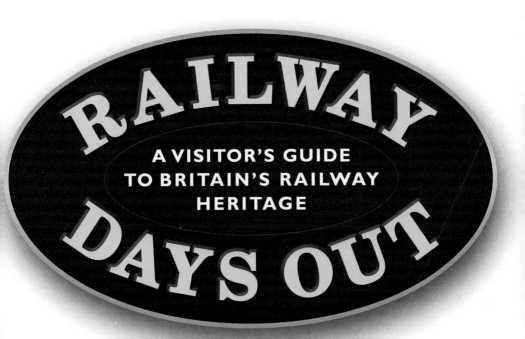

AA

RAILWAY
A VISITOR'S GUIDE TO BRITAIN'S RAILWAY HERITAGE
DAYS OUT

Julian Holland

Published by AA Publishing (a trading name
of AA Media Limited, whose registered office
is Fanum House, Basing View, Basingstoke
RG21 4EA; registered number 06112600).

© AA Media Limited 2012

Written by Julian Holland
Text © Julian Holland 2012

Editor: David Popey
Designers: Austin Taylor and Tracey Butler
Picture Researcher: Julian Holland
Image retouching and internal repro:
  Jacqueline Street
Proofreader: Jennifer Wood
Production: Stephanie Taylor

Cartography provided by the Mapping Services
Department of AA Publishing

Contains Ordnance Survey data © Crown
copyright and database right 2012

ISBN: 978-0-7495-7337-9

The contents of this book are believed correct
at the time of printing. Nevertheless, the
publishers cannot be held responsible for any
errors or omissions or for changes in the details
given in this book or for the consequences of
any reliance on the information provided by the
same. This does not affect your statutory rights.

We have tried to ensure accuracy, but things
do change, so please let us know if you have
any comments or corrections. Always check
a location's website or call before visiting
to avoid disappointment.

Printed and bound in China by C&C

A04791

Visit AA Publishing at **theAA.com/shop**

Opposite, left Preserved 'Britannia' Class 4-6-2 No. 70013 'Oliver Cromwell' heads
a London to Bristol charter train near Bradford-on-Avon.
Opposite, right Preserved 'Merchant Navy' 4-6-2 No. 35028 'Clan Line' hauls the
'Blackmoor Vale Express' up Micheldever Bank on 16 July 2011.

CONTENTS

INTRODUCTION

As THE BIRTHPLACE OF the steam railway locomotive and railways, Britain has always been justifiably proud of its rich railway heritage. Remembering and preserving our railway heritage dates back to 1857 when George and Robert Stephenson's 'Locomotion No. 1', built for the opening of the Stockton & Darlington Railway in 1825, was preserved at a workshop in Hopetown, Darlington – from 1892 to 1975 it was displayed on a plinth at Darlington's Bank Top station. Other famous and even earlier steam locomotives were soon to follow the preservation route. In 1862 the colliery owners of George Stephenson's world-famous 'Rocket' donated the locomotive to the Patent Office in South Kensington. In the same year William Hedley's groundbreaking steam locomotive 'Puffing Billy', of 1813, was lent to the Patent Office. Later to become the Science Museum, the Patent Office eventually bought the locomotive for £200. Both locos are still on display today.

Fortunately for later generations, other historic steam locomotives were preserved during the years preceding the Second World War – the London & North Eastern Railway was so proud of its heritage that it opened a railway museum in York. Following nationalisation of Britain's railways at the beginning of 1948, the newly-formed British Transport Commission inherited a hotch potch of a collection, much of which was later displayed at the Museum of British Transport in Clapham until 1975. In that year the new National Railway Museum at York was opened – the 20-acre site now houses an ever-growing collection of railway locomotives (steam, diesel and electric), rolling stock and all kinds of railway ephemera. The NRM at York is now the most visited museum of any kind outside of London, with over 800,000 visitors each year passing through its doors (see page 210).

The railway preservation movement in Britain (and the world) had its beginnings in 1951 when a group of railway enthusiasts, led by author L. T. C. Rolt amongst others, saved the narrow gauge Talyllyn Railway in West Wales from almost certain closure. The Talyllyn project was the first railway preservation scheme in the world and over the last 60 years the railway preservation movement in Britain has grown from strength to strength. Today there

are scores of these railways dotted around Britain, all supported by an enormous band of dedicated volunteers, visited by millions of visitors each year and greatly boosting the country's tourist economy. From major players such as the West Somerset Railway, the North Yorkshire Moors Railway and the recently reopened 25-mile Welsh Highland Railway, to much smaller but just as fascinating historic attractions such as the Rhyl Miniature Railway in North Wales and the North Bay Miniature Railway in Scarborough and even some schemes still in their infancy, the railway enthusiast and the general public alike have a virtual cornucopia of nostalgic railway attractions to visit and enjoy.

Above Ex-Corris Railway 0-4-2T No. 3 'Sir Haydn' heads a short mixed train on the Talyllyn Railway.
Opposite BR Standard Class '9F' 2-10-0 No. 92220 'Evening Star' at the National Railway Museum, York.

With over 340 entries and nearly 300 photographs and regional location maps, *Railway Days Out* pulls together the various strands of Britain's fascinating railway heritage in one handy-sized volume. Not only does it include preserved standard gauge and narrow gauge railways but also miniature railways, cliff railways, tramways, railway museums and even model railways. To complete the picture, main-line railtours and railway paths and cycleways are listed at the back of the book (see pages 246–252).

VISITING A LOCATION

Railway Days Out is divided into seven regions and the locations in each have icons showing the type(s) of railway they feature (see right). All entries are also listed in alphabetical order in the location index (see pages 253–255).

Address, phone and website contacts are given where available, as are basic opening periods. Always check a location's website or call before visiting to confirm opening hours and timetable details, and to avoid disappointment. Many places may close at short notice due to weather conditions. Entries also provide details about the route, length, gauge and history of the railway. Where nearby, a main-line station is given.

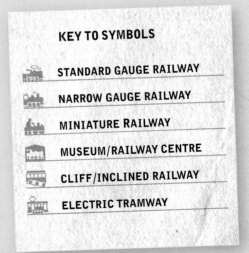

KEY TO SYMBOLS

STANDARD GAUGE RAILWAY

NARROW GAUGE RAILWAY

MINIATURE RAILWAY

MUSEUM/RAILWAY CENTRE

CLIFF/INCLINED RAILWAY

ELECTRIC TRAMWAY

WEST COUNTRY & CHANNEL ISLANDS

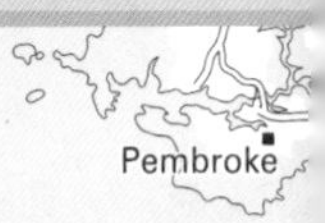

Pembroke

Wadeb
40
Bodmi
Newquay
Lostw
18
St Au
Redruth
Truro
26
Camborne
Penzance
17
Falmouth
Helston

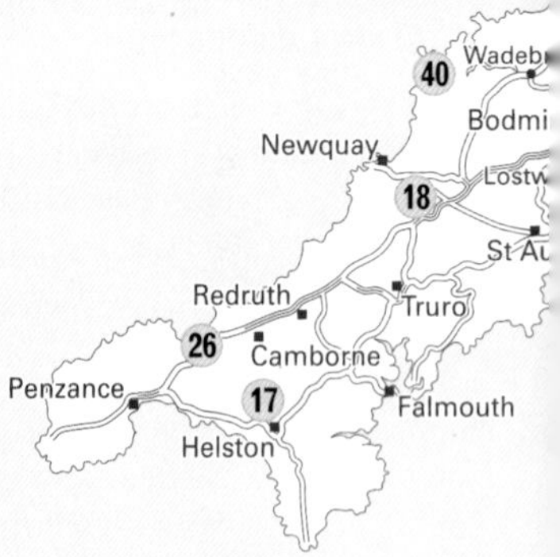

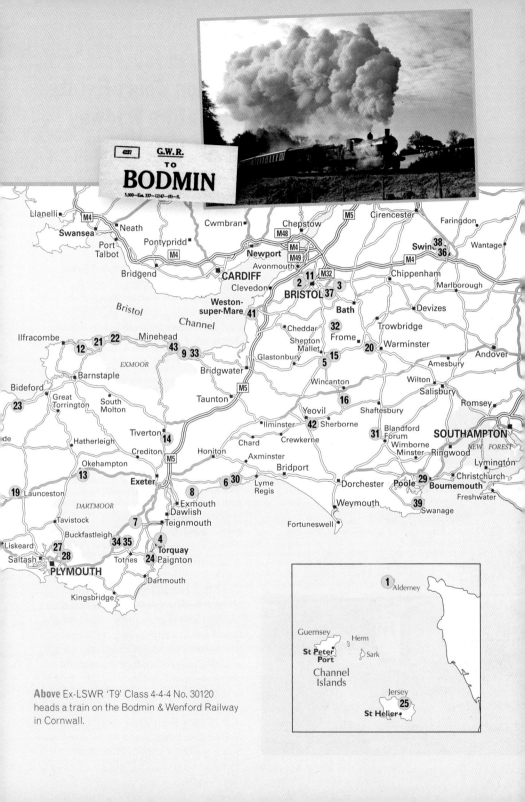

G.W.R.
TO
BODMIN
4237
5,000—Est. 337—12/47—(8)—S.

Llanelli
M4
Swansea
Neath
Pontypridd
Port Talbot
M4
Bridgend
Cwmbran
Chepstow
M48
Newport
M4
M49
Avonmouth
CARDIFF
Clevedon
Weston-super-Mare
2 **11**
M32
BRISTOL **37** **3**
41
Cirencester
M5
Faringdon
Swin...
38
36
Wantage
M4
Chippenham
Marlborough
Bath
Devizes
Cheddar
32
Shepton Mallet
Frome
Trowbridge
20
Warminster
Glastonbury
5 **15**
Amesbury
Bristol
Channel
Ilfracombe
12 **21** **22**
Minehead
43 **9** **33**
EXMOOR
Barnstaple
Bridgwater
Wincanton
Wilton
Andover
Salisbury
Romsey
Bideford
Great Torrington
South Molton
Taunton
M5
Yeovil
16
Shaftesbury
SOUTHAMPTON
23
Ilminster
42 Sherborne
Blandford Forum
31
Wimborne Minster
NEW FOREST
Hatherleigh
Tiverton
14
Crediton
M5
Chard
Crewkerne
Ringwood
Lymington
Christchurch
Okehampton
13
Honiton
Axminster
Bridport
Dorchester
Poole
29
Bournemouth
Freshwater
Exeter
8
6 **30**
Lyme Regis
Weymouth
39
Swanage
19 Launceston
DARTMOOR
Exmouth
Dawlish
Teignmouth
Fortuneswell
Tavistock
7
Buckfastleigh
34 35
4
Torquay
Paignton
Liskeard
27
28
Totnes
24
Saltash
PLYMOUTH
Dartmouth
Kingsbridge

1 Alderney

Guernsey
Herm
St Peter Port
Sark
Channel Islands

Jersey
25
St Helier

Above Ex-LSWR 'T9' Class 4-4-4 No. 30120 heads a train on the Bodmin & Wenford Railway in Cornwall.

Alderney Railway

PO Box 75, Alderney GY9 3DA
Channel Islands

WEBSITE www.alderneyrailway.com
ROUTE Braye Road to Mannez Quarry
LENGTH 2 miles | **GAUGE** Standard
OPEN Sun, Bank Holidays and other selected days,
Easter to end Sep; Santa Specials in Dec

THE ONLY RAILWAY IN the Channel Islands,
this short standard gauge line was opened by
the Admiralty in 1847 to convey stone from
Mannez Quarry to build a breakwater and
fortifications. Queen Victoria and Prince
Albert visited in 1854 and became the first
passengers on this normally freight-only line.
In 1980, the Alderney Railway Society leased
the line from the Ministry of Defence and
the first steam services started in 1982. Trains
are now operated by a Vulcan Drewry 0-4-0
diesel, 'Elizabeth', and a Ruston 0-4-0 diesel,
'Molly 2'. They haul two Metro-Cammell ex-
London Underground tube cars dating from
1959, or six Wickham Type 27 railcars.

A 7¼in gauge miniature railway operates
on most Sundays during July and August at
Mannez Quarry.

Below Braye Road station is the current western
limit of operations for the Alderney Railway.

Ashton Court Estate Miniature Railway

Ashton Court Estate, Long Ashton,
North Somerset BS8 3PX

WEBSITE www.bristolmodelengineers.co.uk
ROUTE Within Ashton Court Estate
LENGTH c.600yds | **GAUGES** 3½in, 5in and 7¼in
OPEN Certain Sun, Mar to Oct; Santa Specials
in Dec (see website for details)

OWNED AND OPERATED BY the Bristol
Society of Model and Experimental
Engineers, this miniature railway features
fully signalled, continuous running
tracks and a recently built tunnel. Steam
locomotives are provided by the members
of the Society.

Avon Valley Railway

Bitton Station, Bath Road, Bitton,
Bristol BS30 6HD

TEL 0117 932 5538
WEBSITE www.avonvalleyrailway.org
ROUTE Oldland to Avon Riverside, via Bitton
LENGTH 3 miles | **GAUGE** Standard
OPEN Selected days during school holidays,
Feb to Oct; most weekends, Apr to Oct
(see website for details)

THE MIDLAND RAILWAY'S LINE from
Mangotsfield, where there was a triangular
junction with that company's mainline
from Bristol to Birmingham, to Bath Queen
Square (later renamed Green Park) opened
in 1869. From the south, the northward
extension from Evercreech Junction of the
near-bankrupt Somerset & Dorset Railway
reached the Midland Railway's terminus in
Bath in 1874. Soon trains were running from
the North of England and the Midlands to
Bournemouth, via the Midland Railway's

Above Built by Robert Stephenson & Hawthorns, 0-6-0T No. 7151 heads a train along the Avon Valley Railway near Bath.

route to Bath and the S&D's line southwards over the Mendips. This state of affairs lasted until 1962, when through trains were withdrawn from the S&D route. Listed for closure in the 'Beeching Report' of 1963, the S&D and the former MR line from Mangotsfield to Bath struggled on until March 1966, although coal trains to Bath Gas Works continued to use the line until 1971.

Initially set up to restore train services between Bristol and Bath, the Bristol Suburban Railway Society held its first open day at Bitton station in 1983. The first trains ran along a mile of line to Oldland in 1987. Oldland station opened in 1991 and in 2004 the section eastwards from Bitton to Avon Riverside was opened. The railway's long term plan is to reach Bath once again, but this entails rebuilding five bridges over the meandering River Avon. Cyclists and walkers can use the Bristol & Bath Railway Path along most of the route of the closed railway; the first green traffic-free route for cyclists in Britain, opened by Sustrans in 1984.

Babbacombe Cliff Railway

Downs Station, Babbacombe, Torquay, Devon TQ1 3LF

TEL 01803 328750
WEBSITE www.babbacombecliffrailway.co.uk
ROUTE Babbacombe Downs to Oddicombe Beach
LENGTH 718ft | **GAUGE** 5ft 10in
OPEN Daily, late Feb half-term to Oct; weekends, Nov to mid–Dec

OWNED AND OPERATED BY the Friends of Babbacombe Cliff Railway, who took over from Torbay Council, this electric-powered funicular railway has a gradient of 1 in 2.83 and was built by Weygood-Otis, opening in 1926. Closure during the Second World War came in 1941. It was reopened following modernisation in 1951. The railway was refurbished and given new cars and track between 2005 and 2007.

Above Hauled by 'Sara', a train at the Royal Bath & West Showground, near Shepton Mallet.

Bath & West Miniature Railway

The Royal Bath & West Showground,
Shepton Mallet, Somerset BA4 6QN

TEL see website
WEBSITE www.essmee.org.uk
ROUTE Within Royal Bath & West Showground
LENGTH c.800yds | GAUGES 5in and 7¼in
OPEN Operates when showground is open to
   the public for events, such as the Royal Bath
   & West Show in Jun, the Truckfest in Jul,
   New Wine end Jul/early Aug, Gardening Show
   and Motor Caravan Show in Sep. The railway's
   open weekend is held in late Sep (see website
   for details)

OWNED AND OPERATED BY the East
Somerset Society of Model & Experimental
Engineers, this mixed gauge circular line
features a new station, recently opened by
the Countess of Wessex.

Beer Heights Light Railway

Pecorama, Underleys, Beer,
Nr Seaton, Devon EX12 3NA

TEL 01297 21542
WEBSITE www.pecorama.info
ROUTE Long return loop within Pecorama
LENGTH 1 mile | GAUGE 7¼in
OPEN Daily, Easter to Oct (closed Sun off-peak)

OPENED IN 1975 BY the Rev W. Awdry,
creator of Thomas the Tank Engine, this
miniature railway was built to complement
the permanent Peco Model Railway
Exhibition. The railway has been extended
in stages and is widely regarded as one of the
most impressive 7¼in lines in the country.
In best Welsh narrow gauge tradition, the
line is built partly on a shelf on the hillside
and follows a circuitous route through deep
cuttings and embankments, over bridges and
through a 180ft-long tunnel. Seven narrow
gauge steam locomotives and two diesels, all
built to one-third full size, operate the trains.
An extensive model railway exhibition is
housed in the adjacent Pecorama building.

Below The Beer Heights Light Railway, set high
on a hill, gives a superb view towards Lyme Bay.

Bickington Steam Railway

Trago Mills Shopping & Leisure Centre, Stover, Devon TQ12 6JD

TEL 01626 821111
WEBSITE www.trago.co.uk
ROUTE Around lakes within Trago Mills complex
LENGTH 1¼ miles | **GAUGE** 10¼in
OPEN Daily throughout the year

THE MINIATURE BICKINGTON STEAM Railway is situated at the famous Trago Mills Shopping and Leisure Centre. The railway opened in 1988 using equipment from Suffolk Wildlife Park and originally comprised of two tracks, each of which was ¾-mile in length. During 1993, part of the inner circuit was lifted and used to extend the line to its current length. Trago Central is the main station, complete with ticket office, covered waiting area and two platforms linked by a footbridge. The new Riverside Station opened in 2006. The railway incorporates a 23-pier viaduct, six bridges, three level crossings and a second station serving a Supakart track. On leaving the station, trains encounter gradients of 1 in 49 as the line meanders through woodland, a nature reserve and around or across several lakes and streams, affording panoramic views of the Devonshire countryside. The railway is capable of operating up to four trains at any one time, being controlled by a three-aspect colour signalling system, operated by four computers. The motive power for the railway is provided by four steam locomotives, 'Blanche of Lancaster', 'E. R. Calthrop', 'Alice' and 'No. 24 Sandy River', and one diesel. Rolling stock comprises four sets of four articulated coaches, each set capable of carrying 50 passengers. The railway has a large workshop with storage facilities and a 20ft turntable.

Bicton Woodland Railway

Bicton Park Botanical Gardens, East Budleigh, Devon EX9 7BG

TEL 01395 568465
WEBSITE www.bictongardens.co.uk
ROUTE Within grounds of Bicton Park
LENGTH 1½ miles | **GAUGE** 18in
OPEN Daily throughout the year

COMPLETED IN 1963, THIS narrow gauge line runs through beautiful gardens, passing by a lake and through woodland, in the grounds of Bicton Park. Until 1998, motive power consisted of 0-4-0 steam locomotive, 'Woolwich', built by Avonside in 1916, with some of the rolling stock, dating from the First World War, from the Woolwich Arsenal Railway. Several other diesel locos and rolling stock originated from War Department and Air Ministry lines. In 1998, the gardens were put up for sale and the new owners sold the railway's existing stock. Trains are now hauled by 0-4-0 diesel-powered replica tank locomotive, 'Sir Walter Raleigh'.

Blue Anchor Railway Museum

Blue Anchor Station, Nr Minehead, Somerset TA24 6LG

WEBSITE www.wssrt.co.uk
OPEN Sun and Bank Holidays, Easter to Sep
STATION Heritage railway station Blue Anchor

RUN BY THE WEST Somerset Steam Railway Trust, this small museum contains over 500 items of GWR ephemera and artefacts. It is housed in the old Great Western station building at Blue Anchor, on the West Somerset Railway (see pages 34–35).

Bodmin & Wenford Railway

Bodmin General Station, Bodmin, Cornwall PL31 1AQ

TEL 0845 125 9678 or 01208 73555
WEBSITE www.bodminandwenfordrailway.co.uk
ROUTE Bodmin General to Boscarne Junction and Bodmin General to Bodmin Parkway
LENGTH 6½ miles | **GAUGE** Standard
OPEN Most days, Easter to end Oct; Santa Specials in Dec; see website for details
STATION National rail network station Bodmin Parkway

ONE OF THE EARLIEST railways in Britain, the Bodmin & Wadebridge Railway opened between Wadebridge Quay, Bodmin and Wenford Bridge in 1834. Built primarily to carry sand, stone and agricultural produce, it was the first steam-operated line in Cornwall. Although taken over by the London & South Western Railway in 1846, it remained isolated from the rest of the expanding national rail network until as late as 1888, when the Great Western Railway opened its branch line from Bodmin Road, on the main Plymouth to Penzance line, to Bodmin General with a link to the B&W at Boscarne Junction. However, the Bodmin & Wadebridge was

only connected to its parent company, the LSWR, in 1895, when the line from Halwill and Delabole opened to Wadebridge.

Much to the sadness of Poet Laureate John Betjeman, passenger services ceased between Bodmin Road, Bodmin, Wadebridge and Padstow in early 1967. Freight traffic, particularly china clay from Wenford Bridge, lingered on until 1983, when the line from Bodmin Road closed completely. The following year, the Bodmin Railway Preservation Society was formed and in 1989 a Light Railway Order was granted, with passenger services recommencing between

Above Ex-LSWR Class '0298' 2-4-0WT No. 30587 heads a chartered china clay train away from Boscarne Junction, on the Bodmin & Wenford Railway.
Opposite Part of the National Collection, ex-LSWR Class 'T9' 4-4-0 No. 30120 heads a passenger train on the Bodmin & Wenford Railway.

Bodmin Parkway (previously named Bodmin Road) and Bodmin General in 1990. An intermediate station at Colesloggett Halt was also opened, giving passengers access to Cardinham Woods with its waymarked trails, café, picnic area and cycle hire facilities. The line from Bodmin General to Boscarne Junction (for the Camel Trail footpath and cycleway) was re-opened in 1996. Trains are mainly steam-hauled, with gradients as steep as 1 in 37. Motive power is provided by a selection of former GWR, LSWR and industrial steam locomotives, along with main-line diesel locos and a multiple unit.

Future plans include a controversial extension of the railway from Boscarne Junction to Wadebridge, alongside the existing Camel Trail.

Bristol Harbour Railway

Princes Wharf, City Docks, Bristol BS1 4RN

TEL 0117 352 6600
WEBSITE www.mshed.org
ROUTE Along south side of Bristol Harbour
LENGTH 1 mile | GAUGE Standard
OPEN Some weekends May until Oct
STATION National rail network station
   Bristol Temple Meads

Above Built in 1937, Peckett 0-6-0ST 'Henbury' heads a short train along Bristol Harbour.

BRITAIN'S ONLY DOCKSIDE STEAM railway, the Bristol Harbour Railway is operated by Bristol M Shed. The Bristol Harbour Railway originally opened to the quayside in 1866 and the present operation started in 1978. Steam trains operate on certain dates along the south side of Bristol Harbour from Princes Wharf Industrial Museum to the Create Centre (Butterfly Junction), via the SS *Great Britain*. The two restored steam locomotives, that originally worked at Avonmouth Docks, are 0-6-0 saddle tanks No. 1764 'Portbury', built by Avonside in 1917, and No. 1940 'Henbury', built by Peckett in 1937. Passengers are carried in converted open wagons and a GWR 'Toad' brakevan. Brunel's SS *Great Britain* is nearby at the Great Western Dry Dock.

Combe Martin Wildlife Park Railway

Higher Leigh, Combe Martin, Devon EX34 0NG

TEL 01271 882486
WEBSITE www.devonthemepark.co.uk
ROUTE Within wildlife park
LENGTH 500yds | GAUGE 15in
OPEN Daily, mid-Feb to early Nov

FIRST OPENED IN 1989, the line was extended to its present length in 1991. Motive power is in the form of a diesel-powered US steam outline locomotive, 'Rio Grande'.

Dartmoor Railway

Okehampton Station, Okehampton, Devon EX20 1EJ

TEL 01837 55164
WEBSITE www.dartmoor-railway.co.uk
ROUTE Sampford Courtenay to Meldon Quarry,
   via Okehampton
LENGTH 5½ miles | GAUGE Standard
OPEN Buffet and model shop – Fri and
weekends; see website for train operating days
STATION National rail network station
   Okehampton; summer Sunday service operated
   by First Great Western from Exeter St Davids,
   between late May and mid-Sep.

WHAT WAS TO EVENTUALLY become part of the LSWR's growing empire west of Exeter, the Okehampton Railway, opened throughout from Coleford (on the North Devon Railway) to Okehampton in 1871. Three years later, with the completion of the 120ft-high Meldon Viaduct, it was extended to Lydford, where it met the broad gauge Launceston & South Devon Railway (an extension of the South Devon & Tavistock Railway). Financially backed by the LSWR, the Okehampton Railway had already changed its name to the Devon & Cornwall Railway in 1870. In 1872, the LSWR acquired the company and in 1879 opened a branch from Okehampton to Holsworthy, later extending it over Holsworthy Viaduct to the small resort of Bude in 1898. What became the LSWR main line to Plymouth opened between Lydford and Devonport in 1890.

Closure west of Okehampton came in 1966, but despite the line from Yeoford to Okehampton not being listed for closure in the 'Beeching Report', it lost its passenger services in 1972. However the line, by now singled, remained open for stone traffic from Meldon Quarry.

Opened in 1997, the Dartmoor Railway is a mainly diesel-hauled heritage line that currently operates on this normally freight-only route between Meldon Quarry and Sampford Courtenay, via Okehampton. Work is currently in hand to extend services to an interchange station at Yeoford, on the Exeter to Barnstaple Tarka Line. In 2010, the Devon & Cornwall Railway Ltd (a subsidiary of Iowa Pacific Holdings, which bought the Dartmoor Railway in 2008) announced plans to reinstate a through passenger service between Okehampton and Exeter.

Devon Railway Centre

**Station House, Bickleigh,
Tiverton, Devon EX16 8RG**

TEL 01884 855671
WEBSITE www.devonrailwaycentre.co.uk
ROUTE Within landscaped grounds in centre
LENGTH Two separate lines c.½ mile each
  GAUGES 7¼in and 2ft
OPEN Most days, Apr to Sep plus Oct half-term;
  Santa Specials also run in Dec

ORIGINALLY BUILT FOR THE South Devon Railway in 1885, Bickleigh station was served by trains on the Exe Valley line until closure in 1963. Restoration of the station and the laying of the 2ft gauge track commenced in 1997, and the Devon Railway Centre opened the following year. The 7¼in-gauge miniature railway opened in 2000 and was extended in 2004. It runs for ½ mile in the centre grounds. Six ex-BR coaches house a large model railway exhibition, featuring over 15 layouts.

Below Meldon Viaduct, near the western limit of the Dartmoor Railway's line from Okehampton.

East Somerset Railway

Cranmore Station, Shepton Mallet,
Somerset BA4 4QP

TEL 01749 880417
WEBSITE www.eastsomersetrailway.com
ROUTE Cranmore to Mendip Vale
LENGTH 2½ miles | GAUGE Standard
OPEN Easter; weekends, May to Oct; some
   Wed, Jun to Sep

THE EAST SOMERSET RAILWAY was founded
in 1973 by David Shepherd, the famous
wildlife and railway artist, to provide a home
for his steam locomotives. These included
BR Standard Class 4MT 4-6-0 No. 75029
'The Green Knight' and Class 9F 2-10-0
No. 92203 'Black Prince' – two locomotives
which have since found new homes.

Trains presently operate from the
attractive Cranmore station to Mendip
Vale, on the outskirts of Shepton Mallet,
along part of the old Great Western Railway
branch, affectionately known as 'The

Below Ex-GWR 0-6-2T No. 5637 at Cranmore
station, on the East Somerset Railway.

Strawberry Line' (named after the local
produce that it used to convey to market),
from Witham Priory to Yatton, opened as
a broad gauge route in 1858 and closed by
British Railways in 1963. Cranmore station
continued to be used by bitumen trains until
1985. Occasional specials once visited the
railway from other parts of the system via
the junction at Witham Priory, on the main
Westbury to Taunton line, and the freight-
only line currently used by stone trains from
Merehead Quarry. This physical connection
is not currently in use.

The two-road engine shed at Cranmore,
built to a traditional GWR design, was
opened in 1976 and a new station building
housing a restaurant and shop opened in
1991. Future plans include extending the line
westwards from Mendip Vale, to the outskirts
of Shepton Mallet at Cannards Grave.

Gartell Light Railway

Common Lane, Yenston,
Nr Templecombe, Somerset BA8 0NB

TEL 01963 370752
WEBSITE www.glr-online.co.uk
ROUTE Common Lane to Park Lane
LENGTH 1 mile | GAUGE 2ft
OPEN Open days on selected Sun from end Jul
   to end Oct (see website)

THIS SUPERB 2FT-GAUGE LINE runs partly
along the trackbed of the old Somerset &
Dorset Joint Railway, closed in 1966, a mile
south of Templecombe. It is run by three
generations of the Gartell family. From small
beginnings in 1982, the first public open day
was held in 1990. Motive power is provided
by both steam and diesel locomotives, and
passengers can travel in either open-sided
or covered bogie carriages. The line is fully
signalled, using ex-BR equipment, and
employs two fully operational signalboxes.

Above A busy scene at Pinesway Junction, on the fully signalled Gartell Light Railway.

Helston Railway

**Trevarno Manor, Crowntown,
Helston, Cornwall TR13 0RU**

WEBSITE www.helstonrailway.co.uk
ROUTE Trevarno to Gansey Farm
LENGTH ½ mile | **GAUGE** Standard
OPEN Daily, except 25 and 26 Dec

OPENED IN 1887, THE 8¾-mile branch line from Gwinear Road to Helston (famous for its GWR connecting bus service to The Lizard) closed to passengers in 1962 and completely in 1964. The trackbed, viaduct and bridges of the line disappeared into the undergrowth until 2005, when a group of volunteers started restoring a short length of track in Trevarno Gardens. Trains currently operate for ½ mile north of Trevarno to Gansey Farm. The Helston Railway Preservation Company has also cleared about ¾ mile of the trackbed south of Trevarno to Truthall Halt. They currently have a shop and exhibition of railway memorabilia in a converted mail van at their new station in Trevarno Gardens. Steam operations are planned to return in late 2012. Access to the railway is only available via Trevarno Gardens main entrance.

Lappa Valley Railway

**Benny Halt, St Newlyn East,
Newquay, Cornwall TR8 5LX**

TEL 01872 510317
WEBSITE www.lappavalley.co.uk
ROUTE Benny Halt to East Wheal Rose Mine and
    Newlyn Downs Halt
LENGTH 1½ miles | **GAUGES** 7¼in, 10¼in and 15in
OPEN Daily, Easter to Oct

THIS MINIATURE RAILWAY OPERATES along part of the trackbed of the former GWR Chacewater to Newquay branch, opened in 1849 as the Treffry Tramway and closed in 1963. The 15in-gauge line opened in 1974 and runs for one mile from Benny Halt to East Wheal Rose. It includes a gradient of 1 in 100, a turntable at Benny and a large loop round a boating lake at East Wheal Rose. A 10¼in-gauge line runs for ½ mile from East Wheal Rose to Newlyn Downs, with a gradient of 1 in 70. There is also a 7¼in-gauge circuit at East Wheal Rose, operated by a Mardyke APT set.

Below Locomotive No. 1 'Zebedee', on the 15in-gauge Lappa Valley Railway near Newquay.

Launceston Steam Railway

St Thomas Road, Launceston, Cornwall PL15 8DA

TEL 01566 775665
WEBSITE www.launcestonsr.co.uk
ROUTE Launceston to Newmills
LENGTH 2½ miles | **GAUGE** 2ft
OPEN Easter, May and Whitsun Bank Holiday weekends; Sun, Mon and Tue in Jun; daily, early Jul to late Sep; Oct half-term

LAUNCESTON NORTH STATION WAS opened by the broad gauge Launceston & South Devon Railway in 1865, later becoming part of the Great Western Railway. The standard gauge North Cornwall Railway from Halwill Junction reached Launceston in 1886 and by 1899 through trains between London Waterloo and Padstow were calling at the company's separate station, known as Launceston South. North station was closed in 1952 when trains along the former GWR line from Plymouth were re-routed into South station. Trains along the GWR line via Tavistock ceased in 1962 and along the LSWR line in 1966.

Below 0-4-0ST 'Lilian' waits to depart from Launceston station on the steam railway.

Opened in 1985, the Launceston Railway is a narrow gauge line that runs along part of the trackbed of the old London & South Western Railway's line from Halwill Junction to Padstow. Locomotives, including 'Lilian' and 'Covertcoat', built by Hunslet in 1883 and 1898 respectively, are beautifully restored steam engines that formerly worked in the North Wales slate quarries at Penrhyn and Dinorwic. Passengers are taken through the scenic Kensey Valley in replicas of Victorian narrow gauge carriages. The 19th-century workshop at Launceston, once used by the Launceston Gas Company, is an example of a belt-driven machine shop in daily use, and the British Engineering Exhibition gives an opportunity to view those locomotives not in service. The station features the canopy previously used at the GWR's North station, while the café and booking office are located in a building that was originally built in 1919 for the first Ideal Home Exhibition and then erected as a three-bedroom bungalow in Surrey! A westward extension to the village of Egloskerry is under serious consideration.

Longleat Railway

Longleat House, Nr Warminster, Wiltshire BA12 7NW

TEL 01985 844400
WEBSITE www.longleat.co.uk or
   (unofficial) www.longleat-railway.com
ROUTE Alongside lake in Longleat House grounds
LENGTH 1¼ miles | **GAUGE** 15in
OPEN Daily, Mar to end Oct

SET IN THE EXTENSIVE grounds of Longleat House, the Longleat Railway was opened as an end-to-end line in 1965 and was rebuilt as an out and back loop in 1977. Passengers are carried in a fleet of nine coaches (one with wheelchair access) on the Jungle Express (as it has recently been rebranded). Motive power includes two steam locomotives, as well as various diesel engines and a railcar.

Above The replica Manning Wardle 2-6-2T 'Lyd' visited the Lynton & Barnstaple Railway in 2010.

Lynton & Barnstaple Railway

Woody Bay Station, Martinhoe Cross, Parracombe, Devon EX31 4RA

TEL 01598 763487
WEBSITE www.lynton-rail.co.uk
ROUTE Woody Bay station to Killington Lane
LENGTH 1 mile | **GAUGE** 1ft 11½in
OPEN Most weekends throughout the year; daily, Apr to Oct; Santa Specials in Dec

WHAT WAS TO BECOME a much-loved but short-lived institution, the Lynton & Barnstaple narrow gauge railway, opened in 1898. Financially backed by millionaire publisher Sir George Newnes, the 1ft 11½in-gauge line ran from its standard gauge interchange station alongside the River Taw at Barnstaple Town to the up-and-coming clifftop resort of Lynton. Winding its way up through the hills and valleys of North Devon, this scenic line featured stations built in a Swiss-chalet style. The First World War brought an end to its popularity and with financial difficulties, brought on by increasing competition from road transport, it was taken over by the newly formed Southern Railway in 1923. Despite much

investment from its new owner, the little Lynton & Barnstaple struggled to pay its way and succumbed to closure in 1935 – a wreath laid at Barnstaple Town on the very last day read 'Perchance it's not dead but sleepeth'. How very apt, as 60 years later the Lynton & Barnstaple Railway Association purchased the former Woody Bay station in 1995. Since then about a mile of track has been laid to a temporary terminus at Killington Lane. With views towards the North Devon coast, most trains are steam hauled during the period from April to October. Extensions to Lynton in the north and Wistpoundland Reservoir in the south are serious long-term plans as the Lynton & Barnstaple Trust now owns much of the former trackbed.

Much of the route of the railway can still be followed today, while the attractive Swiss-style former stations can still be seen at Chelfham, Blackmoor Gate and Lynton. The superb 70ft-high Chelfham Viaduct has been waterproofed and will hopefully see steam trains crossing it once again in the future.

Lynton & Lynmouth Cliff Railway

Lynmouth, Devon EX35 6EQ

TEL 01598 753908
WEBSITE www.cliffrailwaylynton.co.uk
ROUTE Lynton to Lynmouth
LENGTH 862ft | **GAUGE** 3ft 9in
OPEN Daily, Feb half-term to early Nov

PROBABLY THE MOST FAMOUS of the British cliff railways, the Lynton & Lynmouth was the brainchild of the millionaire publisher Sir George Newnes and was opened in 1890. With a gradient of 1 in 1.75, the funicular railway carries passengers a height of 490ft and operates by gravity, or the water-balance method. Each of the two linked coaches carries a 700-gallon water tank that is emptied at the bottom and filled at the top.

continued overleaf

Above The ascending carriage vents water from its tank on the Lynton & Lynmouth Cliff Railway.

By this method the heavier coach at the top slowly descends, pulling the lighter, lower coach uphill by way of a linking wire rope. Passengers are treated to great sea views on their short journey between the two towns.

Milky Way Railway

**Downland Farm, near Clovelly,
North Devon EX39 5RY**

TEL 01237 431255
WEBSITE www.themilkyway.co.uk/railway
ROUTE Within countryside centre
LENGTH ½ mile | **GAUGE** 1ft 11 ½in
OPEN Daily, Apr to Oct; weekends in winter

THIS NARROW GAUGE RAILWAY is part of a large family entertainment complex and operates two steam-outline diesels with three bogie carriages. Visitors are given a free ride on the railway, which was once a fundraising project operated by the Lynton & Barnstaple Railway Association when it was known as the Lynbarn Railway.

Paignton & Dartmouth Steam Railway

**Queens Park Station, Torbay Road,
Paignton, Devon TQ4 6AF**

TEL 01803 555 872
WEBSITE www.dartmouthrailriver.co.uk
ROUTE Paignton Queens Park to Kingswear
LENGTH 7 miles | **GAUGE** Standard
OPEN Daily, April to end Oct; Santa Specials in Dec
STATION National rail network station Paignton

PRESERVED AS A TYPICAL GWR seaside branch line, the Paignton & Dartmouth Steam Railway has a fascinating history. A broad gauge line from Torquay was built by the Dartmouth & Torbay Railway Company, reaching Paignton in 1859 and Churston in 1861. A branch to Brixham was opened in 1867. Although originally intending to bridge the River Dart to reach Dartmouth, the railway was finally terminated at Kingswear in 1864, being converted to standard gauge by the Great Western Railway in 1892. A railway booking office also operated on the opposite side of the river at Dartmouth.

Scheduled for closure by British Rail in 1972 (the Brixham branch having succumbed in 1963), the line was taken over by the Dart Valley Light Railway Ltd at the end of that year. Services began in January 1973 and were worked by the company until 1991. Since then the operating company has been the Paignton & Dartmouth Steam Railway and it has the advantage of being linked with the national system at Paignton. At the other end of the line, Kingswear, passengers from the trains can take a ferry across to Dartmouth or take a pleasure cruise up the scenic River Dart. A journey along the line offers a variety of scenic attractions, including three viaducts and a tunnel, passing sandy beaches and a river estuary. Motive power is provided by three ex-GWR steam locomotives – No. 4277 'Hercules', No. 5239 'Goliath' and No. 7827 'Lydham Manor' – in addition to BR Standard Class 4 No. 75014 'Braveheart', and a Class 25 ex-BR diesel. A service of regular trains operates along this attractive route, with an ex-'Devon Belle' observation car being attached to certain trains. The 'Dartmouth Express' dining train is also provided on certain evenings and for Sunday lunches (telephone for details).

Above Ex-GWR 2-6-2T No. 4555 arrives at Kingswear station alongside the River Dart, on the Paignton & Dartmouth Steam Railway, with a train from Paignton.

Below Ex-GWR 2-6-2T No. 4588 heads for Kingswear past a busy Goodrington Sands; holidaymakers use the station at Goodrington to access the beach and the nearby Quaywest Water Park.

Pallot Heritage Steam Museum

Rue de Bechet, Trinity, Jersey
JE3 5BE Channel Islands

TEL 01534 865307
WEBSITE www.pallotmuseum.co.uk
OPEN Daily except Sun, Apr to Oct

OPENED IN 1990, THIS museum is devoted to the age of steam and includes a large private collection of industrial, agricultural and railway exhibits. A Victorian-style station and engine shed, loosely styled on the Jersey Eastern Railway terminus at Snow Hill, St Helier, have been built, and it is intended to operate trains on both standard gauge and 2ft-gauge track. Included in the collection are four standard gauge steam tank locomotives, two North London Railway coaches, a Jersey Eastern Railway brake van and passenger coach, and part of a JER Sentinel-Cammell railcar. 2ft-gauge stock includes a Simplex diesel, carriages and a brakevan. Peckett 0-4-0ST 'Kestrel' and the North London Railway coaches operate a steam-hauled service on a short standard gauge demonstration track each Thursday.

Above Peckett 0-4-0ST No. 2129 'Kestrel' at the Pallot Steam Heritage Museum on Jersey.

Paradise Railway

Paradise Park, Hayle, Cornwall TR27 4HB

TEL 01736 753365
WEBSITE www.paradisepark.org.uk
ROUTE Within the grounds of a bird garden
LENGTH c.250yds | GAUGE 15in
OPEN Daily, Apr to Oct

Above The 'Jungle Express' going through the tropical bird gardens at Paradise Park.

KNOWN AS THE 'Jungle Express', a miniature diesel-hauled train carries passengers on a circular tour around the grounds of Glanmor House in the Paradise Park tropical bird garden.

Plymouth Miniature Steam

Goodwin Park, Pendeen Crescent, Plymouth, Devon PL6 6RE

TEL 01752 778083
WEBSITE www.plymouthminiaturesteam.co.uk
ROUTE Within Goodwin Park
LENGTH ½ mile | GAUGES 3½in, 5in and 7¼in
OPEN First and third Sun each month, Apr to Oct

OWNED AND OPERATED BY Plymouth Miniature Steam, this club track was formally opened on its present landscaped site on the outskirts of Plymouth in 1990. The double-circuit mixed gauge ground-level track includes bridges and a tunnel. Once a landfill site, the park has now been designated a Nature Reserve.

Plym Valley Railway

Marsh Mills Station, Colypool Road, Plymouth, Devon PL7 4NW

WEBSITE www.plymrail.co.uk
ROUTE Marsh Mills to Lee Moor Crossing
LENGTH ¾ mile | **GAUGE** Standard
OPEN Selected Sun, Apr to Oct; Christmas Specials
  (see website for details)

THE BROAD GAUGE SOUTH Devon & Tavistock Railway opened in 1859. In 1865 the railway amalgamated with the South Devon Railway, before becoming part of the Great Western Railway in 1876. In the same year, a mixed gauge line was laid to enable standard gauge trains of the London & South Western Railway to reach Plymouth. This was used by the LSWR until their own line was completed between Lydford and Devonport in 1890. Passenger trains were axed between Plymouth and Tavistock at the end of 1962, although freight traffic continued along part of the line until 1966.

Above Andrew Barclay 0-4-0ST 'Albert' with a fine rake of ex-BR carriages at the Plym Valley.

Marsh Mills is now home to the Plym Valley Railway and at present the short section from Marsh Mills to Lee Moor Crossing sees steam-hauled trains on selected Sundays. The eventual aim of the railway is to extend the line to Plym Bridge station. Fully operational locomotives working on the line include ex-Falmouth Docks 0-4-0 saddle tank No. 3, former British Sugar Corporation 0-4-0ST 'Albert', ex-BR Class 08 0-6-0 diesel No. 13002 (the oldest working Class 08 diesel shunter in the country, built in 1952) and an ex-BR Class 117 diesel multiple unit.

North of Plym Bridge, much of the trackbed of the line to Tavistock is now a designated 13½-mile footpath and cycleway. Known as the Plym Valley Cycle Path, it features Cann and Bickleigh viaducts, and Brunel's broad gauge Shaugh Tunnel.

Poole Park Railway

Poole Park, Parkstone Road, Poole, Dorset BH15 2SF

TEL 01202 683701 (evenings)
WEBSITE www.pooleparktrains.co.uk
ROUTE Within Poole Park
LENGTH ½ mile | **GAUGE** 10¼in
OPEN Daily throughout the year

THIS MINIATURE RAILWAY STARTED life as Southern Miniature Railways in 1949 and was one of a number of similar railways owned by the same company at Stokes Bay, Bognor Regis and Southsea. The line was originally constructed and operated by George Vimpany until 1979, when a new partnership took over, changing hands again in 2005. The route of the line is circular, around the perimeter of a wildfowl lake within this Victorian park, and includes a basic station building and engine shed. Diesel outline locomotive 'Desmond' and 0-4-0 steam loco 'George' operate the line throughout the year.

Seaton Tramway

Riverside Depot, Harbour Road,
Seaton, Devon EX12 2NQ

TEL 01297 20375
WEBSITE www.tram.co.uk
ROUTE Seaton to Colyton
LENGTH 3 miles | **GAUGE** 2ft 9in
OPEN Selected days, Feb–Mar; daily, Apr to Oct;
    Specials in Dec

Above Tramcars No. 12 and No. 6 at the Victorian
terminus of the Seaton Electric Tramway.

THE 4¼-MILE BRANCH LINE from Seaton
Junction, on the London & Southern
Railway's main line from Waterloo to Exeter,
to the seaside resort of Seaton, opened in
1868 and closed in 1966. In 1969, Modern
Electric Tramways of Eastbourne took over
the trackbed and stock was moved to Seaton
in 1970. The present 2ft 9in-gauge line was
finally completed in 1980 and now miniature
replica electric trams take passengers on a
delightful trip, firstly alongside the estuary
of the River Axe and then, from Colyford
station, along the valley of the River Coly
to the present terminus (the original 1868
railway station) at Colyton. The fleet consists
of five open-top double-deck trams, two
enclosed trams, one toast-rack for disabled
people and one illuminated tram for evening
operating. A new Victorian tram-style
terminus at Seaton was opened in 1995.

Shillingstone Station Project

North Dorset Railway Trust
Shillingstone Station, St Patricks Industrial
Estate, Station Road, Shillingstone,
Dorset DT11 0SA

TEL 01258 860696
WEBSITE www.shillingstone.addr.com
GAUGE Standard
OPEN Daily during peak summer holiday season;
    Wed, Sat and Sun at other times of the year

SHILLINGSTONE STATION OPENED IN
1863 on the line formed by the 1862
amalgamation of the Somerset Central and
Dorset Central railways. The station was
occasionally frequented by King Edward
VII on his visits to nearby Iwerne Minster
House and was closed along with the rest of
the S&DJR on 7 March 1966. The signal box
and down platform shelters were demolished
in 1967 but the main station building
and platform have survived. After several
industrial owners, the station was leased
to the North Dorset Railway Trust in 2003
and has since been restored and had a short
length of track relaid. BR Standard Class
9F 2-10-0 No. 92207 is currently awaiting
restoration at Shillingstone.

Below BR Standard Class '9F' 2-10-0 is currently
being restored at Shillingstone station in Dorset.

Somerset & Dorset Railway Heritage Trust

Midsomer Norton Station, Silver Street, Midsomer Norton, Somerset BA3 2EY

TEL 01761 411221 (Sun & Mon)
WEBSITE www.sdjr.co.uk
ROUTE South from Midsomer Norton station
LENGTH ½ mile | **GAUGE** Standard
OPEN Sun for all facilities including station tour; Mon afternoons for sales and viewing; see website for special events

THE SOMERSET & DORSET RAILWAY'S heavily engineered northerly extension from Evercreech Junction to Bath Green Park opened in 1874. Due to the high cost of building the line, the S&D was already facing serious financial difficulties and a year later was bailed out by the London & South Western Railway and the Midland Railway, who jointly took on a lease of the line for 999 years. Providing an important north–south freight route during the two World Wars, the steeply graded line also became synonymous with numerous holiday expresses from the north of England and the Midlands to Bournemouth, in particular the famous 'Pines Express', which passed through Midsomer Norton on summer Saturdays until 1962. Scheduled for closure in the 'Beeching Report', it lingered a slow death by cuts until final closure in March 1966.

Since then the Somerset & Dorset Railway Heritage Trust has restored the station at Midsomer Norton, along with the former stable block and goods shed, and reconstructed the signalbox, adjacent greenhouse and vegetable garden. Track has been laid southwards from the station towards Masbury and it is hoped that steam-hauled passenger trains over this short section will start soon – a Sentinel 0-4-0 vertical-boilered steam loco that once worked on the S&D is currently undergoing restoration. The station site is currently open to the public on Sundays and Mondays, and diesel-hauled brakevan rides are operated on selected days. Extension of the line to Chilcompton is seen as a long-term goal for the Trust.

Below A visiting 0-4-0ST hauls a short goods train at the Somerset & Dorset Railway Heritage Trust's restored station at Midsomer Norton.

Somerset & Dorset Railway Trust Museum

Washford Station, Nr Watchet,
Somerset TA23 0PP

TEL 01984 640869
WEBSITE www.sdrt.org
OPEN See page 34 for West Somerset Railway times
STATION Heritage railway station Washford

Above Demonstration steam trains at the Somerset & Dorset Railway Trust Museum.

ORIGINALLY LOCATED AT RADSTOCK, the museum moved to its present site in 1975/6. Situated next to Washford Station on the West Somerset Railway (see page 34), the Somerset & Dorset Railway Trust Museum contains artefacts and archives primarily, but not exclusively, from the S&DJR. These include a replica of the Midford signalbox and the actual signalbox from Burnham-on-Sea. In the goods yard opposite the station, there is ¼-mile of track with a display of rolling stock. Former S&DJR 2-8-0 No. 88, owned by the Trust, is currently operating on the adjoining West Somerset Railway, while Peckett 0-4-0ST 'Kilmersdon' is regularly steamed to shunt the yard. Three former S&DJR six-wheeled coaches, including two built at Highbridge Works in the late 19th century, are under restoration.

Above Ex-GWR 0-6-0PT No. 5786 enters Staverton station on the South Devon Railway.

South Devon Railway

The Station, Dart Bridge Road,
Buckfastleigh, Devon TQ11 0DZ

TEL 0845 3451420 or 01364 642338
WEBSITE www.southdevonrailway.co.uk
ROUTE Buckfastleigh to Totnes (Littlehempston)
LENGTH 7 miles | **GAUGE** Standard
OPEN Daily, Feb half-term; weekends, Mar; daily, Apr to Oct; Dec weekends and New Year
STATION National rail network station Totnes

ORIGINALLY CONSTRUCTED AS A broad gauge railway, the Buckfastleigh, Totnes & South Devon Railway opened in 1872. Worked from the outset by the South Devon Railway, the Ashburton branch was taken over by the Great Western Railway in 1897. Passenger services ceased in 1958 but freight traffic continued until 1962 when the line finally closed.

Reopened by Lord Richard Beeching in 1969, the South Devon Railway evokes all the atmosphere of a sleepy GWR West Country branch line as it follows the winding valley of the River Dart. One of the earliest preserved lines, it was eventually jointly operated with its seaside cousin, the Paignton & Dartmouth, by the Dart Valley Light Railway Ltd. For a few years trains could still operate north of Buckfastleigh to Ashburton but the building of the A38 dual carriageway in

1971 effectively severed the line just north of the present terminus. However, one of the main drawbacks to the success of the preserved railway was the lack of access for passengers at the Totnes end of the line. For a short period between 1985 and 1988, Dart Valley trains were able to run into the BR station at Totnes but, due partly to the high charges made by the then state operator for this privilege, the practice was abandoned, although the line is still physically linked to the national rail system at Totnes. In 1991 the South Devon Railway Trust took over the running of the railway and this change of ownership has been a great success. One of the highlights of recent years has been the opening of the South Devon Railway station at Totnes (Littlehempston), which is connected via a new footbridge over the River Dart to the car park of the nearby mainline station. Trains are currently mainly steam-hauled and rolling stock includes superbly restored vintage GWR carriages. A railway museum, adjoining Buckfastleigh station, contains many fascinating railway artefacts and relics, including the only surviving broad gauge locomotive, 'Tiny'. The South Devon Miniature Railway (see page 28) also operates on a site adjacent to Buckfastleigh station.

Below Ex-GWR 0-6-0 No. 3205 heads along the Dart Valley with a milk train on the South Devon Railway.

South Devon Miniature Railway

Buckfastleigh Station, Dart Bridge Road, Buckfastleigh, Devon TQ11 0DZ

WEBSITE www.sdmr.me.uk
ROUTE Adjacent to South Devon Railway car park
LENGTH ¾ mile | GAUGE 7¼in
OPEN Weekends and school holidays, Apr to Sep
STATION Heritage railway station Buckfastleigh

THIS PASSENGER-CARRYING MINIATURE railway, situated adjacent to the South Devon Railway's car park at Buckfastleigh, uses steam and internal combustion locomotives to haul its trains on a meandering, circular route. Track was relaid using aluminium rail from the closed Forest Railroad at Dobwalls.

Steam – Museum of the GWR

Kemble Drive, Swindon, Wiltshire SN2 2TA

TEL 01793 466637
WEBSITE www.swindon.gov.uk/steam
OPEN Daily throughout the year (except Christmas Day, Boxing Day and New Years Day)
STATION National rail network station Swindon

HOUSED IN PART OF the former GWR's Works, the museum opened in 2000 and contains many interesting exhibits, including locomotives, rolling stock, a series of reconstructed work areas and an enormous collection of GWR archive material. Locomotives on display include replica broad gauge loco 2-2-2 'North Star', a Dean Goods 0-6-0, 'Star' Class 4-6-0 No. 4003 'Lode Star', 'King' Class 4-6-0 No. 6000 'King George V', 'Castle' Class 4-6-0 No. 4073 'Caerphilly Castle', and streamlined diesel railcar (or 'Flying Banana') No. 4.

Above GWR 'Castle' Class 4-6-0 No. 4073 'Caerphilly Castle' on display at Steam.

Strawberry Line Miniature Railway

Avon Valley Country Park, Pixash Lane, Keynsham, Bristol BS31 1TS

TEL 0117 986 0124
WEBSITE www.strawberryminirail.co.uk
ROUTE Within Avon Valley Country Park
LENGTH ⅔ mile | GAUGE 5in
OPEN Daily, end Mar to early Nov

DEVELOPED SINCE 1999, THIS fully signalled double-track miniature railway includes a turntable, tunnel, motive power depot, signal box and goods yard. Passengers are hauled around the line by a superb fleet of battery-

Below A line-up of 5in-gauge miniature trains on the Strawberry Line, Keynsham.

Above Ex-GWR 2-6-2T No. 5542 halts at sleepy Blunsdon station on the Swindon & Cricklade Railway.

operated, scale model diesel outline locos and several steam locos. A model railway and model shop complete the attractions at this very popular miniature railway venue.

Swanage Railway

See page 30

Swindon & Cricklade Railway

Blunsdon Station, Tadpole Lane, Blunsdon, Swindon, Wiltshire SN25 2DA

TEL 01793 771615 (weekends)
WEBSITE www.swindon-cricklade-railway.org
ROUTE Northwards from Blunsdon to South Meadow Lane; southward extension from Blunsdon to Mouldon Hill Country Park is nearing completion
LENGTH 2 miles | **GAUGE** Standard
OPEN Weekends and Bank Holidays, all year; Wed during school holidays; see website for special events and timetables

AFFECTIONATELY KNOWN AS THE 'Tiddley Dyke', the Midland & South Western Junction Railway was formed in 1884 by the amalgamation of the Swindon, Marlborough & Andover Railway and the Swindon & Cheltenham Extension Railway. Rescued from near bankruptcy, the railway offered an alternative north-south route between the north of England and the Midlands and Southampton. However, journey times on the single-track railway between Andoversford Junction (east of Cheltenham) and Andover Junction were painfully slow, and by the 1950s saw only one through train each weekday between Cheltenham and Southampton. It was completely closed in September 1961, apart from a short section which is still open from Andover Junction to the military depot at Ludgershall. Blunsdon station actually closed as early as 1937. A preservation group took over the station site in 1979 and now operate mainly steam-hauled trains along a short section of reinstated track, northwards towards Cricklade. A southward extension from Blunsdon to Mouldon Hill Country Park is nearing completion, while a northward extension from South Meadow Lane to Cricklade is planned.

Swanage Railway

**Station House, Swanage,
Dorset BH19 1HB**

TEL 01929 425800
WEBSITE www.swanagerailway.co.uk
ROUTE Swanage to Norden
LENGTH 6 miles | **GAUGE** Standard
OPEN Weekends throughout the year; daily,
    Feb half-term and Apr to Oct; Specials in Dec
    (see website)

THIS FORMER LONDON & SOUTH Western
Railway branch line on the Isle of Purbeck
was opened from Worgret Junction, a
mile west of Wareham, to Swanage in
1885. The opening of the line transformed
Swanage from a small harbour town to a
thriving seaside resort. Goods traffic was
also important, with large amounts of clay
being carried from the Furzebrook area to
the Potteries. Passenger traffic was heavy,
especially during the summer months and
included through carriages to and from
Waterloo on summer Saturdays. Despite
not being listed for closure in the 'Beeching
Report', the line was controversially closed
by BR in 1972, although the section from
Worgret Junction to the Wytch Farm oil
terminal (now mothballed) was retained.

A preservation group started to re-open
the line from Swanage and first trains ran

along a short section from the station in 1979. By August 1995 the line had been extended to Corfe Castle and Norden, and on its first week of extended operation packed trains carried over 20,000 passengers. A park-and-ride scheme is in operation from Norden, which should help to ease road traffic congestion in the Corfe Castle and Swanage areas. Although the railway has now extended to Worgret Junction no regular trains run through to Wareham at the moment, although the link is used by special trains from the national rail network. Trains are mainly steam-hauled by a variety of locomotives, and the 'Wessex Belle' Pullman dining train service is operated on certain Saturday evenings. Locomotives operating on the line include Southern Railway 'Battle of Britain' class 4-6-2 No. 34070 'Manston', 'West Country' Class 4-6-2 No. 34028 'Eddystone', Class M7 0-4-4T No. 30053 and BR Standard Class 4 2-6-4T No. 80104.

Below left Ex-SR Class 'M7' 0-4-4T No. 30053 trundles its two-coach train through Purbeck countryside on the Swanage Railway.

Below and bottom Unrebuilt ex-SR 'Battle of Britain' class 4-6-2 No. 34070 'Manston' storms into Corfe Castle station and, elsewhere on the Swanage Railway, is silhouetted against the setting sun.

Above Happy days on Weston-super-Mare's seafront miniature railway.

Tamarisk Miniature Railway

Old MacDonald's Farm, Porthcothan Bay, Padstow, Cornwall PL28 8LW

TEL 01841 540829
WEBSITE www.oldmacdonalds.co.uk
ROUTE Within farm park
LENGTH ⅓ mile | **GAUGE** 7¼in
OPEN Daily, Easter to Sep (closed Mon, May/Jun)

PASSENGERS ARE HAULED AROUND this circular track in a children's farm park by a diesel outline locomotive. This location is a campsite and farm park; a ride on the railway is included in the entrance fee.

West Somerset Railway

See page 34

Weston Miniature Railway

Marine Parade, Weston-super-Mare, Somerset BS23 1AL

TEL 01934 643510
WEBSITE www.westonminiaturerailway.co.uk
ROUTE On Beach Lawns
LENGTH ½ mile | **GAUGE** 7¼in
OPEN Weekends and school holidays, Feb to Nov; daily, Spring Bank Holiday to mid-Sep
STATION National rail station Weston-super-Mare

OPENING IN 1981, THIS miniature railway has been under the same ownership for the last 27 years. Motive power for trains along Weston's 19th-century Beach Lawns is provided by a steam-outline loco, 'Dylan', American-style diesel, 'Dennis', and on summer weekends by 2-4-0 steam loco, 'Petra', originally built in 1989 for the Moors Valley Railway (see page 70). The future of the railway is in doubt because the site lease expires at the end of the 2012 season.

Yeovil Railway Centre

Yeovil Junction Station, Stoford,
Nr Yeovil, Somerset BA22 9UU

TEL 01935 410420
WEBSITE www.yeovilrailway.freeservers.com
ROUTE Within site along Clifton Maybank spur
LENGTH ¼ mile | GAUGE Standard
OPEN Selected Sun, March to Oct; for Santa Specials
   in Dec; see website for special events, such as
   visiting mainline steam locomotives
STATION National rail network station
   Yeovil Junction

OPERATED BY THE SOUTH West Main Line
Steam Company, the Yeovil Railway Centre
was founded in 1993, when it was discovered
that British Rail was about to remove the
turntable at Yeovil Junction. Since then
a 99-year lease has been agreed for the site,
the turntable restored to working order, a
15,000-gallon water tower and a two-road
engine shed erected, and trackwork along
the former GWR Clifton Maybank spur
relaid. More recently the Centre has
acquired the former GWR broad gauge
goods transfer shed, a listed building dating
back to the 1860s, which now houses a café
and art gallery.

Open days at the centre see a variety of
activity, including brakevan rides behind
beautifully restored Peckett 0-4-0 saddle
tank, 'Pectin', a miniature railway and model
railways. The centre's popularity vastly
increases on days when visiting mainline
steam locomotives from as far afield as
Exeter and Weymouth make use of the only
working locomotive turntable in the region.

Below Peckett 0-4-0 saddle tank, 'Pectin', gives a demonstration on the restored turntable
at the Yeovil Junction base of the Yeovil Railway Centre.

West Somerset Railway

**The Railway Station, Minehead,
Somerset TA24 5BG**

TEL 01643 704996
WEBSITE www.west-somerset-railway.co.uk
ROUTE Minehead to Bishops Lydeard and
    Norton Fitzwarren
LENGTH 22¾ miles | **GAUGE** Standard
OPEN Selected days Feb, Mar, Dec; Daily, Apr to Oct,
    except selected Mon and Fri (see website); for
    numerous special events see website
STATION National rail network station bus link
    from Taunton to Bishops Lydeard station

THE WEST SOMERSET RAILWAY was
originally opened as a broad gauge line from
Norton Fitzwarren, on the main Taunton to
Exeter line, to Watchet in 1862 and extended

to Minehead in 1874. The line was initially
operated by the Bristol & Exeter Railway
and then by its successor, the Great Western
Railway, who converted it to standard gauge
over two days in 1882. The coming of the
railway to Minehead saw what was once a
small fishing village develop into a major
seaside town and by the 20th century it was
a popular destination for holidaymakers
from the Midlands and London. Summer
Saturdays saw through trains running to
the resort from various destinations and
the increased traffic saw the construction
of additional passing loops, the doubling of
the line from Norton Fitzwarren to Bishops
Lydeard and the extension of the platforms at
Minehead to cater for lengthy holiday trains.

Despite the opening of Butlin's holiday
camp at Minehead in 1962, and the
subsequent increase in passenger traffic,
the line was still listed for closure in the
'Beeching Report' of 1963. Despite this,
Minehead station was one of the locations

Above Ex-SR 'King Arthur' Class 4-6-0 No. 30777 'Sir Lamiel', on the new turntable at Minehead.

Left Ex-GWR 2-6-2T No. 4160 heads a train through rolling Somerset countryside.

Below Diesel enthusiasts are also well catered for at Williton on the West Somerset Railway.

used in the filming of The Beatles' film *Hard Days Night* in early March 1964. Over the following years, the Minehead branch was deliberately run-down (losing its freight services as early as July 1964) and finally closed by British Railways in 1971, much to the consternation of local people and businesses.

The line was partly reopened, from Minehead to Williton, in 1976 by the newly formed West Somerset Railway Company, who leased it from Somerset County Council – the council had had the foresight to purchase the closed line in 1973. By 1979, services had been extended to the present 'terminus' at Bishops Lydeard. The section from here to Norton Fitzwarren is not currently used on a regular basis but there is a physical connection with the national network, with a number of special through trains being run from the national system on to the WSR via the new turning triangle here. Plans to run a regular service to Taunton have been obstructed for many years,

originally by opposition from the National Union of Railwaymen and then by official state-run railway bureaucracy. Although a bus service currently links Bishops Lydeard with Taunton station, it would be the 'icing on the cake' if WSR trains were once more allowed to run into the county town.

Britain's longest standard gauge heritage railway, the West Somerset Railway is home to a wide variety of steam and diesel locomotives (the diesel preservation group being based at Williton), as well as the Somerset & Dorset Trust's museum at Washford. Steam locomotives include S&DJR Class 7F 2-8-0 No. 88 and a wide variety of former GWR types. Visiting locomotives can regularly be seen at work on the line on Gala Days (see website), making use of the turntable (originally from Pwllheli) that has recently been installed at Minehead. The 'Quantock Belle' dining train is very popular and advance booking is essential. The ten picturesque stations on the line have all been painstakingly preserved and a journey through rolling Somerset countryside in the shadow of the Quantock Hills and along the coast to Minehead evokes all the atmosphere of a GWR country railway, and must surely rate as one of the best railway journeys in England.

MAIN-LINE STEAM

Rarely a week goes by without some form of main-line steam special somewhere on Britain's rail network. Here are some highlights from the West Country.

Left Commemorating the 175th anniversary of the Great Western Railway, 'Castle' Class 4-6-0 No. 5043 'Earl of Mount Edgcumbe' on the 1 in 75 climb out of Bristol up to Filton Junction with the return journey of 'The Bristolian' back to Paddington on 17 April 2010.

Below Record-breaking GWR 'City' Class 4-4-0 No. 3440 'City of Truro' heads to Truro on 30 November 2004 to commemorate the re-doubling of the Burngullow section of the Cornish mainline.

Above 'Hall' Class 4-6-0 No. 4965 'Rood Ashton Hall' and 'Castle' Class 4-6-0 No. 5043 'Earl of Mount Edgcumbe' on the 1 in 90 climb towards Whiteball Tunnel, on the Somerset-Devon border, with the Vintage Trains tour from Bristol to Plymouth and back, on 15th May 2010.

Below Organised by Steam Dreams to mark the GW175 anniversary, the 'Cornish Riviera Express' heads along the coast at Horse Cove near Dawlish, behind 'Castle' Class 4-6-0 No, 5029 'Nunney Castle' and 'King' Class 4-6-0 No. 6024 'King Edward I', on 26 June 2010.

SOUTH & SOUTH EAST ENGLAND

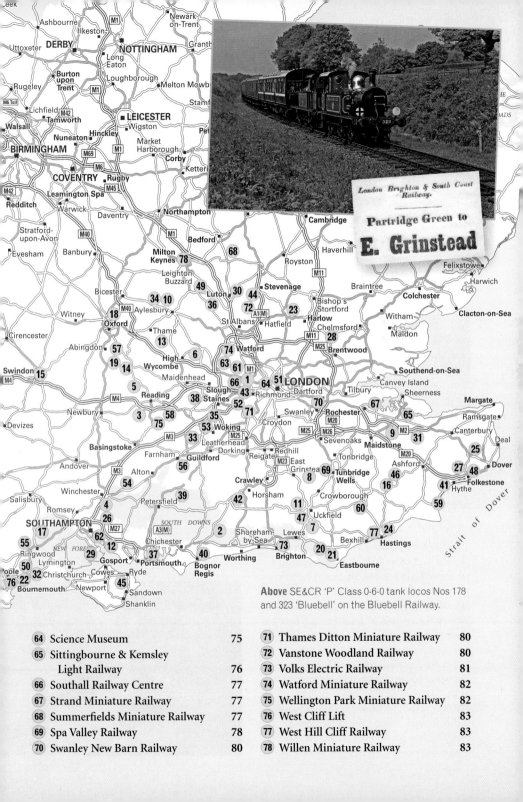

London Brighton & South Coast Railway.

Partridge Green to E. Grinstead

Above SE&CR 'P' Class 0-6-0 tank locos Nos 178 and 323 'Bluebell' on the Bluebell Railway.

Acton Miniature Railway

London Transport Museum Depot,
2 Museum Way, 118–120 Gunnersbury Lane,
London W3 9BQ

TEL 0207 565 7299 (Museum Depot)
WEBSITES www.ltmuseum.co.uk and
    www.actonminiaturerailway.co.uk (unofficial)
ROUTE Within grounds of museum depot
LENGTH c.100yds | GAUGE 7¼in
OPEN During Depot Museum open weekends
    (see website)

Above A battery-powered London Underground
train on the Acton Miniature Railway.

THIS SHORT END-TO-END miniature railway
opened in 2005 and features rides behind a
variety of scale London Transport battery-
powered and steam locos and rolling stock.
Signalling will soon be controlled by an LTE
Westinghouse style 'N' lever frame. There are
plans to extend the railway to Ealing End,
next to the entrance to Ealing Common
Depot. The adjoining 6,000sq ft London
Transport Museum Depot holds the majority
of the Museum's collections (totalling
370,000 items), which are not on display in
the main museum in Covent Garden (see
page 66). It is open to the public for special
events, including themed open weekends.

Amberley Museum & Heritage Centre

Houghton Bridge, Amberley, Arundel,
West Sussex BN18 9LT

TEL 01798 831370
WEBSITES www.amberleymuseum.co.uk
    (museum) and www.amberleynarrowgauge.co.uk
    (Industrial Railway Collection)
ROUTE Within 36-acre outdoor museum site
LENGTH 500yds | GAUGE 2ft
OPEN Wed to Sun and Bank Holidays, end Mar to
    early Nov; daily during West Sussex school hols
STATION National rail network station Amberley

THE NARROW GAUGE & INDUSTRIAL
Railway Collection, part of a larger industrial
museum, is set in an old chalk pit near to the
national rail station at Amberley. Exhibits
include a large collection of 2ft-gauge diesel
and steam industrial locomotives from
Britain and abroad, including Bagnall 2-4-0T
'Polar Bear' (ex-Groudle Glen Railways, see
page 199), Bagnall 0-4-0ST 'Peter', built in
1918, and Hunslet 0-4-0ST 'Cloister' (on loan
from the Hampshire Narrow Gauge Railway
Trust, see page 46). The railway consists
of 500yds of passenger line and a complex
of industrial lines over which works and

Below "Polar Bear" (1905), "Wendy" (1919)
and "Barbouilleur" (1947) at Amberley.

demonstration trains are run. The 2ft-gauge passenger-carrying line operates steam trains most Sundays and Bank Holiday Mondays. Historic passenger rolling stock consists of an ex-RAF Hudson bogie coach, two Penrhyn Quarrymen's coaches and three Groudle Glen four-wheeled coaches.

Amnerfield Miniature Railway

Amners Farm, Amners Farm Road, Burghfield, Reading, Berkshire RG30 3UE

TEL 01189 833437
WEBSITE www.amnersfarm.co.uk
ROUTE Within farm site
LENGTH ¾ mile | **GAUGES** 5in and 7¼in
OPEN Selected Sun, April to Oct (see website)

OPENED IN 1999, THIS mixed gauge miniature railway features a continuous circuit of ¾ mile, which includes crossing a pond on a steel bridge. A good selection of members' steam and diesel outline locos haul passengers around on open days.

Bankside Miniature Railway

Brambridge Park Garden Centre, Kiln Lane, Eastleigh, Hampshire SO50 6HT

TEL 01962 713707 (Garden Centre)
ROUTE Close to River Itchen, adjacent to garden centre
LENGTH c.300yds | **GAUGE** 8¼in
OPEN Weekends and Bank Holidays, Apr to Oct

THE ONLY 8¼IN-GAUGE MINIATURE railway in the UK, the Bankside Miniature Railway carries passengers for a short return journey on raised tracks close to the Itchen Navigation, and adjacent to the Brambridge

Park Garden Centre. Motive power is provided by 1924-built steam locomotive, 'Carolyn', and complete trains are turned on a turntable.

Beale Railway

Beale Park, Lower Basildon, Reading, Berkshire RG8 9NH

TEL 0844 826 1761
WEBSITE www.bealepark.co.uk
ROUTE Within family park
LENGTH 1 mile | **GAUGE** 10.5in
OPEN Daily, mid-Feb to end Oct

OPENED IN 1989, THIS miniature railway, featuring a Mercedes Benz diesel-powered loco and open carriages, carries passengers for a trip around a conservation wildlife park, founded as a charitable trust by Gilbert Beale in 1956.

Below The Beale Railway's Mercedes Benz-powered diesel in Berkshire.

Bekonscot Model Village & Railway

Warwick Road, Beaconsfield,
Buckinghamshire HP9 2PL

TEL 01494 672919
WEBSITE www.bekonscot.co.uk
ROUTE Around model village and gardens
LENGTH 250yds | **GAUGES** 7¼in and Gauge '1'
OPEN Daily, Feb half-term to early Nov

OPENED IN 1929, BEKONSCOT Model Village
and Railway is the world's oldest original
model village. It was created by the late
Roland Callingham as a feature for his back
garden, with the Gauge '1' model railway
built at 10 scale miles by modelmakers
Bassett-Lowke. With seven stations, the
railway is controlled by a computerised block
signalling system, allowing up to 12 trains to
run at any time. Some of the historic locos
and rolling stock operating on the railway are
over 60 years old.

The village also features a 7¼in-gauge
line, opened in 2001, that carries visitors for
a short return ride behind the model village
and around a pond. Trains are hauled by
battery electric locomotives.

Below A train calls at Greenhaily station on the
beautifully detailed Gauge '1' model railway.

Above 'Jasmine' on the Uckfield Model Railway
Club's dual gauge Bentley Miniature Railway.

Bentley Miniature Railway

Bentley Wildfowl & Motor Museum, Halland,
Nr Lewes, East Sussex BN8 5AF

TEL 0845 867 2583
WEBSITE www.bentleyrailway.co.uk
ROUTE In the grounds of the Bentley Wildfowl Park
LENGTH ½ mile | **GAUGES** 5in and 7¼in
OPEN Sun, all year; Sat and Bank Holidays, Apr
   to end Oct; daily, during school holidays
   (except Christmas)

A MIXED GAUGE PASSENGER-CARRYING
miniature railway, operated by Uckfield
Model Railway Club. First built in 1985 as
a small circuit of 600ft, it was later extended
to give a ½-mile run. The ground-level
line runs beside fields and woodland, and
includes a deep cutting, three bridges and a
30ft tunnel. Two stations are situated on the
line, one near the picnic area and the other at
the edge of Glyndebourne Wood. Owned by
club members, a wide variety of both steam
and diesel outline locos can be seen at work.

Bluebell Railway

See page 44

Bolebroke Castle Miniature Railway

Bolebroke Castle, Edenbridge Road,
Hartfield, East Sussex TN7 4JJ

TEL 01892 770061
WEBSITE www.bolebrokecastle.co.uk
ROUTE Around 3-acre lake in grounds of castle
LENGTH ½ mile | GAUGE 7¼in
OPEN Weekends, Apr to Sep; daily, during school
   holidays; for special events see website

SET IN THE GROUNDS of 15th-century
Bolebroke Castle (one of Henry VIII's
hunting lodges), this miniature railway takes
passengers on a scenic trip around a three-
acre lake. Motive power is provided by a
range of steam and diesel outline locos.

Bredgar & Wormshill Light Railway

The Warren, Bredgar, Sittingbourne,
Kent ME9 8AT

TEL 01622 884254
WEBSITE www.bwlr.co.uk
ROUTE Warren Wood, Bredgar to Stony Shaw,
   Wormshill
LENGTH ½ mile | GAUGE 2ft
OPEN Easter Sun; every first Sun, May to Oct

A SMALL PICTURESQUE NARROW gauge line
and vintage transport collection that has
been developed since the 1970s. Trains are
hauled by a fascinating variety of narrow
gauge steam and diesel locomotives from
around the world. Passengers are carried
in a collection of traditional narrow gauge
coaches. A restored Thomas Horne beam
engine, built in 1870 for the Ashford Water
Company, and an extensive 'G' Scale model
railway can also be seen on open days.

Buckinghamshire Railway Centre

Quainton Road Station, Quainton,
Nr Aylesbury, Buckinghamshire HP22 4BY

TEL 01296 655720
WEBSITE www.bucksrailcentre.org
ROUTE Within site
LENGTH ½ mile | GAUGE Standard
OPEN Feb half-term; most days, Apr to end Oct;
   weekends, Dec

THIS 25-ACRE WORKING STEAM museum
incorporates two demonstration lines
based on the former Metropolitan Railway
country station at Quainton Road. Opened
in 1899, the London Extension of the
Great Central Railway from Marylebone to
Nottingham, Leicester and Sheffield closed
in 1966, although trains still operate between
Marylebone and Aylesbury.

   Opened in 1969, the centre houses a
very large collection of steam and diesel
locomotives, which operate trains along
two short sections of track within the
site. Occasional specials also work from
Quainton Road to Aylesbury Town along
the freight-only line still operated by
Network Rail. Engines and rolling stock are
restored to working order in well-equipped
workshops which are open to public
viewing. Locomotives and rolling stock
include Metropolitan Railway 0-4-4T No.
1, London & South Western Railway 2-4-0
Beattie well tank No. 0314, ex-GWR/London
Transport 0-6-0 pannier tank No. L99, GWR
'Castle' Class 4-6-0 No. 5080 'Defiant', WR/
BR 'Modified Hall' Class 4-6-0 No. 6989
'Wightwick Hall', a London & North Western
Railway first class royal dining car and
vintage coaching stock examples from the
London Chatham & Dover Railway, Great
Northern Railway and Manchester, Sheffield
& Lincolnshire Railway. A reconnection to
the national network has been proposed.

Bluebell Railway

Sheffield Park Station, Nr Uckfield, East Sussex TN22 3QL

TEL 01825 720800
WEBSITE www.bluebell-railway.com
ROUTE Sheffield Park to Kingscote
LENGTH 9 miles | **GAUGE** Standard
OPEN Weekends, all year; daily, Feb half-term and Apr to Oct; Santa Specials in Dec

OPENED IN 1882 as part of the Lewes & East Grinstead Railway, this line was once a rural through route linking East Grinstead and Lewes. The following year the railway was taken over by the London, Brighton & South Coast Railway. Passenger traffic was never heavy on the line as most of the stations were built to serve the homes of the railway's sponsors, often miles from any village. After two inquiries British Railways closed the line in 1955. However, it was soon discovered that the closure was illegal and services re-commenced in 1956, with final closure following on 17 March 1958.

The Bluebell Railway Preservation Society was founded in 1959, and services started between Horsted Keynes and Sheffield Park on 7 August 1960, becoming the first preserved standard gauge steam-operated passenger railway in the world to operate a public service. Although originally linked to the national system via the Haywards Heath to Horsted Keynes branch,

this connection was severed in 1963 when that line was closed. Bluebell Railway steam locos were even used by the contractor lifting the track on this line. The Bluebell Railway has since purchased the trackbed of this link between Horsted Keynes and the freight depot at Ardingly, with a long-term plan to reconnect with the national rail system at Copyhold Junction in the future.

The northward extension to Kingscote through West Hoathly tunnel was opened in 1994. Work is now in progress to extend the line across the spectacular Mill Place viaduct from Kingscote to East Grinstead, where it will make an important link again with the national network. A 30ft-deep cutting along this section of line had previously been used as a landfill site and 300,000 cubic metres of

spoil has had to be removed via the national rail connection at East Grinstead before the final section to the town can be opened.

With one of the largest collections of preserved steam locomotives in Britain, trains of beautifully restored vintage carriages presently terminate at Kingscote, two miles short of the railway's eventual northern terminus at East Grinstead. A wide range of historic steam locomotives operate on the line, including examples from the LBSCR, SECR, LSWR, NLR, GWR, SR and BR. The Bluebell Railway is widely used by film and TV companies seeking authentic period locations, and this in turn has led to a great public awareness of the line.

The Bluebell Railway Museum (website www.bluebell-railway-museum.co.uk) at Sheffield Park station houses a large railway archive and ephemera collection, while at Horsted Keynes station the Carriage Works has a visitor centre where coach restoration can be viewed.

Left London Brighton & South Coast Railway 'Terrier' 0-6-0T No. 672 'Fenchurch' heads a Santa Special on the Bluebell Railway.

Below Ex-Great Western Railway 4-4-0 No. 3440 'City of Truro' heads a lunchtime Pullman dining train on the Bluebell Railway.

Burlesdon Light Railway

Burlesdon Brickworks, Coal Park Lane, Swanwick, Southampton, Hants SO31 7GW

TEL 01489 576248
WEBSITES www.burlesdonbrickworks.org.uk
and www.hngrt.org.uk
ROUTE Within brickworks museum site
LENGTH 450yds | GAUGE 2ft
OPEN On selected open days (see website)

OPENED IN 2010 AND operated by the Hampshire Narrow Gauge Railway Trust, this narrow gauge brickworks railway is currently being extended. Burlesdon Brickworks Industrial Museum is thought to be the only remaining steam-driven brickworks in the UK. A 7¼in miniature line also gives passenger rides on open days.

Chinnor & Princes Risborough Railway

Station Approach, Station Road, Chinnor, Oxfordshire OX39 4ER

TEL 01844 353535 (talking timetable)
WEBSITE www.chinnorrailway.co.uk
ROUTE Chinnor to Thame Junction
LENGTH 3½ miles | GAUGE Standard
OPEN Most Sat, Sun and Bank Holidays, mid-Mar
to end Oct; weekends, Dec

THE CHINNOR & PRINCES RISBOROUGH Railway has re-opened part of the closed Great Western Railway Watlington branch, from Chinnor to its connection with the main network at Princes Risborough. The line was originally opened in 1872 and taken over by the GWR in 1883. Passenger traffic ceased in 1957 but the section to Chinnor

Below Ex-GWR 0-6-0PT No. 5786 hauls a train at Wainhill, on the picturesque Chinnor & Princes Risborough Railway in Oxfordshire.

remained open until 1989 to serve the cement works.

Trains currently run from Chinnor to the junction with the former Thame branch. The line parallels the Icknield Way and passes through attractive countryside with views across the Vale of Whiteleaf. Once the link with the Chiltern line has been made at Princes Risborough, the long-term plan is to extend the line back to Aston Rowant. A new ticket office and waiting room, using a Cambrian Railway six-wheel coach dating from 1895, was opened at Chinnor station in 1995. There is no station at Thame Junction, so passengers can only board and alight at Chinnor.

Above Visiting ex-LBSCR 'Terrier' 0-6-0T No. 662 'Martello' on the 'Cholsey & Wallingford Railway.

Cholsey & Wallingford Railway

Hithercroft Road, Wallingford, Oxfordshire OX10 9GQ

TEL 01491 835067
WEBSITE www.cholsey-wallingford-railway.com
ROUTE Cholsey to Wallingford
LENGTH 2¼ miles | **GAUGE** Standard
OPEN Selected weekends and Bank Holidays, Apr to Oct; weekends, Dec
STATION National rail network station Cholsey

OPENED IN 1866, THE ex-GWR branch line to Wallingford was closed to passengers in 1959 and to goods in 1965, although part of the line was left open to serve a mill until 1981. Since then a preservation society has re-opened the line, and limited services with a borrowed locomotive ran until 1990, when the line bought its first engine. A Light Railway Order was granted in 1995 and trains now connect with the national network at Cholsey, on the main line to Paddington. Although the railway does not currently own a resident steam locomotive, visiting engines are a regular feature (see website for more information).

Coate Water Park Miniature Railway

Coate Water Country Park, Marlborough Road, Swindon, Wiltshire SN3 6AA

WEBSITE www.coatewaterrailway.webs.com
ROUTE Within Coate Water Park
LENGTH ½ mile | **GAUGES** 5in and 7¼in
OPEN Sun throughout the year

OPERATED BY THE NORTH Wilts Model Engineers Society, this popular dual-gauge miniature railway started life in 1961 on raised track. Rebuilt at ground level in 1966, it has been gradually extended over the years to its present layout of one outer circuit with an inner figure-of-eight. The line boasts a signalbox, signalling, a steaming bay and club house, with a wide range of steam and diesel outline locos supplied by members. Passengers are carried on sit-on carriages based on a GWR design.

The Colonel Stephens Railway Museum

Tenterden Town Station, The John Miller Building, Station Road, Tenterden, Kent TN30 6HE

TEL 01580 765155
WEBSITE www.hfstephens-museum.org.uk
OPEN During Kent & East Sussex Railway operating days until Oct (see page 62)
STATION Heritage railway station Tenterden Town

THIS FAIRLY NEW MUSEUM, which opened in 1996 (the centenary year of the 1896 Light Railways Act), replaced the Colonel Stephens Railway Collection previously exhibited at the Tenterden & District Museum. The new museum gives an account of Colonel Stephens' family background (his father was a member of the pre-Raphaelite Brotherhood of painters); his career as light railway promoter, engineer and manager; and Stephens' career as a Territorial Army officer. Included is Stephens' assistant and eventual successor W. H. Austen, whose son was instrumental in gathering together much of the material exhibited in the museum. The exhibition covers the 16 railways with which Stephens was associated, including the nearby Kent & East Sussex, and those lines proposed but not built. Exhibits include relics, posters, maps, models and ephemera, a reconstruction of Stephens' office in Tonbridge, and various tableaux showing aspects of light railway activity. The photographic archive contains around 4,000 photographs, while the smallest standard gauge locomotive in Britain, the 'Gazelle' from Stephens' Shropshire & Montgomeryshire Light Railway, is the star exhibit.

Cuckoo Hill Railway

Avon Valley Nurseries, South Gorley, Fordingbridge, Hampshire SP6 2PP

TEL 01425 650408
ROUTE Within grounds of fruit farm
LENGTH ¾ mile | GAUGE 7¼in
OPEN Telephone for details

THIS STEAM-HAULED CIRCULAR miniature railway takes visitors on a journey around this pick-your-own-fruit farm. Passengers are carried in open wagons on a six-minute journey which features two passing loops, a station and a short tunnel.

Cutteslowe Park Miniature Railway

Harbord Road, Oxford OX2 8LH

TEL 01367 700550
WEBSITE www.cosme.org.uk
ROUTE Within Cutteslowe Park
LENGTH two lines total c.660yds |
   GAUGES 5in and 7¼in
OPEN Afternoons, 1st, 3rd and 5th Sun of summer months; Bank Holiday Mon; Wed afternoons during school summer holidays

OWNED AND OPERATED BY the City of Oxford Society of Model Engineers, these two miniature railways have been operating in Cutteslowe Park since 1988. Prior to that the society had operated a miniature railway in the grounds of Blenheim House. A popular venue for families on Sundays, the railway carried its 250,000 passenger in 2005. A wide variety of steam and diesel outline locos are supplied by members.

Opposite Resplendent in early BR blue livery, ex-GWR 'King' Class 4-6-0 No. 6023 'King Edward II' gets up steam at the Didcot Railway Centre.

Didcot Railway Centre

Didcot, Oxfordshire OX11 7NJ

TEL 01235 817200
WEBSITE www.didcotrailwaycentre.org.uk
ROUTE Within site
LENGTH ¼ mile | **GAUGES** Standard and broad
OPEN Weekends, all year; daily, during school
   holidays and Jun to mid-Sep; see website for
   steam days and special events
STATION National rail network station Didcot

THE GREAT WESTERN SOCIETY, founded in 1961, moved its base to the former engine shed at Didcot in 1967 and now evokes all the atmosphere of a working 1930s GWR running shed, with turntable and coaling stage. Now housing the largest collection of GWR locos and rolling stock in Britain, the centre is also frequently visited by other locomotives employed on mainline steam

specials. Locomotives on display include 'Castle' Class 4-6-0s No. 4079 'Pendennis Castle' and No. 5051 'Drysllwyn Castle', 'Hall' Class 4-6-0 No. 5900 'Hinderton Hall', blue-liveried 'King' Class 4-6-0 No. 6023 'King Edward II', 'Modified Hall', Class 4-6-0 No. 6998 'Burton Agnes Hall' and 'Manor' Class 4-6-0 No. 7808 'Cookham Manor', along with former Wantage Tramway 0-4-0 well tank 'Shannon', built in 1857.

Short rides are given on two demonstration lines within the site, which also boasts a rebuilt small country station (Didcot Halt), complete with the working signalbox originally used at Frome Mineral Junction. A short section of Brunel's broad gauge (7ft ¼in) has also been built, where replica locomotive 'Firefly' can be seen on selected days. On Steam Days, demonstrations are given using the restored Travelling Post Office. A library houses the Society's collection of books and papers relating to the Great Western Railway.

Drusillas Zoo Park Railway

Alfriston Road, Alfriston,
East Sussex BN26 5QS

TEL 01323 874100
WEBSITE www.drusillas.co.uk
ROUTE Within Zoo Park
LENGTH 400yds | **GAUGE** 2ft
OPEN Daily, except Christmas

A NARROW GAUGE RAILWAY that runs through Drusillas Zoo Park, home to a collection of rare breeds of cattle and other farm animals. The Zoo Park was founded by Douglas Ann in 1930 and a 9¼in-gauge railway was opened in 1935 but was closed during the Second World War. Following the end of the war, the railway was rebuilt to 2ft gauge and has been operating ever since. Until recently, locomotives used were a steam outline Ruston, built in 1943, and two Simplexes built in 1948 and 1965 respectively. However, the line has now been given a 'Thomas & Friends' makeover, complete with a Fat Controller. Passengers are taken on a journey behind 'Thomas the Tank Engine', through the llama paddock with excellent views of the South Downs.

Above 'Thomas the Tank Engine' at work on the Drusillas Zoo Park Railway at Alfriston.

Eastbourne Miniature Steam Railway

Lottbridge Drove, Eastbourne,
East Sussex BN23 6QJ

TEL 01323 520229
WEBSITE www.emsr.co.uk
ROUTE Circular within site
LENGTH 1 mile | **GAUGE** 7¼in
OPEN Daily, April to Sep; weekends, Oct

THIS POPULAR MINIATURE RAILWAY was opened by the Wadey family in 1992. The single-track route is predominantly flat and meanders around a 5-acre fishing lake through newly-planted woodland, cuttings, bridges, a tunnel and over an automatic pedestrian level crossing, passing the engine shed, turntable and sidings. A wide variety of scale locomotives operate including coal-fired 4-6-0 'Royal Green Jackets', 'Black Five' 4-6-0 'Ayrshire Yeomanry', two 'Britannia' 4-6-2s, 2-10-0 'Evening Star' and several diesel outline locos.

East Cliff Lift

East Overcliff Drive, Bournemouth,
Dorset BH1 3DD

TEL 01202 451451
WEBSITE www.bournemouth.gov.uk
ROUTE East Overcliff Drive to Undercliff Drive
LENGTH 170ft | **GAUGE** 5ft 6in
OPEN Weekends, Mar; daily, April to Oct

OPENED IN 1908, THIS funicular railway is the oldest, and the busiest of Bournemouth's three cliff railways (all owned and operated by Bournemouth Borough Council), linking the cliff top with the beach. An electric-powered winding drum at the top station raises and lowers the two passenger coaches 117ft on a gradient of 1 in 1.5.

East Herts Miniature Railway

Above Steam locomotive 'Ellan Bee' on the 7¼in-gauge East Herts Miniature Railway.

East Herts Miniature Railway

Van Hage Garden Centre, Great Amwell,
Nr Ware, Hertfordshire SG12 9RP

WEBSITE www.ehmr.org.uk
ROUTE Behind garden centre
LENGTH ¼ mile | **GAUGE** 7¼in
OPEN Weekends and Bank Holidays, all year;
also Tue and Thu during school holidays

Opened in 1977, this miniature railway has carried over one million passengers and raised £25,000 for local children's charities. The route is a double oval of track with a diamond crossing and is situated in a field in the outer garden centre area. Motive power consists of three steam locomotives and two petrol hydrostatic locomotives, with passengers carried on seven sit-astride and two sit-in coaches. The line features a station, bridge, tunnel, level crossing, turntable and ex-London Underground signalbox.

East Hill Cliff Railway

Rock-a-Nore Road, Hastings,
East Sussex TN34 3DW

ROUTE Rock-a-Nore Road to Old Town
LENGTH 267ft | **GAUGE** 5ft
OPEN Daily, Apr to Oct

Owned and operated by Hastings Borough Council, the East Hill funicular railway was the second such line to open in Hastings (see page 83). Completed in 1903, it was built in a deep cutting in the cliff face on a gradient of 1 in 1.28 (the steepest in Britain) and was operated by the water-balance method until 1973. The twin towers of the grand castellated top station once contained tanks holding 1,200 gallons of water, which was fed into tanks beneath the cars. During the Second World War, the railway was commandeered to service anti-aircraft installations on the cliff top. Today, the railway is powered by electricity and carries visitors to the Hastings Country Park.

East Kent Railway

Station Road, Shepherdswell,
Nr Dover, Kent CT15 7PD

TEL 01304 832042
WEBSITE www.eastkentlightrailway.moonfruit.com
ROUTE Shepherdswell to Eythome
LENGTH 2 miles | **GAUGE** Standard
OPEN Sun and Bank Holidays, Apr to Oct;
weekends, Aug and Dec
STATION National rail network station
Shepherdswell

The East Kent Light Railway was constructed between 1911 and 1924 to serve the Kent coalfield and originally ran from Shepherdswell, on the main Dover to Canterbury line, to the port of Richborough. The latter was not reached until 1928, by which time the port was already in decline. The line was built by Colonel H. F. Stephens, the famous railway engineer and supporter

continued overleaf

of light railways (see Colonel Stephens Museum on page 48), and passengers were first carried in 1916. However, the decline of the coal industry after the Second World War had a severe impact on the railway's revenue. Passenger services ceased in 1948 and by 1953 the railway beyond Tilmanstone had been closed. The remaining three-mile section was kept open for colliery traffic until 1984 and the line was finally closed in 1987.

A preservation group was formed in 1985 and work started on restoring Shepherdswell station and clearing the overgrown line in 1989. By 1993, a Light Railway Order was granted and BR agreed to sell the trackbed to the Society. Regular train services now run over the two miles through Golgotha Tunnel to Eythorne and future plans include extending the line to Tilmanstone Colliery. Motive power includes a diesel multiple unit and various diesels, while former 0-6-0 colliery engine 'St Dunstan' is currently awaiting restoration.

Eastleigh Lakeside Steam Railway

Lakeside Country Park, Doncaster Drove, Off Wide Lane, Eastleigh, Hampshire SO50 5PE

TEL 023 8061 2020
WEBSITE www.steamtrain.co.uk
ROUTE Around lakes
LENGTH 1¼ miles | GAUGES 7¼in and 10¼in
OPEN Weekends all year; daily during school hols

THIS MINIATURE MIXED GAUGE railway crosses Lakeside Park and skirts a large lake, all within sight of Eastleigh railway works. Opened in 1992 and extended to its present length in 2000, it features a shop, café, two stations, a signal gantry, a 355ft tunnel and maintenance facilities. The locomotive fleet consists of 19 steam locos (several dating back to the 1930s), two diesel hydraulics and a battery-powered Eurostar train.

Elham Valley Railway Museum

Peene Yard, Peene, Newington, Folkestone, Kent CT18 8BA

TEL 01303 273690
WEBSITE www.elhamvalleylinetrust.org
OPEN Weekends and Bank Holidays, Apr to Aug

THIS RAILWAY MUSEUM, DEVOTED to the former South Eastern & Chatham Railway line from Canterbury to Folkestone (built in 1884 and closed in 1947), is situated in a recreated 1934 station building. It contains SECR artefacts and ephemera, and a 50ft-long 'N' gauge model railway depicting the 16½ miles from Folkestone to Canterbury through the Elham Valley in the 1930s. Also on display are a replica of an SECR Class 'E1' 0-6-0 tank locomotive, a fully working signalbox and a scale working model of the Channel Tunnel (Folkestone Terminal).

Epping-Ongar Railway

Ongar Station, Station Approach, Ongar, Essex CM5 9BN

TEL 01277 365200
WEBSITE www.eorailway.co.uk
ROUTE Epping to Ongar
LENGTH 6½ miles | GAUGE Standard
OPEN See website for details
STATION London Underground station Epping

AN EXTENSION OF THE Great Eastern Railway's Stratford to Loughton line was opened from Loughton to Ongar in 1865. The section from Loughton to Epping was later doubled. Following the end of the Second World War, London Transport's Central Line had reached Loughton by 1948, although steam trains continued to operate from here to Ongar until 1949 when the section to Epping was electrified. At the same time, the London Transport Executive took over the Epping to Ongar steam push-pull service from British Railways. Eventually, this last section was electrified in 1957 but passenger numbers had declined so much that it was finally closed in 1994.

The line was purchased by the Epping-Ongar Railway Volunteer Society in the same year and it ran a diesel multiple unit service on Sundays from 2004 until 2008. Following a change in ownership in 2009, train services were suspended to allow engineering work prior to eventually reopening the line with steam haulage. The railway now has a fleet of diesel locomotives (including 03, 08, 25, 31 and 37), a steam engine ('Isabel'), Class 117 DMU and a Class 205 'Thumper', and offers the closest heritage line to London, within easy reach of the M11 and A12. On operating days there is a frequent heritage bus service (running RT's, RM's & RF's) from Epping Tube station (on the Central Line) to North Weald station, with combined bus and rail tickets available.

Below Ongar Station, the headquarters of the reborn Epping-Ongar Railway in Essex.

Exbury Gardens Railway

Exbury Gardens, The Estate Office, Exbury, Southampton, Hampshire SO45 1AZ

TEL 023 8089 1203
WEBSITE www.exbury.co.uk
ROUTE Within Exbury Gardens
LENGTH 1¼ miles | GAUGE 12¼in
OPEN Daily, late Mar to early Nov; Santa Specials in Dec (see website)

OPENED IN 2001, THIS railway follows a circular journey through the 200-acre gardens owned by Leopold de Rothschild. Motive power for the blue-liveried trains is by three steam locomotives and one diesel hydraulic, all built by Exmoor Steam Railway since 2001. Loco 'Mariloo' was named by the Queen in 2008. Visitors can also see the engine shed and an exhibition about the line.

Fancott Miniature Railway

Luton Road, Luton, Bedfordshire LU5 6HT

TEL 07917 756237
WEBSITE www.fancottrailway.tk
ROUTE Around beer gardens of the Fancott Pub
LENGTH 350yds | GAUGE 7¼in
OPEN Weekends and Bank Holidays, Apr to Sep; daily, during school holidays (closed Mon)

A 10¼IN-GAUGE MINIATURE RAILWAY operated at the Fancott Pub between 1975 and 1986. A new 7¼in line was opened in 1996 and since then has seen new owners and been completely rebuilt. Trains are currently hauled by diesel outline locos, although visiting steam locos also make regular appearances. Its success has gone hand-in-hand with that of the adjacent pub.

Faversham Miniature Railway

Brogdale Farm, Brogdale Road,
Faversham, Kent ME13 8XZ

TEL 01795 474211 (Chairman)
WEBSITE www.favershamminiaturerailway.co.uk
ROUTE Within farm grounds
LENGTH ¼ mile | GAUGE 9in
OPEN Sun, Bank Holidays and special events,
    Mar to Nov

THE ONLY 9IN-GAUGE PUBLIC railway in the
UK, operated by the Faversham Miniature
Railway Society. Now at its third home after
opening in Leysdown on the Isle of Sheppey
in 1985, moving to Norton Ash Garden
Centre in 1987 and then to its present
location in 2001. A total of nine locomotives
complete the roster, including steam engine
'Robin' and petrol-engined Class 35 Hymek,
while passengers are carried in four sit-
astride coaches. A major track extension
programme is now underway.

Above A battery-powered loco at Brogdale
Central on the Faversham Miniature Railway.

Fisherman's Walk Cliff Lift

Southbourne, Bournemouth BH6

TEL 01202 451451
WEBSITE www.bournemouth.gov.uk
ROUTE Fisherman's Walk, Southbourne to
    Boscombe and Southbourne promenades
LENGTH 128ft | GAUGE 5ft 8in
OPEN Daily, Easter to Oct

OPENED IN 1935, THIS electric-powered
funicular railway is the youngest of its
type in Britain and rises 86ft on a gradient
of 1 in 1.49.

Frimley Lodge Miniature Railway

Frimley Lodge Park, Sturt Road,
Frimley Green, Camberley,
Surrey GU16 6HT

TEL 07710 606461 (Weds and Sun)
WEBSITE www.flmr.org
ROUTE Within Frimley Lodge Park
LENGTH c.1200yds | GAUGES 3½in, 5in and 7¼in
OPEN First Sun of each month, Mar to Nov; see
    website for extra days and special events in Aug

OWNED AND OPERATED BY the Frimley
& Ascot Locomotive Club, this extensive
ground-level, mixed gauge, continuous
miniature railway runs alongside the
Basingstoke Canal and through the
59-acre wooded Frimley Lodge Park.
The line features signalling, an engine
traverser, turntable and two stations.
A wide variety of member's scale steam
and internal combustion locomotives can
be seen in action on open days. There is
a café in the pavilion of Frimley Lodge
Park, nearby.

Golding Spring Miniature Railway

Quainton Road Station, Quainton, Nr Aylesbury, Buckinghamshire HP22 4BY

TEL 01296 655720 (Buckinghamshire
    Railway Centre)
WEBSITE www.vames.co.uk
ROUTE Adjacent to Quainton Road station
LENGTH 1,100yds | **GAUGES** 3½in, 5in and 7¼in
OPEN During opening times of neighbouring
    Buckinghamshire Railway Centre (see page 43)

OWNED AND OPERATED BY the Vale of
Aylesbury Model Engineering Society, this
mixed gauge, ground-level miniature railway
opened on its present site in the mid-1970s.
Major remodelling of the layout took place in
the late 1990s and the railway is now capable
of carrying 3,000 passengers on open days.
A wide range of locomotives are supplied by
members, while miniature steam traction
engines and a popular 'G' scale model railway
also feature.

Great Cockcrow Railway

Hardwick Lane, Lyne, Nr Chertsey, Surrey KT16 0AD

TEL 01932 565474 (Sun afternoons)
WEBSITE www.cockcrow.co.uk
ROUTE Hardwick Central to Cockrow Hill
LENGTH 2 miles | **GAUGE** 7¼in
OPEN Sun afternoons, May to Oct

ORIGINALLY NAMED THE GREYWOOD
Central Railway, this unique miniature
passenger-carrying line was established
by Sir John Samuel, of Burwood Park,
Walton-on-Thames, in 1946. On his death
in 1962, the entire line was purchased by the

Above A 7¼in-gauge model of Southern Railway
Class 'S15' 4-6-0 No. 837, at Hardwick Central.

Below Locomotives being prepared for work
on the 7¼in-gauge Great Cockcrow Railway.

publisher Ian Allan, who transferred it to its
present location at Lyne. It was re-opened
on its new site in 1968 and since then has
been much expanded to its present layout,
which includes three distinctive train rides
and a 45ft-long viaduct. The 'Gladesman'
train is normally double-headed by two
steam locomotives and departs at 16.30
each Sunday – bookings are advisable. A
total of 25 steam locomotives are on the
roster and at least seven of these should be
on duty on any operating day. Turntables at
each terminus enable all the engines to be
turned after each journey and passengers are
carried on four-seater vehicles. The railway
is fully signalled, using both semaphore and
colour-light signals, with three signalboxes
and four stations. The booking office at
Hardwick Central was originally situated at
Ravenscourt Park, on the District Line.

Great Whipsnade Railway

Whipsnade Zoo, Dunstable, Beds LU6 2LF

TEL 01582 872171
WEBSITE www.zsl.org
ROUTE Circuit within wild animal paddocks
LENGTH 2 miles | **GAUGE** 2ft 6in
OPEN Daily during summer months (during zoo opening times)

BUILT IN 1970 BY William McAlpine, of the McAlpine Construction company, for Pleasurerail, this line was originally named the Whipsnade & Umfolozi Light Railway and carried visitors through the white rhino herd at Whipsnade Zoo. In 1985, when the rhinos were relocated, the name changed to the Great Whipsnade Railway, and in 1990 Pleasurerail was taken over by the zoo operators. The station is situated near the dolphinarium and the line now runs through paddocks containing the animals of Asia. The majority of the railway equipment, including two steam locomotives ('Excelsior' and 'Superior') built earlier this century, came from the former Bowaters Papermill Railway in Kent (see Sittingbourne & Kemsley Light Railway, page 76) and passengers are carried on coaches built from former wood pulp wagon bogie frames.

Below A triple-headed steam train on the 2ft 6in-gauge Great Whipsnade Railway.

Hayling Seaside Railway

Beachlands Station, Beachlands, Hayling Island, Hampshire PO11 0AG

TEL 07775 696912
WEBSITE www.haylingseasiderailway.com
ROUTE Eastoke to Beachlands
LENGTH 1 mile | **GAUGE** 2ft
OPEN Weekends and Wed throughout the year; daily during all school and public holidays

SUPPORTED BY THE EAST Hayling Light Railway Society, the Hayling Seaside Railway opened in 2003 and is now a popular seaside attraction. Narrow gauge trains, hauled by former industrial diesel locos and a steam outline loco powered by a Ford Transit engine, operate from Eastoke through sand dunes and along the Hayling Island seafront, to a western terminus at the Beachlands Amusement Park. Visiting steam locos can be seen in action on a Gala weekend in June.

Hill Railway

Legoland, Winkfield Road, Windsor, Berkshire SL4 4AY

TEL 0871 2222 001
WEBSITE www.legoland.co.uk
ROUTE 'The Beginning' to 'Traffic'
LENGTH 1,000ft | **GAUGE** 3ft 6in
OPEN Daily, Mar to Oct

THIS CURVING FUNICULAR RAILWAY with an average gradient of 1 in 8.5 was originally built to operate in the Windsor Safari Park in 1991. The Park closed in October 1992 and was reopened, along with railway, as Legoland in 1996. In true Lego style, two brightly coloured three-car trains carry visitors from the main entrance to the heart of the park.

Above 1895-built Hunslet 0-4-0ST 'Jerry M', at work on the 2ft-gauge Quarry Railway at the Hollycombe Working Steam Museum in Hampshire.

Hollycombe Working Steam Museum

Iron Hill, Liphook, Hampshire GU30 7LP

TEL 01428 724900
WEBSITE www.hollycombe.co.uk
ROUTE Within grounds of Hollycombe House
LENGTH 1½ miles | **GAUGES** Standard, 2ft and 7¼in
OPEN Sun and Bank Holidays, Easter to Oct; daily,
    Whitsun week; Wed to Sun, Aug

THE 2FT-GAUGE STEAM-OPERATED Quarry Railway climbs through woodland within the grounds of Hollycombe House, before giving passengers wonderful views of the South Downs. Trains are normally hauled by 1895-built Hunslet 0-4-0ST 'Jerry M' and 1931-built Barclay 0-4-0WT 'Caledonia', both formerly from the Dinorwic Slate Quarry in North Wales. Passenger carriages are from the long-closed Ramsgate Electric Tunnel Railway. The shorter, standard gauge Hollycombe Tramway features rides behind 0-4-0VBT locomotive, 'Yankee'. A miniature railway also operates on a 600yd continuous loop within the grounds, where a large collection of traction engines and fairground rides are operated for the public.

Hotham Park Miniature Railway

Hotham Park, Bognor Regis, West Sussex PO21 1HN

TEL 01903 527321
WEBSITE www.hothamparkrailway.co.uk
ROUTE Within landscaped Hotham Park
LENGTH ½ mile | **GAUGE** 12¼in
OPEN Weekends, Mar to Oct; daily during School
    and Bank Holidays (weather permitting)

REPLACING AN EARLIER 10¼IN-GAUGE line opened in 1969 by Ian Allan, the present line opened in 2007 and features a circular ride around Hotham Park. Motive power is provided by 0-6-0T steam outline loco 'Boris', built in 2007 and powered by a Perkins Diesel with hydraulic drive. Passengers are carried in four covered bogie carriages, including one with disabled facilities.

Above A 1922 vintage Brush electric locomotive on the Hythe Pier Railway.

Hythe Pier Railway

The Ferry Office, Prospect Place, Hythe, Hampshire SO45 6AU

TEL 02380 840722
WEBSITE www.hytheferry.co.uk (includes webcam of pier railway)
ROUTE Along the length of Hythe Pier
LENGTH 2,100ft | GAUGE 2ft
OPEN Daily, throughout the year

THIS HISTORIC LITTLE ELECTRIC railway carries passengers along the length of Hythe Pier to connect with ferries to Southampton Town Quay. Hythe Pier was opened in 1880 and in 1909 a tramway, using a hand-propelled trolley, was built to convey luggage to and from the ferry. In 1922 the line was electrified on the third-rail principle and now the small three-coach trains, powered by a diminutive electric locomotive, still ply to and fro along the pier with their load of ferry passengers. Operating the service are two vintage Brush four-wheel, three-speed 100 volt DC motor units and four timber-framed, 18-seat coaches.

Ingfield Light Railway

Ingfield Manor School, Five Oaks, Billingshurst, Kent RH14 9AX

TEL 01403 865427
WEBSITE www.ingfieldrailway.co.uk
ROUTE Within Ingfield Manor School grounds
LENGTH c.600yds | GAUGE 10¼in
OPEN Please contact railway in advance to arrange a visit

THIS SUPERBLY DETAILED, PRIVATELY-RUN 10¼in miniature railway is set in the grounds of one of the leading British schools for children with cerebral palsy. Dating back to 1973, when it was first established as the Manor Railway by the late Keith Stratton, the end-to-end line now has two termini, two intermediate stations and four halts. The main loco shed and a turntable are located at Bramble Hill station, midway along the line. Powerful visiting steam locomotives, including several from the

Above 10¼in-gauge 4-4-0 Midland Compound No. 1102, on the Ingfield Light Railway in Kent.

now-closed Oakhill Manor and Berkeley Light railways, make light work of the Ingfield's 1 in 29 and 1 in 36 gradients. Other engines regularly visit.

Isle of Wight Steam Railway

See page 60

Kent & East Sussex Railway

See page 62

Kew Bridge Steam Museum

Green Dragon Lane, Brentford TW8 0EN

TEL 020 8568 4757
WEBSITE www.kbsm.org
ROUTE Within museum site
LENGTH 400yds | **GAUGE** 2ft
OPEN Museum open Tue to Sun, all year except Christmas. Railway operates Sun and Bank Holidays, Apr to Oct

LONDON'S ONLY OPERATING STEAM railway, the 2ft-gauge Waterworks Railway operates at this museum, originally a 19th-century pumping station for London's water supply network. The museum is also home to five working Cornish steam beam engines – built in 1846, 'Grand Junction 90' is the world's largest working beam engine. Passenger trains are operated by 'Wren' Class 0-4-0 steam locomotive, 'Thomas Wickstead', built as recently as 2009, and 3-cylinder Lister diesel, 'Alister', of 1957 vintage.

Above 'Wren' Class 0-4-0 'Thomas Wickstead' heads a short train at Kew Bridge Museum.

Knebworth Park Railway

Knebworth House, Knebworth, Nr Stevenage, Hertfordshire SG3 6PY

TEL 01438 812661
WEBSITE www.knebworthhouse.com
ROUTE Within grounds of Knebworth House
LENGTH 1,200yds | **GAUGE** 10¼in
OPEN Weekends and school holidays, Apr to Sep; see website for closures; 2012 will be last season

A SMALL COLLECTION OF steam, diesel and petrol locomotives are employed on this miniature passenger-carrying railway that runs around an adventure playground in the grounds of historic Knebworth House. The present line was opened in 1991 and replaced a previous steam-hauled 2ft-gauge system. Motive power is provided by three historic locos: steam 0-6-0T 'Pilgrim', formerly of the Wells & Walsingham Railway, diesel 'Uncle Jim' from the Hastings Miniature Railway, and petrol loco 'Jungle Express' from the Paignton Zoo Railway.

Isle of Wight Steam Railway

**The Railway Station, Havenstreet,
Isle of Wight PO33 4DS**

TEL 01983 882204
WEBSITE www.iwsteamrailway.co.uk
ROUTE Smallbrook Junction to Wootton
LENGTH 5 miles | **GAUGE** Standard
OPEN Selected days Feb to Dec (see website);
 daily, Jun to Sep
STATION National rail network station
 Smallbrook Junction

THE RYDE & NEWPORT RAILWAY opened on the Isle of Wight in 1875. In 1887 it amalgamated with the bankrupt Isle of Wight (Newport Junction) Railway and the Cowes & Newport Railway, to form the Isle of Wight Central Railway. This company also took over the running of the last railway to be built on the island, the Newport, Godshill & St Lawrence Railway, when it opened in 1900, eventually absorbing it in 1913. All of the railways on the island became part of the newly formed Southern Railway in 1923, which found that it had essentially inherited a working Victorian museum and set about modernising the system. New Class '02' 0-4-4s and new rolling stock were shipped in and these remained the backbone of the island system until 1966. In that year the remaining lines on the island were closed, apart from the section from Ryde Pierhead to Shanklin. This was electrified with the third-rail system using redundant London Underground stock.

Right 'Terrier' Class 'A1X' 0-6-0T No. W8 'Freshwater' arrives at Havenstreet station with a train for Wootton (top). The driver exchanges the single line token (bottom).

Opposite Ex-Southern Railway Class '02' 0-4-4T No. W24 'Calbourne' builds up steam as it heads a train of vintage carriages.

A preservation group moved in to Havenstreet, on the former Ryde & Newport Railway's line between Smallbrook Junction and Newport, in 1971. Services to Wootton restarted in 1977, and to Ashey and a new station at Smallbrook Junction in 1991, where connection can be made with the electrified Island Line. The ancient and beautifully preserved locomotives and rolling stock, some dating back to the 19th century, all contribute to the Victorian atmosphere. Included in the line-up are former London Brighton & South Coast Railway Class 'A1X' 0-6-0 tanks, No. W8 'Freshwater' and No. W11 'Newport', built in 1876 and 1878 respectively, and Southern Railway Class '02' 0-4-4 tank No. W24 'Calbourne', recently restored in resplendent BR black livery.

Kent & East Sussex Railway

Tenterden Town Station, Station Road, Tenterden, Kent TN30 6HE

TEL 01580 765155
WEBSITE www.kesr.org.uk
ROUTE Tenterden to Bodiam
LENGTH 10½ miles | **GAUGE** Standard
OPEN Daily, school holidays; most weekends all
   year; see website for details and special events

ORIGINALLY KNOWN AS THE Rother Valley Railway, the first light railway in the world was built and owned by the legendary Colonel Holman Stephens. Opened in sections from Robertsbridge to Rolvenden in 1900, to the Cinque Port of Tenterden in 1903, and eventually reaching Headcorn in 1905, the line changed its name to the Kent & East Sussex Railway in 1904. It is one of England's classic railways, epitomised by sharp curves, steep gradients and remote country stations. As was usual with all of Colonel Stephens' 16 railways, the Kent & East Sussex always led a very precarious financial existence, but managed to survive through to British Railways ownership in 1948, before being closed in 1961.

Following closure, a preservation group, eventually based at Tenterden, was quickly formed but it was not until 1974 that services were up and running. Wittersham

Road station was opened in 1978, Northiam in 1990 and Bodiam in 2000. Trains are mainly steam-hauled and the railway owns a collection of superbly restored four-and six-wheeled Victorian coaches. Locomotives include the diminutive former SECR 'P' Class 0-6-0T No. 31556, built in 1909, two Stroudley LBSCR 'Terrier' 0-6-0Ts, powerful ex-War Department 'Austerity' types and a Norwegian 2-6-0 tender engine. The Colonel Stephens Museum, which opened in 1996 and contains a photo archive, is located at Tenterden Town station (see page 48).

A separate railway preservation group, the Rother Valley Railway (see page 74), is restoring the line near Bodiam towards Robertsbridge, where it is hoped it will once again connect with the national rail network.

Above Visiting ex-SECR 'C' Class 0-6-0 No. 592 heads a passenger train.
Below Ex-LBSCR 'Terrier' Class 'A1X' 0-6-0T No. 32662 heads a short workmen's train.

Lavender Line

Isfield Station, Nr Uckfield,
East Sussex TN22 5XB

TEL 01825 750515
WEBSITE www.lavender-line.co.uk
ROUTE Isfield to Little Horsted
LENGTH 1 mile | **GAUGE** Standard
OPEN Sun throughout the year; Bank Holidays
and special events (see website)

SITUATED ONLY A FEW miles from the Bluebell Railway (see page 44), the Lavender Line is based at the restored station at Isfield. Originally part of the London Brighton & South Coast Railway's route from Eridge to Lewes, which opened in 1858, Isfield station was closed by British Rail in 1969. It was bought by David Milham in 1983 and, along with the Saxby & Farmer signalbox, was restored to its former Victorian glory. In 1992 it was sold to a preservation group, the Lavender Line Preservation Society, who operate both steam and diesel trains along

a mile of track. During quiet times an ex-British Railways Wickham railbus carries passengers along the line.

Leas Lift

Lower Sandgate Road, Folkestone,
Kent CT20 1PR

TEL 01303 210047
WEBSITE www.leasliftfolkestone.co.uk
ROUTE The Leas to Leas Promenade
LENGTH 164ft | **GAUGE** 5ft 10in
OPEN Daily, Apr to Oct

RECENTLY REOPENED, THE LEAS Lift is the only remaining funicular cliff railway out of four that once operated in Folkestone. Operated by gravity using the water-balance system, the railway opened in 1885. As with other coastal cliff railways, it closed in 1940 for the duration of the Second World War but reopened in 1948. Completely refurbished in 1985, it was taken over by a community organisation in 2010.

Below Peckett 0-4-0ST 'Teddy' and visiting 'AIX' Class 0-6-0T No. 662, at the Lavender Line's engine shed at Isfield.

Above 1922-built Kerr Stuart 0-4-0ST 'Pixie' heads a short train on the Leighton Buzzard Railway in Hertfordshire.

Leighton Buzzard Railway

Page's Park Station, Billington Road, Leighton Buzzard, Bedfordshire LU7 4TN

TEL 01525 373888
WEBSITE www.buzzrail.co.uk
ROUTE Page's Park to Stonehenge Works
LENGTH 2¾ miles | **GAUGE** 2ft
OPEN Most Sun, Mar to Oct; Tues to Thurs, Aug; Santa Specials in Dec; see website for extra days and special events

BUILT DURING THE FIRST World War to transport sand from pits near Leighton Buzzard, this former industrial 2ft-gauge line was saved from closure by a preservation group, who started to operate trains in 1968. Now home to 11 steam and 40 diesel locomotives, originating from West Africa, India, Spain and Britain, trains operate from the railway's headquarters at Page's Park, running behind housing estates and into open country before arriving at Stonehenge Works, a former brickworks. It is here that many items of the railway's historic collection are housed. Sharp curves and steep gradients abound on this fascinating line. The oldest working locomotive on the railway is the 1877-built 0-4-0 vertical-boilered 'Chaloner', and visiting locomotives are a common sight on special events days. The Greensand Railway Museum at Page's Park houses narrow gauge railway artefacts from the First World War, including restored Baldwin-built War Department Light Railways 4-6-0 No. 778 and Simplex petrol locomotive No. 2182, that once worked on railways in the trenches. Restoration of the ¾-mile line to Double Arches is also a long-term objective.

Littledown Miniature Railway

Littledown Park, Chaseside, Castle Lane East, Bournemouth, Hampshire BH7 7DX

WEBSITE www.littledownrailway.co.uk
ROUTE Within Littledown Park
LENGTH c.600yds | GAUGES 3½in, 5in and 7¼in
OPEN Most Sun throughout the year (see website)

OWNED AND OPERATED BY the Bournemouth & District Society of Model Engineers, this mixed gauge miniature railway is located on the western extremity of Littledown Park. The line features continuous running on a raised track set on concrete beams, a station with canopy, and an engine and carriage shed.

London Transport Museum

Covent Garden Piazza, London WC2E 7BB

TEL 020 7379 6344
WEBSITE www.ltmuseum.co.uk
OPEN Daily throughout the year
STATION London Underground station
    Covent Garden

A LARGE COLLECTION OF public transport road and rail vehicles used in London from Victorian times to the present day is housed in the former Flower Market, which dates back to 1870. The museum was extended during 2007 with increased display space and spectacular new mezzanine floors. Included on display are a 1866-built Metropolitan Railway 4-4-0 condensing tank No. 23 and a 1922-built 1,200 horsepower Bo-Bo electric locomotive, 'John Hampden'. There is also Wotton Tramway traction engine locomotive No. 807, built in 1872, as well as examples of

early underground electric trains, such as the 1890-built City & South London Railway 'Padded Cell' car. Visitors to the museum can 'drive' an Underground train on a simulator. Models, artefacts, posters and an audio-visual display are included. The museum has a large photographic and film archive section containing over 100,000 black and white photographs of London Transport and its predecessors. The London Transport Museum Depot at Acton (see page 40) houses the remainder of the Museum's vast collection.

Below and bottom Open on special events days, the London Transport Museum's Depot at Acton (below) and a restored coach interior at the museum in Covent Garden (bottom).

Metropolitan Water Board Railway Society

Kempton Park Steam Museum, Snakey Lane, Kempton, Middlesex TW13 6XH

WEBSITE www.hamptonkemptonrailway.org.uk
ROUTE Work in progress
LENGTH c.¼ mile | **GAUGE** 2ft
OPEN Open Days are on same dates as Kempton Great Engines Steaming Days during Sep, Oct and Nov (see website)

THREE LARGE STEAM-POWERED PUMPING stations were established to draw water from the Thames at Hampton in the mid-19th century. Coal for these enormous beam engines was first delivered by barge to Hampton Court. However, so vast were the amounts of coal required that a 2ft-gauge industrial railway was built linking the wharf at Hampton Court, the pumping engines and the standard gauge main line at Shepperton. Opened in 1915, the 3½-mile Metropolitan Water Board Railway employed three 0-4-2T locos supplied by Kerr, Stuart, which remained in service until closure in 1947.

The Metropolitan Water Board Railway Society was founded in 2003 with the eventual aim of reinstating the railway link between Hampton Riverside and Kempton. Since then, society members have built a new 0-4-0 petrol-engined loco, 'Hounslow', and are currently laying concrete-sleepered track on the Hanworth Loop. For details of progress, visit the society's excellent website.

Mid-Hants Railway Watercress Line

See page 68

Mizens Miniature Railway

Barrs Lane, Knaphill, Woking, Surrey GU21 2JW

TEL 01784 461476 (Hon Secretary)
WEBSITE www.mizensrailway.co.uk
ROUTE Triple circuit within farm
LENGTH 1 mile | **GAUGE** 7¼in
OPEN Sun, Easter to Sep; Santa specials in Dec

OPERATED BY THE WOKING Miniature Railway Society, founded in 1989, this railway once operated at Mizens Farm but in 2004 moved to its present site, where passenger-carrying miniature steam trains operate in a pleasant eight-acre woodland location. The railway also holds Halloween Fright Nights and Santa Specials (see website for details).

Below The Mizens Miniature Railway is operated by the Woking Miniature Railway Society.

Above Ex-Southern Railway 'U' Class 2-6-0 No. 31806 heads a demonstration freight train through Medstead & Four Marks station.

Right British Railways Standard Class '5' 4-6-0 No. 73096 arrives at Medstead & Four Marks station.

Bottom right No. 73096 hard at work in the area known locally as 'The Alps'.

Mid-Hants Railway Watercress Line

The Railway Station, Alresford, Hampshire SO24 9JG

TEL 01962 733810
WEBSITE www.watercressline.co.uk
ROUTE Alton to Alresford
LENGTH 10 miles | **GAUGE** Standard
OPEN Weekends and school holidays, Jan to Oct; daily except Mon and Fri, mid-Apr to end Sep; daily, Aug; Santa Specials in Dec
STATION National rail network station Alton

OPENED IN 1865, THE railway between Alton and Winchester, known as the Mid-Hants (Alton) Railway, was an important link for the armed services between Aldershot and Portsmouth. Operated from the outset by the London & South Western Railway, the line was heavily used in both World Wars and was also an important diversionary route for main-line trains between Woking and Winchester. In the 1950s and early '60s it was not an uncommon sight to see the diverted 'Bournemouth Belle' Pullman train headed by a Bulleid Pacific making its way along this rural line on a Sunday. An important local traffic included the transport of locally grown watercress, which is now used by the present company as its marketing title.

Finally closed by British Railways in 1973, the current section of the line was bought by a preservation group in 1975, which started services, initially from Alresford to Ropley, two years later. Services to Alton, where there is an important link with the national rail network, started in 1985. Steam-hauled trains operate over this

steeply graded line, locally known as 'The Alps'. Its highest point is near Medstead & Four Marks, 652ft above sea level, necessitating the use of large and impressive steam locomotives, including ex-SR Bulleid 'West Country' Class 4-6-2 No. 34007 'Wadebridge' and ex-SR 'U' Class 2-6-0 No. 31806. Visiting locomotives can also be regularly seen hard at work on special event days through the year (see website for details). The stations along the line are all beautifully restored to different periods in the history of the railway, and of special note is the carefully pruned 60-year old topiary at Ropley station, where the Mid-Hants also has its extensive workshops and engine shed.

A miniature railway at Ropley operates every weekend from June to September.

Moors Valley Railway

Moors Valley Country Park,
Horton Road, Ashley Heath,
Nr Ringwood, Dorset BH24 2ET

TEL 01425 471415
WEBSITE www.moorsvalleyrailway.co.uk
ROUTE Within Moors Valley Country Park
LENGTH 1 mile | **GAUGE** 7¼in
OPEN Weekends and school holidays, all year;
daily, Spring Bank Holiday to mid-Sep

Above A train leaves the terminus station
at Kingsbury, on the Moors Valley Railway.

ESTABLISHED IN 1986, USING equipment
from the closed Tucktonia Miniature
Railway in Christchurch, the Moors Valley
Railway operates a large collection of 14
miniature steam locomotives, including
a 2-4-0+0-4-2 Garratt type, 36 passenger
vehicles and a refrigerated ice cream van.
This professionally-run railway includes
four tunnels, signalbox, signalling and a
roundhouse, and the journey along the shore
of a lake takes in a spiral, steep gradients
and tight curves. The main signal lever
frame came from Becton Gas Works in
East London. Special events with visiting
locomotives are held throughout the year
(see website for details).

Moors Valley Country Park, owned by
Dorset District Council, also provides a golf
course, visitor centre, adventure playground,
picnic areas and tree-top forest walk.

Old Kiln Light Railway

Rural Life Centre, Reeds Road,
Tilford, Farnham, Surrey GU10 2DL

WEBSITE www.oldkilnlightrailway.com
ROUTE Along boundary of museum. Mills Wood
to Reeds Road, via Old Kiln
LENGTH 1 mile | **GAUGE** 2ft
OPEN Sun, Mar to end Sep

ESTABLISHED IN 1982, THE Old Kiln Light
Railway has a large and fascinating collection
of narrow gauge petrol, diesel and steam
locomotives and rolling stock. Visitors can
take a pleasant journey through woodland,
close to an RSPB Reserve, on this steeply
graded line. Trains are usually hauled by a
selection of petrol and diesel locos. Steam
lovers are catered for on summer Sundays
and special events days, when 0-6-0T
'Elouise', built by Orenstein & Koppel of
Berlin in 1922, can be seen in action (see
website for details).

Below Orenstein & Koppel 0-6-0 'Elouise' with
a Santa Special on the Old Kiln Light Railway.

Pendon Museum

Long Wittenham, Nr Abingdon,
Oxfordshire OX14 4QD

TEL 01865 407365
WEBSITE www.pendonmuseum.com
OPEN Weekend afternoons, early Jan to end Nov;
Bank Holiday weekends, Easter to Aug; selected
Wed during school holidays

Above A highly detailed railway scene on the
'00'-gauge Dartmoor railway layout at Pendon.

THIS WORLD-FAMOUS MUSEUM was started
in 1954 by Roye England to capture in
miniature the beauty of the Vale of White
Horse landscape and villages as they existed
in the 1930s, and to reveal the excitement of
the Great Western Railway as it was during
the heyday of steam. Since the beginning,
the museum has been a centre for modelling
excellence. There are three major exhibits
at the museum: a 70ft-long model of village
life in the Vale of White Horse; an imaginary
GWR branch line in Dartmoor with
extensive train operations; the formative
Madder Valley model railway, built by
John Ahern.

Although work has been progressing for
over 50 years, the Vale scene is still 'under
construction' and another ten years of work
is not hard to imagine. However, the Vale
is already breathtaking to view, and visitors
who return are always delighted to note the
progress. Not only can you see one of the
finest modelling panoramas in England,
you can see it all being created.

Pinewood Miniature Railway

Pinewood Leisure Centre, Old Wokingham
Road, Wokingham, Berkshire RG40 3AQ

TEL 07587 057885
WEBSITE www.pinewoodrailway.co.uk
ROUTE Within grounds of leisure centre
LENGTH ½ mile | **GAUGES** 5in and 7¼in
OPEN 3rd Sun (afternoon) each month,
Apr to Oct; Santa Specials in Dec

ESTABLISHED ON ITS PRESENT site for 25
years, this dual gauge, continuous ground
level miniature railway takes visitors on a
½-mile journey through a woodland setting
from a recently opened new station. The
railway also features a large loco yard with
traversers and turntable. Motive power
consists of four steam locos, including
two of North American design, along with
one petrol and one battery loco. Visiting
locomotives are supplied by members of
the Pinewood Miniature Railway Society.

Below A Rio Grande 2-8-0 departs from the new
station on the Pinewood Miniature Railway.

Romney, Hythe & Dymchurch Railway

New Romney Station, New Romney, Kent TN28 8PL

TEL 01797 362353
WEBSITE www.rhdr.org.uk
ROUTE Hythe to Dungeness
LENGTH 13½ miles | **GAUGE** 15in
OPEN Most weekends, all year; daily, Easter to end Oct; see website for special events

THE WORLD'S SMALLEST PUBLIC railway, from Hythe to Dungeness, was conceived and built by the wealthy racing driver Captain Jack Howey and even wealthier racing driver Count Louis Zborowski. Their original plan had been to purchase the Ravenglass & Eskale Railway (see page 218) in Cumbria but this fell through. Despite this, the pair ordered two one-third scale LNER 'A3' 4-6-2 locos, designed by Henry Greenly, from Davey Paxman of Colchester in 1925. Before they were delivered, Zborowski was killed in a motor racing accident at Monza and Howey was left to find a home for his two new locomotives, 'Green Goddess' and 'Northern Chief'. With Greenly's help, Howey came up with a proposal for his miniature railway across Romney Marsh – the Romney, Hythe & Dymchurch Railway was born.

No expense was spared to produce an accurate one-third scale working miniature of a main-line railway. As in full-size practice, the line is double-track and signalled, engines are replicas of LNER and Canadian express locomotives, and passengers are carried in bogie carriages. The first section

of the line, from Hythe to New Romney, was opened in 1927 and the then Duke of York, later to become King George VI, had the honour of driving the first train. The line was extended to Dungeness lighthouse, where the line forms a complete loop, in 1929.

In the pre-war years the line was very popular with holidaymakers and during the Second World War, an armoured train was built complete with machine guns. The RHDR also played an important part in transporting materials for Operation Pluto (Pipe Line Under The Ocean) preceding the D-Day landings. Despite a reopening ceremony by Laurel and Hardy, the period after the war brought mixed fortunes for the little railway and, with falling passenger receipts, losses mounted after Howey's death until the line was first put up for sale in 1968. After rumours that the RHDR was going to be moved lock, stock and barrel to the West Country, a consortium headed by Sir William McAlpine bought the line in 1971 and proceeded to restore it to its former glory.

The RHDR currently boasts 11 magnificent steam locomotives (including seven built by Davey Paxman in the 1920s), two diesels (used on the regular school train during term time), and over 65 assorted coaches, including the unique buffet

observation car. To add to the authentic main-line atmosphere, the railway boasts a large engine shed, turntable and workshop at New Romney, and an overall roof covers the three platforms at Hythe terminus. Also at New Romney, an extensive model railway exhibition and museum is open most days. During peak periods trains run every 45 minutes, at speeds up to 25mph.

Above No. 6 'Samson' and No. 10 'Dr Syn' at New Romney station.

Opposite The railway's 4-6-2 No. 8 'Hurricane', built by Davey Paxman of Colchester in 1927.

Below Motive power contrasts: diesel No. 14 'Captain Howey' and 4-6-2 No. 10 'Dr Syn'.

Rother Valley Railway

**Station Road, Robertsbridge,
East Sussex TN32 5DG**

TEL 01580 881833
WEBSITE www.rvr.org.uk
EVENTUAL ROUTE Robertsbridge to Bodiam
LENGTH 3½ miles | **GAUGE** Standard
OPEN RVR shop only while development continues
   (check before visiting)
STATION National rail network station
   Robertsbridge

THE MISSING LINK BETWEEN Robertsbridge
(on the national rail network) to Bodiam
(western terminus of the Kent & East Sussex
Railway – see page 62) is being rebuilt by
volunteer members of the Rother Valley
Railway, which was formed in 1991. Track
laying has already commenced from both
ends, while a visitor centre at Robertsbridge
RVR station is housed in the former Venice-
Simplon-Orient reception lounge from

London's Victoria Station. Also based at
Robertsbridge, the Hastings Tramways
Club is restoring two early 20th-century ex-
Hastings electric tram cars for static display.

Roxbourne Park Miniature Railway

**Roxbourne Park, Field End Road, Eastcote,
Middlesex HA4 9PB**

TEL 020 8953 0098 (Secretary)
WEBSITE www.hwsme.org.uk
ROUTE Within Roxbourne Park
LENGTH ½ mile | **GAUGES** 3½in, 5in and 7¼in
OPEN Sun afternoons during British Summer
   Time; see website for Halloween and Christmas
   special events

OWNED AND OPERATED SINCE 1976 by
the Harrow & Wembley Society of Model
Engineers (formed in 1935), this dual
gauge, ground-level miniature railway gives

Below Ex-LBSCR Class 'A1X' 0-6-0T No. 32670, on the Kent & East Sussex Railway's newly laid westward extension from Bodiam. This will eventually link with the Rother Valley Railway from Robertsbridge.

rides around Roxbourne Park on Sunday afternoons between March and September. A wide variety of members' locomotives can be seen in action on open days.

Royal Victoria Railway

Royal Victoria Country Park, Netley, Southampton, Hampshire SO31 5GA

TEL 02380 456246
WEBSITE www.royalvictoriarailway.co.uk
ROUTE Within grounds of 200-acre country park
LENGTH 1 mile | **GAUGE** 10¼in
OPEN Weekends, all year; daily during school holidays

THE ROYAL VICTORIA RAILWAY runs close to the LSWR Netley to Royal Victoria Hospital branch line, which opened in 1900 and closed in 1955. A few remaining standard gauge rails from this long-lost line are still visible today. The original miniature railway on this site opened in 1989 and was removed in 1995. Track was relaid and very much extended later in the same year. Steam locomotives operating on the line are narrow gauge 2-6-0 'Isambard Kingdom Brunel', built by David Curwen in 1977, 2-6-0+0-6-2 Garratt 'Basil the Brigadier', built by Kitsons in 1938 for the Surrey Border & Camberley Railway, and diminutive 0-6-2T 'Trevithick', built by Marsh in 1976. Two 'Royal Scot' 4-6-0s (including one built by Bassett-Lowke in 1938) are currently being restored to working order. Two superb 'Western' diesel hydraulics also operate trains on the line.

The journey starts at Chapel Road station and involves gradients of 1 in 80, and a tunnel, before reaching Tea Room Halt. It then passes the engine shed and through dense undergrowth before levelling out, providing passengers with good views of Southampton Water, finally returning to the main station.

Ruislip Lido Railway

Reservoir Road, Ruislip, Middlesex HA4 7TY

TEL 01895 622595
WEBSITE www.ruisliplidorailway.org
ROUTE Around Ruislip Lido
LENGTH 1¼ miles | **GAUGE** 12in
OPEN Weekends, Feb to Nov; daily during school holidays; see website for steam operating days and special events

OPERATED ENTIRELY BY VOLUNTEERS, this 12in-gauge miniature railway first started operations at Ruislip Lido as early as 1945. Five diesel locomotives, and half-size Ffestiniog Railway 2-4-0 steam locomotive 'Mad Bess', now operate trains. They run between Woody Bay station and Water's Edge station, close to the car park, within the grounds of Ruislip Lido country park.

Science Museum

Exhibition Road, South Kensington, London SW7 2DD

TEL 0870 870 4868
WEBSITE www.sciencemuseum.org.uk
OPEN Daily, throughout the year

THE SCIENCE MUSEUM ORIGINALLY opened as the South Kensington Museum in 1857, on land purchased with the profits from the 1851 Great Exhibition. The present transport gallery includes a static display of historic locomotives which forms a small part of this famous museum. Exhibits include the Wylam Colliery 'Puffing Billy' (1813), designed by William Hedley, and Stephenson's 'Rocket' (1829) from the Liverpool & Manchester Railway. The National Railway Collection is now based at the National Railway Museum, York (see page 210) and 'Locomotion' at Shildon (see page 211).

Sittingbourne & Kemsley Light Railway

Off Milton Lane, Sittingbourne, Kent ME10 2XD

TEL 01795 424 899
WEBSITE www.sklr.net
ROUTE Sittingbourne (Milton Creek) to
    Kemsley Down
LENGTH 2 miles | **GAUGE** 2ft 6in
OPEN Sun, Easter to Oct; see website for
    other dates

Above Kerr Stuart 0-4-2ST 'Melior' with a train on the Sittingbourne & Kemsley Light Railway.
Below The silhouette of 0-6-2T 'Triumph' running over the viaduct near Kemsley Down.

THIS INDUSTRIAL RAILWAY WAS originally built in 1906 by Edward Lloyd Ltd to carry paper from a wharf on Milton Creek to a mill at Sittingbourne, and later extended to carry logs and woodpulp from a wharf on the River Swale at Ridham to the papermill. In 1924 a further papermill, served by the railway, was opened at Kemsley and more locomotives were purchased to cope with the extra traffic.

In 1948 the Bowater Group purchased the company and its railway, with further locomotive acquisitions, and continued to run it until 1965 when road transport was introduced. The Locomotive Club of Great Britain took over, on loan from Bowaters, the two miles of track between Sittingbourne and Kemsley in 1969 and by Easter 1970 the line was open for passengers. Trains are now mainly steam-hauled using industrial

locomotives and coaches, many from the original railway, including four coaches from the former Chattenden & Upnor Military Railway on the Isle of Grain.

An interesting narrow gauge locomotive line-up includes Kerr Stuart 0-4-2STs 'Premier', 'Melior' and 'Leader', Bagnall 0-6-2Ts 'Apha', 'Triumph' and 'Superb', Bagnall Fireless 'Unique' and three diesels. Several of these can still be seen at work on the line today.

The railway survived a closure threat in 2008/9, as the owners of Sittingbourne Paper Mill were closing the mill and selling off the land. Fortunately, the railway has since been saved from extinction and a limited service recommenced in 2011.

Southall Railway Centre

Southall, Middlesex UB2 4SE

TEL 020 8574 1529
WEBSITE www.gwrpg.co.uk
OPEN Currently closed to the public (see website for details)

FORMERLY BASED IN THE old GWR engine shed at Southall (closed by BR in 1986), the Great Western Railway Preservation Group's collection of standard gauge steam and diesel locomotives and items of rolling stock is now based in the small wheeldrop shed and boiler house building. The site is also used as an operations centre by the West Coast Railway Company for its main line charter trains.

Spa Valley Railway

See page 78

Strand Miniature Railway

Strand Leisure Pool and Park, Gillingham, Medway Town, Kent ME7 1TT

TEL 01634 333925
ROUTE Within Strand Leisure Pool and Park
LENGTH c.¼ mile | GAUGE 7¼in
OPEN Weekends, Easter to Sep

Now OPERATED BY MEDWAY Council, there has been a miniature railway on this site since 1948. It carries passengers on a circular trip around the Strand Leisure Park, with views of the Thames Estuary. Power is provided by two diesel outline locomotives – an HST 125 and a North American type.

Summerfields Miniature Railway

Summerfields Farm, Haynes, Bedfordshire MK45 3BH

TEL 01234 301867
WEBSITE www.bedfordmes.co.uk
ROUTES Three separate routes within grounds
LENGTH See website | GAUGES 2¼in, 3½in, 5in and 7¼in
OPEN See website for public open days

THREE SEPARATE MINIATURE RAILWAYS are operated at Summerfields Farm by members of the Bedford Model Engineering Society. The longest railway is the ground-level 7¼in-gauge Summerfields Railway, which runs from Haynes End, near the car park, to Hammer Hill station. The Winterfield Railway is a raised mixed gauge route of 670yds, catering for 2¼in, 3½in and 5in locos. The dual gauge ground-level Springfield Railway is under construction and will cater for the two larger gauges.

Spa Valley Railway

**West Station, Nevill Terrace,
Royal Tunbridge Wells, Kent TN2 5QY**

TEL 01892 537715
WEBSITE www.spavalleyrailway.co.uk
ROUTE Tunbridge Wells West to Eridge
LENGTH 5½ miles | **GAUGE** Standard
OPEN Weekends, Bank Holidays and selected
   Thu and Fri, Apr to Oct; see website for
   numerous special events
STATION National rail network station Eridge

As PART OF WHAT was to become the
London, Brighton & South Coast Railway's
Three Bridges to Tunbridge Wells Central
line, the East Grinstead, Groombridge &
Tunbridge Wells Railway opened in 1866.
A connecting line from Eridge, on the
Uckfield line, was opened in 1868. Listed
for closure in the 1963 'Beeching Report'
(the author of which lived in nearby East
Grinstead), the section between Three
Bridges and Groombridge was closed at the
beginning of 1967. However, the section
from Groombridge to Tunbridge Wells West
remained open for trains to and from Eridge
until 1985 when that, too, closed.

Formed soon after closure of the line
in 1985, the Tunbridge Wells & Eridge
Preservation Society (TWERPS) began
their long campaign to reopen the line.
From early beginnings in 1996, when the
Society established their base at Tunbridge
Wells West locomotive shed, the line was
completely reopened in 2011 when passenger
trains on the new Spa Valley Railway ran for
the first time in 26 years between Tunbridge
Wells West and Eridge. Here, Spa Valley
trains connect with national network services
on the London to Uckfield line. Heritage
steam and diesel locomotives convey
passengers through the picturesque Kent
and Sussex Weald, stopping off at
Groombridge and High Rocks stations
for a visit to one of the local pubs. The
railway is currently home to 12 steam locos
and a collection of diesels. A miniature
railway operates most Saturdays alongside
Tunbridge Wells West engine shed.

Above Ex-Southern Railway Class 'M7' 0-4-4T No. 53 heads a train for Tunbridge Wells West, between Eridge and Groombridge.

Opposite The Spa Valley Railway at Groombridge station. RSH 0-6-0ST No. 62 "Ugly" waits with a train for Tunbridge Wells West on 9th July 2011.

Above 'Santa Flyer' on the steeply graded 7¼in-gauge Swanley New Barn Railway.

Swanley New Barn Railway

Swanley Park, New Barn Road, Swanley, Kent BR8 7PW

WEBSITE www.snbr.20m.com
ROUTE Within Swanley Park
LENGTH 900yds | **GAUGE** 7¼in
OPEN Weekends, Bank and school holidays, Good Fri to end Oct

THIS STEEPLY GRADED GROUND-level miniature railway was originally run by the local council but was taken over in 1987 by a local society. Trains depart from Lakeside station in the 60-acre Swanley Park, passing the signalbox (containing a 36-lever frame from Gloucester Road), and climb to the summit of the line before reaching New Barn Halt, adjacent to the car park. From here the line runs downhill and back into Lakeside, with its three-platform terminus. A large number of locomotives are available to run the service, including one battery-powered, nine diesels (many of BR outline) and eight steam. Rolling stock consists of a large collection of sit-astride coaches plus various other goods vehicles.

Thames Ditton Miniature Railway

Willowbank, Claygate Lane, Thames Ditton, Surrey KT7 0LE

TEL 020 8398 3985
WEBSITE www.malden-dsme.co.uk
ROUTE Within club grounds
LENGTH Elevated track – 1,620ft; ground-level track – 1,800ft | **GAUGES** 3½in, 5in and 7¼in
OPEN 1st Sun of each month and Bank Holidays, Easter Sun and Mon until early Oct

OWNED AND OPERATED BY the Malden & District Society of Model Engineers since 1949, this miniature railway features two separate continuous routes. A multi-gauge elevated railway in the shape of a figure-of-eight was completed in 1971. The fully signalled, ground-level 7¼in-gauge railway comprises two circuits, with sidings and passing loops, and features a station and a semi roundhouse engine shed. A variety of club members' steam and diesel outline locos can be seen operating on open days.

Vanstone Woodland Railway

Vanstone Park Garden Centre, Hitchin Road, Codicote, Hertfordshire SG4 8TH

TEL 01438 820412 (Garden Centre)
WEBSITE freespace.virgin.net/antony.everett/vanstonerailway
ROUTE Within Vanstone Park Garden Centre
LENGTH 560yd | **GAUGE** 10¼in
OPEN Weekends and Bank Holidays, all year

THIS MINIATURE RAILWAY OPERATES within a garden centre and was opened in 1986, with relocation of the station in 1995. Trains are operated by four freelance diesel-mechanical locomotives and there are three articulated carriages. The route is in the shape of a dumb-bell, with a branch to the station.

Volks Electric Railway

285 Madeira Drive, Brighton, BN2 1EN

TEL 01273 292718
WEBSITE www.volkselectricrailway.co.uk
ROUTE Aquarium (for Brighton Pier) to Black Rock (for Marina)
LENGTH 1¼ miles | **GAUGE** 2ft 8½in
OPEN Daily, early Apr to mid Sep
STATION National rail network station Brighton

OPENED IN 1883 AS a 2ft-gauge railway by the inventor Magnus Volk, the Volks Electric Railway, which was taken over by Brighton Corporation in 1940, was the first electric railway in Britain and runs along the seafront at Brighton. In 1884 it was regauged to 2ft 8½in and extended from the Chain Pier to Banjo Groyne. It was further extended from Banjo Groyne to Black Rock in 1901. Power at 110V DC is supplied by a third rail. Rolling stock includes cars built in 1892 and 1901, and two open toast-rack cars, built in 1898, from the Southend Pier Railway (see page 148). The electric railway, the oldest operating in the world, is a single-line operation with three passing loops and three stations, and a total of 13 pedestrian crossings are marked with red lights. Born in Brighton, Magnus Volk, the son of a German clockmaker, also built the short-lived Brighton & Rottingdean Seashore Electric Railway. In addition, he designed the famous 'Daddy Long Legs', a mixture of tramcar, yacht and seaside pier, which was sadly destroyed in a storm only a few days after its inauguration in 1896.

Below The Volks Electric Railway is the oldest operating electric railway in the world.

Watford Miniature Railway

Cassiobury Park, Watford, Herts WD18 7LH

ROUTE Within Cassiobury Park
LENGTH 1,050yds | **GAUGE** 10¼in
OPEN Weekends and school holidays all year; daily, Jun to Sep; trains run in the afternoons

ESTABLISHED IN 1959, EXTENDED in 1963 and again in 1988, this miniature railway operates three steam locomotives and two diesel hydraulic locos. Passengers are carried on open articulated sets along an out-and-back route from the terminus, situated near the children's paddling pool and playground in Cassiobury Park.

Wellington Park Miniature Railway

Wellington Country Park, Odiham Road, Risely, Nr Reading, Berkshire RG7 1SP

TEL 0118 932 6444
WEBSITE www.wellington-country-park.co.uk
ROUTE Within Wellington Country Park
LENGTH 500yds | **GAUGE** 7¼in
OPEN Daily, Feb half-term to early Nov

THIS MINIATURE RAILWAY WAS opened in 1980 and takes passengers from a four-platform station on a scenic route through the country park, crossing a small lake on a girder bridge and passing through a tunnel. Motive power consists of diesel hydraulic 'Charlotte' and a battery locomotive.

Below Diesel hydraulic loco 'Charlotte' hauls trains through the Wellington Country Park in Berkshire.

Right Bournemouth's West Cliff funicular railway is over a hundred years old.

West Cliff Lift

West Cliff Road, Bournemouth BH2 5DU

TEL 01202 451451
WEBSITE www.bournemouth.gov.uk
ROUTE West Cliff to West Cliff Promenade
LENGTH 145ft | **GAUGE** 5ft 6in
OPEN Daily, Easter to Oct

OWNED AND OPERATED BY Bournemouth Borough Council, this electric-powered funicular railway opened in 1908, just months after Bournemouth's East Cliff Lift (see page 50) and carries passengers a height of 102ft on a gradient of 1 in 1.42.

West Hill Cliff Railway

**George Street, Hastings,
East Sussex TN34 3EG**

ROUTE George Street to Castle Hill
LENGTH 500ft | **GAUGE** 6ft
OPEN Daily, throughout the year

THIS FUNICULAR RAILWAY WAS the first of two such lines to open in Hastings (see page 51). Completed in 1891, it carries visitors up to the ruins of Hastings Castle on a gradient of 1-in-2.9. Most of the line is in a brick-lined tunnel in the cliff and the winding gear was originally powered by a gas engine until 1924 when this was replaced by a diesel engine. The railway was bought by Hastings Borough Council in 1947 and the diesel engine was replaced by electric power in 1971.

Willen Miniature Railway

**Willen Lakeside Park, Milton Keynes,
Buckinghamshire MK15 0SF**

ROUTE Within Willen Lakeside Park
LENGTH 600yds | **GAUGE** 7¼in
OPEN Weekends, all year; daily during school holidays, Apr to end Oct

OPENED IN 1989, THIS short out-and-back miniature line starts at Willen Halt, close to the car park, and runs through woodland past a locomotive shed. Two diesel locomotives operate the trains.

MAIN-LINE STEAM

Rarely a week goes by without some form of main-line steam special somewhere on Britain's rail network. Here are some highlights from South and South East England.

Above Unrebuilt 'Battle of Britain' Class 4-6-2 No. 34067 'Tangmere' crosses the River Arun adjacent to Ford station, on its way to Bristol on 19 March 2011. The train is 'The Bath and Bristol', from Three Bridges to Bristol and back and was operated by the Railway Touring Company.

Left Seen here again, No. 34067 approaches Vauxhall station with a Steam Dreams' Carol Concert Special Cathedrals Express to Salisbury, shortly after leaving London Waterloo on 15 December 2009.

Right Disguised as ex-LNER 'A4' Class 4-6-2 No. 4492 'Dominion of New Zealand', No. 60019 'Bittern' passes St Denys, near Southampton, with a charter train from Swanage to London on 9 August 2011.

Below New-build 'A1' Class 4-6-2 No. 60163 'Tornado' approaches Reigate with a VSOE Surrey Hills lunchtime Pullman Dining train, on 30th September 2011.

CENTRAL ENGLAND

L. & N.W. RY.
Northampton Castle

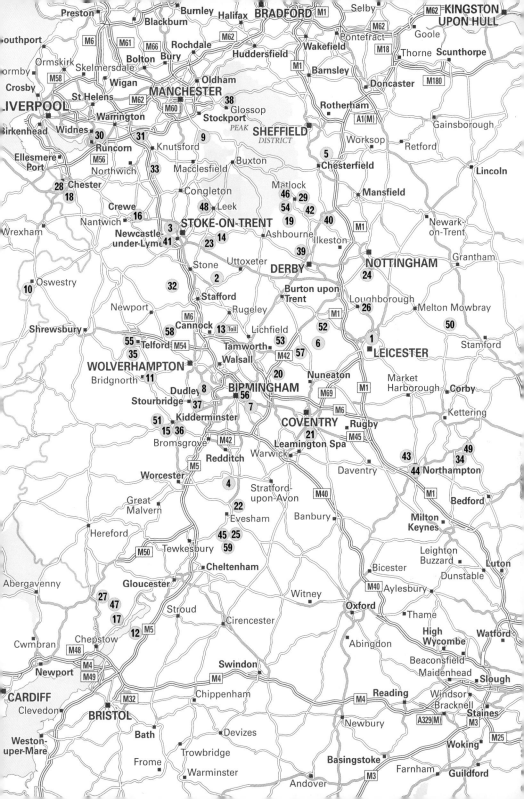

Abbey Pumping Station Railway

Corporation Road, Leicester LE4 5PX

TEL 0116 299 5111
WEBSITE www.leicester.gov.uk
ROUTE Within museum site
LENGTH 300yds | **GAUGE** 2ft
OPEN Selected special events days (see website)

NOW AN INDUSTRIAL MUSEUM operated by Leicester City Council, this massive Victorian pumping station was opened in 1891 to pump raw sewage to treatment works at Beaumont Leys. It closed in 1964 and reopened as a museum in 1972. Three of the four Woolf compound rotative beam engines have been restored to working condition. Opened in the early 1980s, an industrial narrow gauge railway is normally operated by 1918-built Bagnall 0-4-0ST 'Leonard' and it gives rides on special events days.

Amerton Railway

Amerton Working Farm, Stowe-by-Chartley, Nr Weston, Staffordshire ST18 0LA

TEL 01785 850965
WEBSITE www.amertonrailway.co.uk
ROUTE Within site of working farm
LENGTH 1 mile | **GAUGE** 2ft
OPEN Steam trains – Sun and Bank Holidays, Apr to end Oct. Diesel trains – Sat, Easter to Aug; Tue to Thu, Easter holidays and Aug; selected dates in Dec (see website)

THE CONSTRUCTION OF THE Amerton Railway was started on a greenfield site in 1990 by volunteers of the Staffordshire Narrow Gauge Railway Society. The present route was opened in 1992. Passenger trains consist of three modified Baguley toast-rack coaches (ex-Wilson's Pleasure Railway,

Above The 2ft-gauge Amerton Railway in Staffordshire was opened in 1992.

Orpington) and a home-made brakevan. Operating locomotives include Bagnall steam tank 'Isabel', built in Stafford in 1897 (operates Sundays and bank holidays) and diesel 'Gordon' (operates Saturdays). Several others are on display and used on permanent way duties. The ex-Great Northern Railway wooden waiting room from Stowe-by-Chartley station is now a museum.

Apedale Valley Light Railway

Apedale Community Country Park, Nr Newcastle-under-Lyme, Staffordshire ST5 7LB

TEL 0845 094 1953
WEBSITE www.avlr.org.uk
ROUTE Within country park
LENGTH ¼ mile | **GAUGE** 2ft
OPEN Sat, Apr to Oct; selected Sun and Bank Holidays, Apr to Oct; Santa Specials in Dec

FORMERLY KNOWN AS THE Moseley Railway Museum, which was founded in 1969 as a Moseley Hall Grammar School project when the gauge was 1ft 8in (it was

Above The collection of narrow gauge industrial locos and rolling stock from Moseley Hall Grammar School has recently relocated to the Apedale Community Country Park in Staffordshire.

converted to 2ft by 1978). Now relocated to Apedale Community Country Park north of Newcastle-under-Lyme, the museum of the Moseley Railway Trust houses a large collection of industrial narrow gauge railway equipment, including 40 internal combustion locomotives and nearly 100 pieces of rolling stock. The majority of the locos, most in running order, are either diesel or petrol and include unusual examples dating back to the 1920s and rare First World War examples. They include those from most major British manufacturers, including Ruston & Hornsby, Motor Rail and Hunslet. The large rolling stock collection of industrial wagons includes 'V' skips, bomb wagons, peat wagons and mine wagons.

Since 2006, the Trust has been building a new railway at Apedale which will eventually run for one mile through the Country Park from Apedale Heritage Centre to Miry Arena.

Avonvale Miniature Railway

Dunnington Heath Farm, Alcester, Warwickshire B49 5PD

TEL 01527 543350 or 01386 831782
WEBSITE www.hillers.co.uk
ROUTE Within grounds of farm shop
LENGTH c.600yds | **GAUGES** 5in and 7¼in
OPEN Two weekends each month, Apr to Sep; selected Bank Holidays

DESIGNED, BUILT AND OPERATED by the Avonvale Model Engineering Society, this ground-level, dual gauge miniature railway operates both steam and diesel locomotives. The continuous line features a signalbox, station, tunnels, bridges and gradients. A wide variety of members' locomotives can be seen in action on operating days.

Barrow Hill Roundhouse Railway Centre

Campbell Drive, Barrow Hill, Staveley, Chesterfield, Derbyshire S43 2PR

TEL 01246 472450
WEBSITE www.barrowhill.org
OPEN Weekends throughout the year;
  see website for special events

OPENED BY THE MIDLAND Railway next to Staveley Ironworks in 1870, Barrow Hill is the last surviving operational roundhouse engine shed in Britain. It features 24 roads, each between 60ft and 80ft long, and was in continuous use for 121 years until it closed in 1991. In the same year, the Barrow Hill Engine Shed Society persuaded the local council to give the building a Grade 2 Listed Building Status to prevent demolition. Following years of neglect and vandalism, the historic building was eventually purchased by Chesterfield Borough Council from the British Rail Property Board in 1996. Since then the building has been completely restored, opening its doors to the public for the first time in 1998. With physical links to the national rail network, the Roundhouse is now home to a wide range of preserved steam, diesel and electric locomotives, and is frequently visited by main-line railtours and heritage steam locomotives. Steam and diesel trains also operate within the site. The Deltic Preservation Society (see www.thedps.co.uk) has recently built a maintenance depot and museum next to the Roundhouse.

Above and below A line-up of classic London & North Eastern Railway steam locomotives at Barrow Hill Roundhouse (above) and a nostalgic scene inside the former Midland Railway roundhouse (below).

Above An industrial steam locomotive hauls a short demonstration goods train on the Battlefield Line in Leicestershire.

Battlefield Line Railway

Shackerstone Railway Station, Shackerstone, Leicestershire CV13 6NW

TEL 01827 880754
WEBSITE www.battlefield-line-railway.co.uk
ROUTE Shackerstone to Shenton
LENGTH 4¾ miles | **GAUGE** Standard
OPEN Weekends, Easter to Oct; Wed afternoons, Jul and Aug; Christmas Specials in Dec

THE BATTLEFIELD LINE, NAMED after the nearby site of the Battle of Bosworth (1485), is situated on the old LNW & Midland Joint Railway line between Nuneaton and Coalville. It opened in 1873, closed to passengers in 1931 and was finally closed by British Railways in 1968. A preservation group took over in 1969 and has since extended the operating line from Market Bosworth to Shenton. A large collection of diesel multiple units and industrial steam and diesel locomotives are used on this typical English rural railway, running through delightful countryside alongside the Ashby Canal, which originally opened in 1804.

Operational steam locomotives include ex-LNER Class 'B1' 4-6-0 No. 1306 'Mayflower', while a large number of main-line diesels can also be seen in action here. Three industrial steam locos are currently being restored. Various ex-BR preserved steam locomotives also visit the line. The 'Tudor Rose' dining train runs on the third Sunday of each month and the Bosworth Battlefield Country Park can be reached on foot from Shenton station, this building being originally situated at Leicester Humberstone Road.

Birmingham Railway Museum

670 Warwick Road, Tyseley, Birmingham B11 2HL

TEL 0121 708 4960
WEBSITES www.shakespeareexpress.com and
   www.tyseleylocoworks.co.uk
OPEN Selected open days (see website for details)
STATION National rail network station Tyseley

OWNED AND OPERATED BY the Birmingham Railway Museum Trust, this large collection of engines and rolling stock is based in the former Great Western Railway repair shop at Tyseley. The site is fully equipped for locomotive preservation and overhaul, and is home to seven GWR locomotives, including three 'Castles' and a 'Hall', an LMS 'Jubilee' and various diesel and industrial locos. A varied collection of rolling stock includes a travelling post office and a steam crane. The museum also arranges driving and firing lessons on steam locomotives, which operate along the 600yds of track within the site. Open Days feature train rides, locomotive line-ups, demonstrations with locomotive cavalcades, turntable operation and shunting. Vintage Trains (see page 248) also operate out of Tyseley, with tours such as steam-hauled 'Shakespeare Express' to Stratford-upon-Avon.

Above and below A GWR night-time line-up of 0-6-0PT No. 9600 and 4-6-0 No. 4003 'Lode Star' (above) and former GWR locomotives around the turntable at the Birmingham Railway Museum (below).

Black Country Living Museum

Tipton Road, Dudley,
West Midlands DY1 4SQ

TEL 0121 557 9643
WEBSITE www.bclm.co.uk
OPEN Daily throughout the year

Above Using restored tramcars, a 3ft 6in-gauge electric tramway links the numerous attractions.

THIS OPEN AIR MUSEUM, situated next to the northern end of the Dudley Canal Tunnel, is devoted to exhibits from the age of the industrial revolution in this part of the Midlands, commonly known as 'The Black Country'. The 26-acre site contains 50 authentic shops, canal boats, a boatyard, bakery, 19th-century houses, a chainmaking shop, a colliery steam winding engine, a working replica of the 1712 Newcomen pumping engine and an underground mining exhibition. All of these attractions can be visited in a restored 1920s tramcar which travels on a 3ft 6in-gauge electric tramway that runs across the site. The Albion Tram Depot is based on Handsworth Tram Depot, built in the 1880s, while the trams include Dudley & Stourbridge single deck No. 5 and Wolverhampton & Dudley Tramway's No. 19.

Brookside Miniature Railway

Brookside Garden Centre,
London Road North, Poynton,
Cheshire SK12 1BY

WEBSITE www.brooksideminiaturerailway.co.uk
ROUTE Within grounds of garden centre
LENGTH ½ mile | GAUGE 7¼in
OPEN Weekends throughout the year; Wed,
    Apr to Sep; daily, Jul and Aug

DEVELOPED FROM A 5IN-GAUGE line built in 1972, this miniature railway was rebuilt to its present gauge in 1989. A steady acquisition of redundant railway artefacts makes for an interesting display. Trains depart from a four-platform station, Brookside Central, complete with turntables. They run over river bridges and climb steadily through woodland and a 65ft tunnel to the summit of the line, before returning via the same route. Four steam locomotives and five diesels operate trains, which are made up from ten sit-astride coaches and four Pullman covered coaches. Signalling operations are controlled from a full-size Midland Railway signalbox (originally situated at Southport Aughton Road). A museum of railway artefacts is housed in a re-created GWR waiting room.

Below Brookside Miniature Railway features a large terminus station, signalbox and museum.

Cambrian Heritage Railways

Cambrian Visitor Centre, Oswald Road,
Oswestry, Shropshire SY11 IRE

TEL 01691 688763
WEBSITES www.cambrianrailways.com and
  www.cambrianrailwayssociety.co.uk
ROUTE Oswestry station; Llynclys South
  to Penygarreg Lane
LENGTH 1 mile | GAUGE Standard
OPEN Weekends and Bank Holidays,
  Apr to Oct; Santa Specials in Dec

CAMBRIAN HERITAGE RAILWAYS is the
umbrella banner for the Cambrian Railways
Society and the Cambrian Railways Trust.
The former has plans to reopen the ex-CR
Tanat Valley line from Blodwell to Llynclys
Junction; the latter plans to reopen the ex-
CR line from Oswestry to Llynclys, where
the two railways will link up. The purchase
of the mothballed track from Gobowen
to Blodwell Quarry, via Oswestry, by
Shropshire County Council was completed
in 2008, thus paving the way for the eventual
reopening of the line. At Oswestry, the
Cambrian Railways Trust's railway museum
and depot were once part of a major railway
complex in the town that, until takeover
by the GWR in 1922, was the headquarters
of the Cambrian Railways. As late as the
1960s, Oswestry was the headquarters for
the Central Wales Division of BR Western
Region and the workshops were one of the
last locations to undertake steam locomotive
repairs. On display in the old railway
building are artefacts from the Cambrian
Railways, with some arranged in a former
GWR autocar.

Trains currently operate at weekends
from two separate locations at Oswestry
station and for ¾ mile from Llynclys South
station to Penygarreg Lane. See both websites
(above) for further details.

Castle Hill Railway

6A Castle Terrace, Bridgnorth,
Shropshire WV16 4AH

TEL 01746 762052
WEBSITE www.bridgnorthcliffrailway.co.uk
ROUTE High Town to Low Town
LENGTH 201ft | GAUGE 3ft 8½in
OPEN Daily throughout the year
STATION Heritage railway station Bridgnorth

ORIGINALLY OPERATED WITH A water-
balance system, this funicular railway
opened in 1892. As with the Lynton &
Lynmouth Cliff Railway (see page 19), it was
the brainchild of millionaire publisher Sir
George Newnes. Visitors are carried a height
of 111ft in a cutting in sandstone cliffs, on
a gradient of 1 in 1.81. The water-balance
system was replaced by an electric-powered
winding mechanism in 1944 and the two
passenger carriages replaced in 1955 by the
present 'streamlined' versions that resemble
shortened road motor coach bodies.

Cattle Country Miniature Railway

Cattle Country Adventure Park,
Berkeley Heath Farm, Berkeley,
Gloucestershire GL13 9EW

TEL 01453 810510
WEBSITE www.cattlecountry.co.uk
ROUTE Within adventure park
LENGTH 1 mile | GAUGE 10¼in
OPEN Daily during school holidays and Bank
  Holidays, Feb to Oct; Sun, Mar and Dec

OPENED IN 2005, THIS miniature railway
takes visitors on a journey around Cattle
Country Adventure Park and to the
Animal Encounters area. A diesel hydraulic
locomotive provides motive power.

Above A demonstration goods train on the Chasewater Light Railway.

Chasewater Light Railway & Museum

Chasewater Country Park, Pool Road, Nr Brownhills, Staffordshire WS8 7NL

TEL 01543 452623
WEBSITE www.chasewaterrailway.co.uk
ROUTE Chasetown (Church Street) to Brownhills West
LENGTH 2 miles | **GAUGE** Standard
OPEN Sun, Feb to Nov; Sat, Apr to Oct; Tue and Thu, Aug

THE CHASEWATER LIGHT RAILWAY is situated on part of the old Midland Railway's Brownhills branch line, a colliery line north of Birmingham, which was opened in 1883 and closed by the London Midland and Scottish Railway in 1930. One of the earliest preservation projects, founded in 1959 as a static museum run by the Railway Preservation Society, it had its first steam day in 1968 and was represented at the Stockton & Darlington Railway 150th anniversary celebrations in 1975. However, by 1982 the line had almost closed and it was not until 1988 that it reopened with a new terminus at Brownhills West. A short extension was opened in 1992, with a further one in December 1995 which took the railway over the causeway in Chasewater Pleasure Park. Since then the line has been extended to a new easterly terminus at Chasetown (Church Street). Passenger services on the line are handled by a BR diesel multiple unit and the railway is home to a large collection of steam and diesel industrial locomotives. A 2ft narrow gauge railway is being built close to the museum at Brownhills West.

Churnet Valley Railway

Kingsley & Froghall Station, Froghall, Staffordshire ST10 2HA

TEL 01538 750755
WEBSITE www.churnet-valley-railway.co.uk
ROUTE Leekbrook Junction to Kingsley & Froghall
LENGTH 5¼ miles | **GAUGE** Standard
OPEN Sun, Mar to early Oct; weekends and Bank
  Holidays, Easter to end Sep; Wed, Aug; see
  website for special events

THE NORTH STAFFORDSHIRE RAILWAY, locally nicknamed the 'Knotty', was one of the most successful and independent pre-grouping railway companies in Britain. While the majority of its lines served the industrialised Potteries region, a few were also famed for their scenic beauty. One of these was the double-track Churnet Valley line, which opened between North Rode and Uttoxeter in 1849. Promoted heavily by the NSR for tourism, the line survived until 1960, when through passenger services ceased between Macclesfield and Uttoxeter. A workman's service continued to run between Leek and Uttoxeter until 1965. However, the by-then single-line section from Oakamoor northwards to Leekbrook Junction (and thence to Stoke) stayed open for industrial sand traffic until 1988.

Meanwhile, the Cheddleton Railway Centre was opened by a group of preservationists in 1973, who restored the ornate station building at Cheddleton, installed a museum and gave steam train rides along the short length of track. In 1994 the Society signed a contract to purchase the seven miles of redundant trackbed between Oakamoor and Leekbrook Junction, and launched a share issue in 1995 to raise capital for the reopening of the line. Since then the railway has opened between Leekbrook Junction (no public access) to Kingsley & Froghall, via Cheddleton and Consall stations. The line south of Kingsley

to Oakamoor has also been reopened but there is currently no station here. Locomotives based at Cheddleton include former Eastleigh-built Stanier Class 8F 2-8-0 No. 8624, BR Standard 9F 2-10-0 No. 92134 and several main line diesels and DMUs. Future plans include a northward extension to Leek and southwards to Alton Towers. The recently opened Moorland & City Railway (see page 114) extends certain train journeys from the Churnet Valley Railway to Cauldon Low and runs via Leekbrook Junction.

Opposite An ex-LMS 'Jinty' 0-6-0T crosses the Caldon Canal near Consall, on the Churnet Valley Railway in Staffordshire.

Above & below Ex-GWR 2-6-2Ts No. 5542 and No. 5199 make a fine sight as they double-head a heavily laden train on the Churnet Valley Railway.

Coalyard Miniature Railway

Severn Valley Railway Station,
Comberton Hill, Kidderminster,
Worcestershire DY10 1QX

TEL 01562 827232 (Kidderminster SVR station)
ROUTE Parallel to Severn Valley Railway at
    Kidderminster station
LENGTH 500yds | **GAUGE** 7¼in
OPEN Weekends and Bank Holidays throughout
    the year
STATION Heritage railway and national rail
    network station Kidderminster

FIRST OPENED AS A dual gauge miniature
railway in 1988, the Coalyard Railway runs
alongside the Severn Valley Railway's main
line (see page 120), through the site of a
former coal yard. Trains are normally hauled
by petrol or battery locomotives, although
steam is also in action on selected dates.

Crewe Heritage Centre

Vernon Way, Crewe,
Cheshire CW1 2DB

TEL 01270 212130
WEBSITE www.creweheritagecentre.co.uk
OPEN Weekends, Easter to end Sep
STATION National rail network station Crewe

THIS STANDARD GAUGE RAILWAY restoration
centre, opened in 1987 as Crewe Railway Age,
adjacent to the West Coast Main Line near
Crewe station, houses a changing collection
of mainly ex-BR main-line steam, diesel and
electric locomotives. At any given time, a
varied selection of privately owned heritage
steam locomotives can be seen at the centre
while awaiting repairs or restoration, or

Above 0-4-0ST 'Mae' waits at Kidderminster
station on the Coalyard Miniature Railway.
Below The interior of the former GWR Exeter
West signalbox, preserved at Crewe.

being serviced in between main-line steam
tours. Passenger rides are given at weekends
in steam-hauled brakevans over the 300yds
of track within the site. Steam locomotives
are also stabled here when working special
trains to the North Wales coast. In addition,
there are three working signalboxes (Exeter
West, Crewe Station A and Crewe North
Junction), a collection of railway artefacts,
model railways and a 600yd, passenger-
carrying, 7¼in-gauge miniature railway.
The centre is also the main operating base
of the 6201 Princess Elizabeth Society (see
www.6201.co.uk for further details).

Dean Forest Railway

Norchard Railway Centre, Forest Road, Lydney, Gloucestershire GL15 4ET

TEL 01594 845840
WEBSITE www.deanforestrailway.co.uk
ROUTE Lydney Junction to Parkend
LENGTH 4¼ miles | **GAUGE** Standard
OPEN Most Sun and Bank Holidays, mid-Feb
  to Dec; most Wed and Sat, Easter to Oct
STATION National rail network station Lydney

THE FOREST OF DEAN had been an important source of iron ore and coal since medieval times. Railways, in the form of horsedrawn tramways, came early to the area, transporting raw materials down to the River Severn. By far the biggest of these operations was the Severn & Wye Railway & Canal Company, which opened in 1813 and eventually linked the Wye at Redbrook with the Severn at Lydney. In 1869, the tramway from Lydney to Speech House Road was reopened as a broad gauge line using steam haulage. Within five years it had been relaid to standard gauge and extended northwards

Below Ex-GWR 0-6-0PT No. 9681, with a Lydney to Parkend train on the Dean Forest Railway.

to Lydbrook Junction and south to Lydney Harbour. The opening of the Severn Bridge in 1879 also provided an important link between the Forest of Dean and the Midland Railway's mainline at Berkeley Road.

After the First World War, the decline of coal mining in the forest soon led to railway closures. The passenger service from Lydney Town to Coleford, Cinderford and Lydbrook Junction was axed in 1929 but, despite this, part of the line north from Lydney stayed open for goods until 1976.

A preservation society first set up its base at Norchard, north of Lydney, in 1978, having been running steam open days at Parkend since 1972. The scenic railway from Lydney to Parkend was purchased from BR in 1985 and has been progressively reopened. Restored steam locomotives operating on the line include GWR 0-4-2 tank No. 1450, GWR 2-6-2 tank No. 5541 and BR 0-6-0 pannier tank No. 9681. A new station at Whitecroft is under construction, while future plans include extending the line northwards.

Eaton Hall Railway

Eaton Estate Office, Eccleston, Chester CH4 9ET

TEL 01244 684400
WEBSITE www.eatonestate.co.uk
ROUTE Loop within grounds of Eaton Hall
LENGTH c.1 mile | **GAUGE** 15in
OPEN Only during Garden Open Days

THE 1ST DUKE OF Westminster commissioned Sir Arthur Heywood to build a working 15in-gauge railway on his estate at Eaton Hall in 1895. Linking with the GWR main line at Balderton, the 4½-mile 'minimum railway' transported coal and stores to various parts of the estate, as well as providing a passenger service for visitors. The railway was dismantled in 1947 but reinstated in 1996, using a replica of the first steam loco ('Katie') to work on the line.

Ecclesbourne Valley Railway

Wirksworth Station, Coldwell Street, Wirksworth, Derbyshire DE4 4FB

TEL 01629 823076
WEBSITE www.e-v-r.com
ROUTE Wirksworth to Duffield and Wirksworth to Ravenstor
LENGTH 10 miles | **GAUGE** Standard
OPEN Weekends and Bank Holidays, Apr to Oct; Tue, Jun to Sep; Sat, Mar and Nov; Santa Specials
STATION National rail network station Duffield

Above Single car diesel unit 'Iris' leaves the tiny platform at Ravenstor.

ORIGINALLY SEEN AS PART of ana independent railway route to the north, the branch line from Duffield (a junction on the Midland Railway's main line north of Derby) to Wirksworth was opened by the Midland Railway in 1867. Bridges on the line were built to accommodate double tracks but, in the event, this never materialised. Following the Second World War, increasing competition from buses led to the suspension of passenger services in 1947 – they were never reinstated. Despite the loss of passenger services, the branch occasionally witnessed brand new lightweight diesel

multiple units from Derby Works being tested in the early 1950s. The line remained open for limestone traffic from Middlepeak Quarry until 1989, thereafter the trackbed and rusting rails were overtaken by nature.

In 1996 the community-owned and locally managed company, Wyvern Rail, was awarded a Light Railway Order for the entire line. Trains started operating the short distance from Wirksworth to Gorsey Bank in 2004, with the steeply graded mineral line to Ravenstor opening a year later. In 2005 Wyvern Rail purchased the entire railway and adopted Duffield station, the junction with the national rail network. The entire line was reopened in 2010 and now tourist passenger services along the scenic branch are operated by restored diesel multiple units. Steam haulage features on special event days. The steeply graded line from Wirksworth to Ravenstor (for the High Peak Trail) is worked separately from the 'main line'.

Echills Wood Railway

Kingsbury Water Park, Bodymoor Heath Road, Sutton Coldfield, West Midlands B76 0DY

WEBSITE www.ewr.org.uk
ROUTE Within grounds of Kingsbury Water Park
LENGTH 1¼ miles | **GAUGE** 7¼in
OPEN Sun and Bank Holiday weekends, Easter to Sep; Wed and Fri during school holidays

UNTIL 2004 THE ECHILLS Wood Railway was one of the permanent attractions of the National Agricultural Centre, home of the Royal Show. It was established in 1972 at the invitation of the NAC and was owned and operated by a group of local enthusiasts. The railway consisted of a staggered platform terminus, Harvesters. From here a single line led to Echills Wood, where there was a circuit which doubled as a return loop. The line operated a comprehensive electro-mechanical signalling system, correctly interlocked, with a single-line token for the section between Harvesters and Echills Wood. The railway's own passenger stock consists of purpose-built bogie vehicles equipped with automatic vacuum brake.

The railway relocated to Kingsbury Water Park in 2005 and a full service resumed in 2011. The new line now features a ride from Harvesters station to Far Leys station, via a twin bore 70yds tunnel. Locomotives are owned by members and are mainly narrow gauge steam prototypes – star of the show in 2011 was the largest 7¼in-gauge locomotive running in the UK; East African Railways 4-8-2+2-8-4 Garratt, 'Mount Kilimanjaro'.

Electric Railway Museum

Rowley Road, Baginton, Coventry, Warwickshire **CV3 4LE**

TEL 02476 997397
WEBSITE www.electricrailwaymuseum.co.uk
OPEN Open day events only (see website)

ALTHOUGH MORE PASSENGER JOURNEYS are made today by electric traction than any other method, this is the only museum in Britain dedicated to this form of rail traction. The large collection ranges from industrial electric locomotives and suburban multiple units to underground train coaches and the Advanced Passenger Train. The oldest exhibits include two City & South London Railway trailer cars dating from the early 20th century, 1928-built Hawthorn Leslie Bo-Bo electric locomotive that once worked at Kearsley Power Station in Lancashire, 1937-built LMS Class 503 'Wirral' multiple unit that once worked through the Mersey Tunnel and a 1954-built Class 416/2 Tyneside EPB multiple unit. In contrast, historic Class 370 electric unit No. 49006 from the ill-fated Advanced Passenger Train is on loan from the National Railway Museum.

Evesham Vale Light Railway

Evesham Country Park, Twyford, Evesham, Worcestershire **WR11 4TP**

TEL 01386 422282
WEBSITE www.evlr.co.uk
ROUTE Within country park
LENGTH 1 mile | **GAUGE** 15in
OPEN Weekends throughout the year;
    daily during school holidays

Above A locomotive line-up featuring two historic 'Atlantic' 4-4-2s from the 1920s.

FIRST OPENED IN 2002, this steam-hauled railway takes visitors on a scenic journey through old apple orchards and around a country park, stopping briefly at Evesham Vale station, close to the River Avon. Of interest to miniature railway enthusiasts is the steam locomotive line-up, which includes two historic 'Atlantic' 4-4-2 locos: No. 32 'Count Louis' was built by Bassett-Lowke for Count Louis Zborowski (see Romney Hythe & Dymchurch Railway, page 72) in 1924 and was used on the Fairbourne Railway (see page 160) until 1985; No. 103 'John' was built by Albert Barnes for the Rhyl Miniature Railway (see page 171) in 1921. Rolling stock features bogie coaches from the Fairbourne Railway and from a French 15in gauge railway in Brittany.

Above Bagnall 1954-built 0-6-0ST 'Florence No. 2' carries out some shunting on the Foxfield Railway, Stoke-on-Trent.

Foxfield Railway

Caverswall Road Station, Blythe Bridge, Stoke-on-Trent, Staffs ST11 9BG

TEL 01782 259667 or 01782 396210
WEBSITE www.foxfieldrailway.co.uk
ROUTE Blythe Bridge to Dilhorne Park
LENGTH 2½ miles | **GAUGE** Standard
OPEN Weekends and Bank Holidays, Apr
  to Oct and Dec; Wed, mid-July to end Aug
STATION National rail network station
  Blythe Bridge

OPERATING ON AN OLD colliery line, opened in 1893 and closed in 1965, the Foxfield Railway is situated very close to Blythe Bridge station on the main Stoke-on-Trent to Derby railway line. After closure, a preservation group took over and passengers were first carried in 1967, with Caverswall Road Station being opened in 1982. Small and powerful industrial steam and diesel locomotives haul trains up fearsome gradients to a summit 705ft above sea level. The large collection of locomotives includes 15 steam, 12 diesel and two battery electric engines. Future plans include opening both ends of the railway to passenger operation, including the 1 in 19 Dilhorne Bank, and creating a mining museum at the old colliery.

Gloucestershire Warwickshire Railway

See page 104

Great Central Railway

See page 106

Great Central Railway (Nottingham)

Ruddington Station, Mere Way, Ruddington, Nottingham NG11 6JS

TEL 0115 940 5705
WEBSITE www.gcrn.co.uk
ROUTE Ruddington to Loughborough
LENGTH 10 miles | **GAUGE** Standard
OPEN Most weekends and Bank Holidays, April to Oct; Santa Specials in Dec

---

FOLLOWING CLOSURE OF THE Great Central main line in 1966, a short section from Nottingham southwards to a Ministry of Defence ordnance depot at Ruddington was kept open until the early 1980s. On closure of the depot, the railway was reopened by a group of enthusiasts and now operates passenger trains between Ruddington and East Leake on most weekends during the year. Trains are normally operated by diesel multiple units, although the railway is also home to a large number of restored main line diesels and a collection of industrial steam locomotives. A few trains continue on to Loughborough but there are currently no facilities to leave or join the train here. Regular freight trains carrying gypsum still use this line between Loughborough and East Leake, making the Great Central Railway (Nottingham) one of few British heritage lines to support freight traffic. A long-term goal of the railway is to reconnect the two Great Central heritage railways, by reinstating a bridge at Loughborough to enable trains to run between Leicester North and the outskirts of Nottingham once more.

Below Headed by former GCR (LNER Class '04') 2-8-0 No. 63601, a breakdown train makes its way along the Great Central Railway (Nottingham).

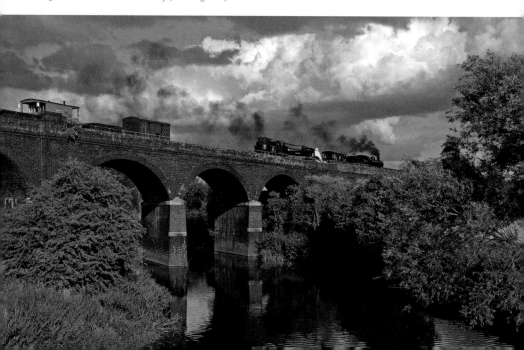

Above Ex-GWR 0-4-2T No. 1450 pulls and pushes its train of auto coaches.

Right Ex-GWR 2-6-0 No. 5322 hauls its train along the Gloucestershire Warwickshire Railway.

Gloucestershire Warwickshire Railway

The Railway Station, Toddington, Gloucestershire GL54 5DT

TEL 01242 621405

WEBSITE www.gwsr.com

ROUTE Toddington to Laverton and Toddington to Cheltenham Racecourse

LENGTH 12 miles | **GAUGE** Standard

OPEN Weekends and Bank Holidays, Apr to Nov; Tue to Thu, Apr to Oct; Santa Specials in Dec

NOTE Landslips, at Gotherington and Chicken Curve, effectively cut the railway in two in 2010. The line at Gotherington has since reopened but that at Chicken Curve still needs very expensive remedial work. See website for train services.

THE NORTH-SOUTH RAILWAY BETWEEN Stratford-upon-Avon and Cheltenham was a very belated attempt by the Great Western Railway to win back traffic from the Midland Railway's route between Birmingham and Bristol. Opened throughout in 1908, it was one of the last stretches of double-track main line to be built in Britain until the Selby cut-off on the East Coast Main Line in 1983. During the 1930s, the line was used by the highly successful GWR's streamlined diesel railcar express between Birmingham and Cardiff. After the Second World War, the route saw the introduction of the 'Cornishman' express from Wolverhampton (LL) to Penzance and iron ore trains bound for South Wales from the Northamptonshire open cast mines. Summer Saturdays also saw a continual stream of steam-hauled holiday specials – a veritable feast for railway photographers during the last year of steam in 1965. Decline soon followed, with the remaining spartan passenger service ceasing in 1966, leaving only freight traffic until 1976 when a derailment north of Cheltenham

brought about complete closure between Stratford and Cheltenham. The double track had been lifted by 1979.

A preservation group moved into Toddington in 1984 and has since relaid the line southwards to Cheltenham Racecourse, and northwards to Laverton. Trains currently run from Toddington to Cheltenham Racecourse with intermediate stations at Winchcombe (originally the station building at Monmouth Troy) and Gotherington, via the 693yd Greet Tunnel. The railway is currently extending its route northwards to Broadway and Honeybourne, with trains currently terminating (no access) at the site of Laverton Halt. Motive power is drawn from a fleet of GWR steam and BR diesel locomotives, while visiting main-line locomotives are a common sight on the railway. A journey along the line takes passengers through the picturesque North Gloucestershire countryside with fine views of the Cotswold escarpment, past Hailes Abbey to the beautifully restored station at Winchcombe (for the Winchcombe Railway Museum, see page 125), and then through the Greet Tunnel to the terminus at Cheltenham Racecourse. A long-term goal of the railway is to extend northward to Honeybourne to provide connection with the national rail network.

The narrow gauge North Gloucestershire Railway (see page 115) operates adjacent to the GWR station site at Toddington.

Great Central Railway

**Great Central Station, Great Central Road,
Loughborough, Leicestershire LE11 1RW**

TEL 01509 632323
WEBSITE www.gcrailway.co.uk
ROUTE Loughborough Central to Leicester North
LENGTH 8 miles | **GAUGE** Standard
OPEN Weekends throughout the year; see website
   for other selected days and special events
STATION National rail network station
   Loughborough

BRITAIN'S LAST MAIN LINE, the London Extension of the Great Central Railway, was opened in 1899 and linked Manchester, Sheffield and Nottingham with Marylebone station in London. Designed for fast traffic with a continental loading gauge and no level crossings, the railway never fulfilled its promoter's dreams of linking up with continental Europe via a Channel Tunnel. Despite, this the route became a highly important artery for heavy freight traffic; in particular, coal via the Woodford Halse to Banbury link. Passenger traffic never really took off due to the railway's duplication of two other existing routes (Midland Railway and Great Northern Railway) from the East Midlands and the North to London. Because of this duplication, the line was listed for closure in the 1963 'Beeching Report'. However, the rot had already set in during 1960, when the London Midland Region took over responsibility and passenger services were seriously downgraded. The end for Marylebone to Nottingham trains came in 1966, although the section from Rugby Central to Nottingham remained open for passengers until 1969.

Following closure of the Great Central, the section from Loughborough to Quorn &

Below Ex-LNWR 'Super D' Class 0-8-0 No. 49395 passes Rothley station on the Great Central Railway with a southbound goods train.

Woodhouse was reopened by the Main Line Steam Trust in 1973, to Rothley in 1976 and finally to a new station at Leicester North in 1991. Uniquely among heritage lines, it is double-track from Loughborough to Rothley, so that the railway can operate with the appearance of a main line. A very large collection of impressive main line preserved steam and diesel locomotives is based on the GCR to provide a variety of train operations, and visiting engines can frequently be seen in action. A restored Travelling Post Office train, complete with mail bag exchanger, is occasionally demonstrated on the railway. Stations have been restored to different periods in the railway's history; Loughborough is typical of the 1960s, Quorn & Woodhouse recreates the 1940s and Rothley captures the Edwardian era. Passengers are conveyed in traditional main-line style through delightful Leicestershire hunting countryside. Volunteers are

Above Former GCR (LNER Class '04') 2-8-0 No. 63601 hard at work on its old stamping ground.

currently relaying the one-mile former industrial branch line from Swithland Sidings to Mount Sorrel with the long-term aim of running branch line passenger trains.

Below British Railways 'Britannia' Class 4-6-2 No. 70013 'Oliver Cromwell' makes its way north to Loughborough with an evening train.

Above Housed in the former goods shed, the GWR Museum at Coleford also features the restored signalbox from Cogload Junction, near Taunton.

Great Western Railway Museum

The Old Railway Station, Railway Drive, Coleford, Gloucestershire GL16 8RH

TEL 01594 833569

WEBSITE www.colefordgwr.150m.com/aboutus

OPEN Fri, Sat and Bank Holidays throughout the year; afternoons only

THE GREAT WESTERN RAILWAY Museum is housed in one of the last remaining railway buildings at the end of the Monmouth to Coleford branch line, which opened in 1883 and closed to passengers in 1916 and goods

in 1967. The former GWR signalbox from Cogload Junction (near Taunton), complete with working lever-frame, has been restored on the site. Exhibits, contained within the former GWR goods station, include Peckett 0-4-0 tank No. 1893, built in 1936 and restored to working order in 2005, a GWR fruit van from 1911 and a six-wheeled LMS Brake Coach. Also displayed is a large collection of photographs of local railways, the Victorian ticket office, station master's office, railway artefacts and railway models ranging from gauge '00' to 5in. A 7¼in-gauge miniature railway operates on the site and trains are worked by either 0-4-0 Bagnall saddle tank 'Victor' or battery electric, 'Little John'. Visiting locomotives are also a regular sight on the miniature railway.

Grosvenor Park Miniature Railway

Grosvenor Park Lodge,
Grosvenor Park Road,
Chester CH1 1QQ

TEL 07530 397079
WEBSITE www.gpmr.co.uk
ROUTE Around lake in Grosvenor Park
LENGTH ¼ mile | **GAUGE** 7¼in
OPEN Sun, Nov to Mar; weekends and Bank
Holidays, Apr to Oct; daily during school
holidays; Tue and Thu, May to Sep

OPENED IN 1996 TO celebrate the centenary
of the Duke of Westminster's railway at
nearby Eaton Hall (see page 99), this ground-
level, circular line takes visitors on a journey
around the lake in Grosvenor Park. Services
are operated by two steam locomotives,
0-4-0 'Brenda Isabella' and 0-4-2 'Thomas II',
and a petrol-driven diesel outline loco.

Hall Leys Park Miniature Railway

Hall Leys Park, Crown Square,
Matlock, Derbyshire DE4 3AT

TEL 01629 583388 (Matlock Tourist Information)
ROUTE Within park
LENGTH 200yds | **GAUGE** 9½in
OPEN Weekends and school holidays,
Easter to Sep

OPENED IN 1948, THIS unusually gauged
end-to-end line features haulage through
a Victorian public park, alongside the River
Derwent in the centre of Matlock. Motive
power is supplied by diesel hydraulic, 'Little
David'. A tram shelter for a cable tramway,
which closed in 1927, is also preserved in
the park.

Halton Miniature Railway

Town Park, Stockham Lane,
Palacefields, Runcorn,
Cheshire WA7 6PT

TEL 01928 574396
WEBSITE www.haltonminirail.weebly.com
ROUTE Within Town Park
LENGTH 1 mile | **GAUGE** 7¼in
OPEN Sun afternoons throughout the year;
see websites for details of limited Easter
Sunday service

THIS MINIATURE RAILWAY OPENED in
1979 and has been gradually extended
to its current extensive continuous layout
within Town Park. The railway owns
four locomotives, all petrol hydraulic,
including a 2-8-0 American-style steam
outline and a 'Hymek'-style diesel Bo-Bo.
Several steam events are held regularly
throughout the year.

High Legh Railway

High Legh Garden Centre,
Halliwells Brow, High Legh,
Cheshire WA16 0QW

TEL 07799 118968
WEBSITE www.cheshirerailways.co.uk/highlegh
ROUTE Within garden centre
LENGTH 400yds | **GAUGE** 7¼in
OPEN Weekends and Bank Holidays throughout
the year; daily during school holidays; Santa
Specials in Dec

OPENED IN 2007, THIS kidney-shaped,
ground-level miniature railway has a fleet
of three battery-electric and three petrol
locomotives that operate within High Legh
Garden Centre. A 0-4-0 Bagnall steam
locomotive operates on Sunday afternoons.

Hilcote Valley Railway

Fletchers Garden Centre,
Bridge Farm, Stone Road, Eccleshall,
Staffordshire ST21 6JY

TEL 01785 284553
WEBSITE www.freewebs.com/hilcotevalleyrailway
ROUTE Through garden centre and around lake
LENGTH 600yds | **GAUGE** 7¼in
OPEN Weekends and Bank Holidays, Easter to Nov;
daily during school hols; see website for events

THIS MINIATURE RAILWAY WAS designed and
built in 1993 by Roger Greatrex and includes
prototype equipment, such as a signalbox,
ticket office, raised platform, turntable,
tunnel, girder bridge and signal gantry. The
line runs around the garden centre, then
into the country at the rear, around a lake
and over a bridge before returning through
a tunnel back into the centre. The bridge is
a replica of one built by the Earl of Dudley's
ironworks in 1907 for J A Holder's miniature
railway at Broome Hall, near Stourbridge.
Motive power includes 0-6-0 Kerr Stuart
'Haig' class tender locomotive, 'Kashmir',
and a Bo-Bo GP40 Union Pacific diesel.

Below 'Lady Madcap' heads a train on the
picturesque Hilcote Valley Railway.

Hill's Miniature Railway

Hills Garden Centre, London Road,
Allostock, Knutsford, Cheshire WA16 9LU

TEL 01565 722567
WEBSITE www.cheshirerailways.co.uk/hills
ROUTE Within garden centre
LENGTH 600yds | **GAUGE** 7¼in
OPEN Weekends, Bank Holidays and school
holidays throughout the year

OPENED IN 2003 AND extended in 2005, this
ground-level miniature railway features two
loops that merge at award-winning Allostock
Junction station. In addition to the famous
station, the line features engine and carriage
sheds, signalbox, turntable and a tunnel.
Loco fleet currently comprises one battery
electric and two diesel outline locos.

Irchester Narrow Gauge Railway Museum

Irchester Country Park, Wellingborough,
Northants NN29 7DL

TEL 01604 675368 or 07955 274249
WEBSITE www.irchester.btinternet.co.uk
OPEN Sun throughout the year

THE MUSEUM IS HOME to industrial steam
and diesel narrow gauge locomotives, and
rolling stock, connected with the ironstone
industries of Northamptonshire and the
East Midlands. Run by the Irchester Narrow
Gauge Railway Trust, the museum has
a lifesize diorama of a working quarry.
Industrial locomotives operate over a 260yd
length of track in the country park on the
last Sunday of every month during summer.

Above The working replica of Richard Trevithick's 'Penydarren', at the Blists Hill site at Ironbridge.

Ironbridge Gorge Museum

The Wharfage, Ironbridge, Telford, Shropshire TF8 7AW

TEL 01952 435900 (Blists Hill 01952 601010)
WEBSITE www.ironbridge.org.uk
OPEN Daily, Easter to end Nov; see website for winter openings

A LARGE OPEN AIR museum, spread over six square miles, devoted to the Industrial Revolution and based near the famous Iron Bridge near Coalbrookdale. Now designated a World Heritage Site, the main museum site is at Blists Hill where exhibits include furnace blowing machines and the Hay inclined plane of the Shropshire Union Canal. Of interest to railway historians is the working replica of Trevithick's first steam railway locomotive, which was built by apprentices of GKN Sankey in Telford. The original locomotive ran on the Coalbrookdale company's 3ft-gauge plateway tracks. The replica weighs 4½ tons, with a top speed of 5mph, and runs on a 100ft-diameter track.

Kidderminster Railway Museum

Station Approach, Comberton Hill, Kidderminster, Worcestershire DY10 1QX

TEL 01562 825316
WEBSITE www.krm.org.uk
OPEN Most days throughout the year (see website)
STATION Heritage railway and national rail network station Kidderminster

A LARGE COLLECTION OF British railway ephemera and artefacts is housed in the beautifully restored former Great Western Railway warehouse, adjacent to the Severn Valley Railway station at Kidderminster. The vast range of railway artefacts includes station totems, signalling instruments, the booking office from Alvechurch station, destination boards, signals, signs and gas lamps, 5in-gauge miniature steam locomotives, platform ticket machines and signs, and a railway telephone exchange. The library also houses photographic and various other railway archive material, that is available for research. Special events are held throughout the year (see website).

Below Part of the Kidderminster Railway Museum's large collection of railway artefacts.

Leasowes Park Miniature Railway

Leasowes Park, Mucklow Hill,
Halesowen, Dudley,
West Midlands B62 8QF

TEL 01562 710614
ROUTE Along canal towpath
LENGTH 450yds | **GAUGE** 7¼in
OPEN Sun and Bank Holiday afternoons, all year

THIS MINIATURE RAILWAY HAS been operating since 1990 along the towpath of Dudley No. 2 Canal on the Birmingham Canal Navigations. The route starts in the car park and, after passing through woodland, arrives at the park lake. Motive power consists of 2-6-2 steam locomotive, 'Prince Edward', built in 1932, and petrol-engined diesel outline locomotive, 'William Shenstone', built in 1989.

Manor Park Miniature Railway

Manor Park Road, Glossop,
Derbyshire SK13 7HS

TEL 07779 601180
ROUTE Within park
LENGTH c.¼ mile | **GAUGE** 7¼in
OPEN Weekends and school holidays,
   Apr to Sep; afternoons

SET IN WHAT WERE the grounds of a former 16th century manor house owned by the Duke of Norfolk, this miniature railway, established in 1970, takes visitors for a ride through the park from the two-platform Manor terminus station. Motive power for the miniature railway is provided across the length of the route by two battery electric diesel outline locomotives.

Markeaton Park Light Railway

Markeaton Park, Derby DE22 4AA

WEBSITE www.markeaton-park-light-railway.
   webs.com
ROUTE Markeaton Station to Mundy Halt
LENGTH 1,400yds | **GAUGE** 15in
OPEN Weekends and school holidays throughout
   the year

OPENED IN 1989 AND extended to its present length in 1996, this end-to-end miniature railway runs around the perimeter of Markeaton Park, close to the remains of Markeaton Village. Previously steam-hauled, trains are now operated by 'Baby Deltic' diesel locomotive D5905 (originally from the Steamtown Miniature railway in Carnforth), with passengers carried in three attractive covered coaches, formerly of the Fairbourne Railway in Wales. A potential sale of the railway was cancelled in 2010. Outdoor model railway enthusiasts are recommended to visit the railway's website links to the Elmtree Line and the Elmside Light Railway.

Above British Railways Standard Class 5 4-6-0 No. 73129 catches the sunshine while crossing Butterley Reservoir at the Midland Railway Centre.

Midland Railway – Butterley

Butterley Station, Nr Ripley, Derbyshire DE5 3QZ

TEL 01773 570140 or 01773 747674
WEBSITE www.midlandrailwaycentre.co.uk
ROUTE Hammersmith to Ironville
LENGTH 3½ miles | **GAUGES** Mainline – Standard;
  narrow gauge–2ft; miniature – 3½in and 5in
OPEN Every weekend, Mar to Oct and Dec;
  every Wed, Apr to Oct; daily, Aug and most
  school holidays

THE MIDLAND RAILWAY – BUTTERLEY (formerly known as the Midland Railway Centre) is situated on part of the former Midland Railway line from Pye Bridge to Ambergate, opened in 1875 and closed by British Railways in 1968. Reopened by a preservation group in 1973, the first passenger trains ran in 1981. With its headquarters at Butterley, the centre, famous for its quality restoration work, occupies a 57-acre site and operates trains along a 3½-mile section of track, including crossing a viaduct over Butterley Reservoir. The centre is home to three registered charities, 39 specialist groups, four museums, a miniature railway and a narrow gauge railway. Locomotives, the majority privately owned, include 16 main-line steam, 18 main-line diesels, 12 diesel multiple units and 21 industrial. Over 100 items of rolling stock are also based here. The Matthew Kirtley Museum, in its large trainshed, contains a varied display of historic steam, diesel and electric locomotives. The standard gauge operating line is authentically signalled and boasts three fully restored Midland Railway signalboxes, originally from Kettering, Ais Gill and Kilby Bridge. The dual gauge (3½in and 5in) Butterley Park Miniature Railway operates on Sundays and Bank holidays from Easter to September. The 2ft-gauge Golden Valley Light Railway runs every weekend from mid-March to late October (see website for other operating days).

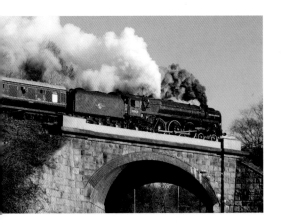

Above BR Standard Class 8 4-6-2 No. 71000 'Duke of Gloucester', on the Moorland & City Railways.

Moorland & City Railways

Office address – Innovation Centre 1, Science & Business Park, Keele University, Newcastle-under-Lyme, Staffordshire ST5 5NB

TEL 01782 621380
WEBSITE www.mcrailways.co.uk

THE RAILWAY FROM STOKE-ON-TRENT to Cauldon Low was opened by the North Staffordshire Railway in two stages from Stoke to Leekbrook Junction and Leek in 1849; from Leekbrook Junction to Waterhouses in 1905. A short branch near Waterhouses served quarries at Cauldon Low. Although passenger services were withdrawn from Leekbrook to Waterhouses in 1935 and from Stoke to Leek in 1956, most of the line remained in use for traffic from the Cauldon Low quarries until 1989.

Formed in 2009, the Moorland & City Railways was set up to buy, restore and return commercial rail traffic to the mothballed Stoke-on-Trent to Cauldon Low railway. This will create a private 30-mile rail network, with a direct connection to the national rail network at Stoke-on-Trent. Benefits will include direct access to stone quarries, Alton Towers Theme Park and the town of Leek, as well as expanding the operations of the Churnet Valley Railway (see page 96). The company purchased the route in 2009 and the eight miles from Leekbrook Junction to Cauldon Low reopened in November 2010, with tourist passenger trains being run in conjunction with the Churnet Valley Railway. Renovation of the remaining section from Stoke to Leekbrook Junction is already underway.

National Tramway Museum

Crich Tramway Village, Nr Matlock, Derbyshire DE4 5DP

TEL 01773 854321
WEBSITE www.tramway.co.uk
ROUTE Crich Town End to Glory Mine
LENGTH 1¼ miles | GAUGE Standard
OPEN Daily, Apr to Oct; weekends, Mar; see website for special events

LOCATED IN A FORMER LIMESTONE quarry, the museum houses Europe's largest collection of street trams, with over 60 examples of vintage electric, steam and horsedrawn examples, a third of which are regularly in passenger-carrying service at the museum. Included are examples from the UK, Prague, Portugal, South Africa and New York. The Tramway Museum Society was formed in 1955, and in 1959 acquired the site at Crich, which once contained a mineral railway built by George Stephenson in 1842. 1963 saw the first horsedrawn public service, and 1964 the first electric public service. A journey along the tramway takes passengers from Town End, through the museum's period street, under the Bowes-Lyon Bridge and into open countryside to the Glory Mine Terminus.

Northampton & Lamport Railway

Pitsford & Brampton Station, Pitsford Road, Chapel Brampton, Northampton NN6 8BA

TEL 01604 820327
WEBSITE www.nlr.org.uk
ROUTE Either side of Pitsford & Brampton station
LENGTH ¾ mile | **GAUGE** Standard
OPEN Bank Holiday weekends, all year; Sun, Mar
to Nov; Santa Specials in Dec

THE NORTHAMPTON TO MARKET Harborough branch was opened by the London & North Western Railway in 1859, and included six stations and two tunnels. It was first closed to passengers in April 1960 but reopened to through traffic in January 1961, closed again in May 1961 and then reopened a second time in July 1972. The passenger service was finally withdrawn in August 1973 and the line completely closed in August 1981.

A preservation society started around the same time as the line closure, moved once and changed its name twice, before finally becoming the Northampton & Lamport Railway. The railway presently extends for ¾ mile, with Pitsford & Brampton station roughly at the centre. The route shares the original track formation with the Brampton Valley Walk, a linear park operated by Northamptonshire County Council. The signalbox at Pitsford Ironstone exchange sidings is an example of a rare 10ft-square LNWR type, which was originally located at Wolverton Works. Another LNWR signalbox, originally from Little Bowden level crossing, controls the station site. The first public steam train operated in 1995 and a Light Railway Order has since been granted northwards to Spratton and south to Boughton Crossing, which will allow the railway to extend to approximately 3½ miles in length. In the more distant future it is hoped to extend to Lamport, giving a total run of seven miles. A good collection of both steam and diesel main-line and industrial locos is on site.

Below Ex-LMS 'Jinty' 0-6-0T No. 47298 waits to depart from Pitsford & Brampton station.

Northamptonshire Ironstone Railway Trust

Hunsbury Hill Country Park,
Hunsbury Hill Road West, Hunsbury,
Northamptonshire NN4 9UW

TEL 01604 702031
WEBSITE www.nirt.co.uk
ROUTE Museum Halt to Tunnel Halt
LENGTH 1¾ miles | **GAUGE** Standard
OPEN Selected weekends and Bank Holidays,
    Apr to Oct; Santa Specials in Dec

THE IRONWORKS AT HUNSBURY were built
in 1873, and to transport the iron ore from
the quarries to the ironworks a horsedrawn
gravity tramway was constructed in 1875. It
was built to a gauge of 3ft 8in and was one
of the earliest ironstone tramways in Britain.
Locomotive power was introduced in 1912
when the gravity system was replaced. The
ironworks closed in 1921 and the tramway
was dismantled in the late 1930s. The
Northamptonshire Ironstone Trust was
formed in 1974 and the present standard
gauge railway runs along part of the original
tramway trackbed. Passenger services started
in 1982 over a loop section, and in 1983

Below Hunslet 0-4-2T 'Chaka's Kraal No. 6',
on the North Gloucestershire Railway.

over the complete section. The main engine
shed and museum building were erected
in 1984 and house the museum display,
workshop and locomotive repair facilities. A
fine collection of Aveling Porter and Sentinel
steam locomotives, along with some former
industrial diesels, give brakevan rides along
a relaid ¼-mile section on operating days.

North Gloucestershire Railway

The Station, Toddington, Cheltenham,
Gloucestershire GL54 5DT

TEL 01452 539062
WEBSITE www.toddington-narrow-gauge.co.uk
ROUTE Toddington (NG) to Didbrook Loop
    (alongside Gloucestershire Warwickshire Railway
    line at Toddington (see page 104)
LENGTH ½ mile | **GAUGE** 2ft
OPEN Bank Holidays and selected weekends,
    Apr to Sep (see website)
STATION Heritage railway station Toddington

A STEAM-OPERATED narrow gauge line
within the station limits at Toddington and
alongside the Gloucestershire Warwickshire
Railway line but at a lower level. It was
formed in 1985 to replace the Dowty Railway
Preservation Society that was based at
Ashchurch from 1962, all stock being moved
to the present site in 1983. Train services
commenced in 1990 and the railway now
owns ten steam and diesel narrow gauge
locomotives, including examples from
Belgium, Poland and South Africa. Track
used on the line came from the Southend
Pier Railway (see page 148) and former
War Department railway installations.
Rolling stock includes a rare Polish covered
coach and three coaches constructed by the
company, using unsprung ex-WD wagon
frames. Also of interest are the signals, which
came from branch lines in and around
Gloucestershire, and the former Midland

Railway signalbox, built in 1920, which was previously situated at California Crossing in Gloucester. Future plans include a possible extension of the line to Didbrook Bridge.

Peak Rail

Matlock Station, Matlock, Derbyshire DE4 3NA

TEL 01629 580381
WEBSITE www.peakrail.co.uk
ROUTE Matlock to Rowsley South
LENGTH 5 miles | **GAUGE** Standard
OPEN Weekends, Apr to Oct; some weekdays during summer (telephone for details)
STATION National rail network station Matlock

THE FORMER MIDLAND RAILWAY main line from London St Pancras to Manchester Central was originally opened through the Peak District in 1849, and closed as a through route by BR between Matlock and Blackwell Mill (near Buxton) in 1968. It was 1975 before a preservation society took over the trackbed of this picturesque line through the heart of the Peak District National Park. Initially work was commenced at both Buxton and Matlock but this was later confined to the latter end, where the railway now makes an end-on connection with the national rail network. Steam and diesel passenger trains started running again to Darley Dale in 1991, with an extension to Rowsley opening in 1996. The last two years have seen significant progress on the railway; a 60ft turntable originally from Mold Junction shed became operational in 2010 and the railway was finally extended from Matlock Riverside station to the national rail network station at Matlock in 2011. Future plans include a further extension to Bakewell, which would involve restoration of a tunnel and viaduct.

There are several added attractions at Rowsley: owned by members of the Heritage Shunters Trust (website www.heritageshunters.co.uk), a large collection of diesel shunter locomotives is now housed in a new shed here; two Class 50 main-line diesels, 'Renown' and 'Repulse', are currently being restored; established in 1998, the Derbyshire Dales Narrow Gauge Railway runs along a short length of track adjacent to the picnic area.

Giving spectacular views of the Wye Valley and Monsal Dale from the top of Headstone Viaduct, the Monsal Trail footpath runs for 8½ miles along the trackbed of the line, from Topley Pike to a mile southeast of Bakewell.

Below Robert Stephenson & Hawthorns 0-6-0ST No. 7136, at Darley Dale station on Peak Rail.

Perrygrove Railway

Perrygrove Farm, Perrygrove Road,
Coleford, Gloucestershire GL16 8QB

TEL 01594 834991
WEBSITE www.perrygrove.co.uk
ROUTE Perrygrove to Oakiron (within
   Perrygrove Farm site)
LENGTH ¾ mile | **GAUGE** 15in
OPEN Daily during school holidays; weekends,
   mid-Feb to Oct; Bank Holidays

OPENED IN 1996, THIS steam-hauled
minimum gauge railway was inspired by
the estate railways built by Sir Arthur
Heywood at Duffield Bank and Eaton Hall
(see page 99) in the late 19th century. The
line features four stations, passing loops,
an engine shed and a museum dedicated
to Heywood's railways. Trains are normally
steam hauled from a line-up of three
locomotives: 0-6-0T 'Spirit of Adventure',
2-6-2T 'Lydia', and a reconstruction of
Duffield Bank Railway loco 0-6-0T 'Ursula'.
Perrygrove Farm also features picnic sites
and play facilities for children, as well as
a treasure hunt in the woodland.

Below 2-6-2T 'Lydia' heads a train of happy
visitors on the Perrygrove Railway.

Rudyard Lake Steam Railway

Rudyard Station, Rudyard,
Nr Leek, Staffordshire ST13 8PF

TEL 01538 306704 (station) and
   01995 672280 (office)
WEBSITE www.rlsr.org
ROUTE Rudyard to Hunthouse Wood
   alongside Rudyard Lake
LENGTH 1½ miles | **GAUGE** 10¼in
OPEN Every Sun except Dec; Sat, Apr to Oct;
   Wed, Jun to Sep; daily during school holidays

THE MINIATURE RAILWAY AT Rudyard lake
conveys passengers along a very scenic
part of the old standard gauge North
Staffordshire Railway's Churnet Valley line
beside Rudyard Lake, opened in 1849 and
closed by BR in 1962. The southern terminus
and headquarters are situated at the site of
the old NSR Rudyard station and consists
of a single platform, run-round loop and
four-road locomotive shed with turntable.
The northern terminus is at Hunthouse
Wood, one mile to the south of the former
NSR Rudyard Lake station. It also has a
single platform, run-round loop and a small
wooden locomotive shed with turntable.
Construction on the line began in 1984 and
limited services started in 1985. The present
route was opened throughout in 1992. Trains
are operated by five steam locomotives, of
which the most recent is 2-4-2 tank No. 7
'Merlin', built in 1993. Built in 1950 by
David Curwen, 4-4-2 'Waverley' had
previously operated at other miniature
railways in Weymouth, Loughborough,
Dinting and on the Isle of Mull. Visiting
steam locomotives can be seen at the annual
gala held in September. A short length of
dual gauge track at Rudyard allows the
running of 7¼in-gauge Talyllyn Railway
trains on special events days (see website for
further details).

Rushden Historical Transport Museum

Rushden Station, Station Approach,
Rushden, Northamptonshire **NN10 0AW**

TEL 01933 318988
WEBSITE www.rhts.co.uk
OPEN Museum – Sat afternoons and Sun, Easter
  to end Oct; see website for special events days

RUSHDEN STATION, NOW A transport museum, was situated on the former Midland Railway branch line from Wellingborough to Higham Ferrers, opened in 1893 and closed completely in 1969. The station was taken over by the Rushden Historical Transport Society in 1984. Included in its collection are many railway artefacts, buses, an Andrew Barclay 0-4-0 steam locomotive and signalling equipment. The former waiting rooms have been converted to a social club, with a Victorian-style real ale bar complete with gas lighting. While the trains currently operate over a ¼ mile of track, the society's long-term aim is to extend the line to a small station halt at Higham.

Rutland Railway Museum

Cottesmore Iron Ore Mines Siding, Ashwell
Road, Cottesmore, Leicestershire **LE15 7BX**

TEL 01572 813203
WEBSITE www.rutlandrailwaymuseum.org.uk
OPEN Tue, Thu and Sun throughout the year

THE IRONSTONE QUARRIES AROUND the village of Cottesmore were opened during 1882 and the Midland Railway constructed a branch line to connect with the quarry system. A 3ft-gauge railway was laid in the quarries to bring tubs of ore down to the standard gauge line via a rope incline. Extensive sidings were put in as quarries were developed at nearby Burley and Exton, served by standard gauge lines. The narrow gauge system was replaced by Euclid dumper trucks in 1957 and the Cottesmore quarries closed in 1965. Closure of the other quarries followed in 1973 and all track was lifted.

A group of railway enthusiasts moved to Cottesmore in 1979 to set up an open-air museum. The museum's collection of industrial steam and diesel locomotives has grown considerably over the years, together with a selection of wagons with which to demonstrate the workings of railways in industry. The collection includes over 20 mainly industrial steam and diesel locomotives, and a very large collection of wagons and vans. Other artefacts, such as a working Ruston Bucyrus dragline and Euclid dumper lorries, as well as visitor facilities, have been added as the museum has developed. Train rides in brakevans, and demonstration freight trains, operate along a ¾-mile length of track within the site.

Below Night-time activity at the Rutland Railway Museum in Cottesmore, Leicestershire.

Severn Valley Railway

The Railway Station, Bewdley, Worcestershire DY12 1BG

TEL 01299 403816
WEBSITE www.svr.co.uk
ROUTE Kidderminster to Bridgnorth
LENGTH 16 miles | **GAUGE** Standard
OPEN Weekends, Feb to Nov; daily, May to Sep and during school holidays; see website for details of numerous special events days
STATION National rail network station Kidderminster

THE PICTURESQUE RAILWAY OF 40¾ miles railway along the Severn Valley opened throughout between Shrewsbury and Hartlebury in 1862. The railway was soon taken over by the Great Western Railway, who opened a link at the southern end of the line from Kidderminster to Bewdley in 1878. Coal traffic was an important source of revenue but after the Second World War, traffic, both passenger and freight, was in serious decline and it closed to through trains in 1963. Parts of the line were kept open for the dwindling coal traffic and passenger services retained until 1970 from Hartlebury and Kidderminster to Bewdley. From that date, only the very short northern section to Ironbridge Power station, reached via the line from Madeley Junction to Coalbrookdale, remained open for coal. It is still used today for this traffic.

Now one of Britain's premier heritage railways, the Severn Valley Railway started life as a fund-raising preservation group in 1965. The first public train ran in 1970, from Bridgnorth to Hampton Loade. The service was extended to Bewdley in 1974 and to Kidderminster in 1984. Since then the line has become a huge success, with its large collection of steam and diesel locomotives and rolling stock. Much restoration work is

Below GWR 'Dukedog' Class 4-4-0 No. 9017 'Earl of Berkeley' heads a vintage train on the Severn Valley Railway in Worcestershire.

carried out by the railway's workshops, which are famed for their high standards of work. The six country stations on the line have all been carefully restored to their former GWR glory and a journey along the scenic route, which closely follows the River Severn, evokes all the atmosphere of the heyday of steam train travel. The major engineering structure on the line is the graceful cast-iron Victoria Bridge, built in 1861, which carries trains on its 200ft span, high above the River Severn. At Highley, the Engine House (opened in 2007) houses the railway's reserve collection of steam locomotives, along with railway-themed exhibitions. The café restaurant has wonderful views across the Severn Valley from its balcony. Numerous enthusiasts weekends are held every year, when visiting steam and diesel locomotives from other heritage railways can be seen in action. Good connections with the main-line network at Kidderminster, with its newly constructed brick-built terminus,

and a frequent steam-operated service have ensured the railway's continuing success. The railway has featured in many cinema and TV films, including the 1979 version of John Buchan's *The Thirty Nine Steps*.

Below Ex-LMS 'Jinty' 0-6-0T No. 47383 crosses Victoria Bridge over the River Severn.

Below GWR 'Castle' Class 4-6-0 No. 5029 'Nunney Castle', at the head of a train of vintage carriages on the Severn Valley Railway.

Snibston Discovery Museum

Ashby Road, Coalville,
Leicestershire LE67 3LN

TEL 01530 278444
WEBSITE www.leics.gov.uk/snibston
OPEN Daily, throughout the year; see website
  for numerous special events

Above A former National Coal Board 0-4-0ST
at work at the Snibston Discovery Museum.

OWNED AND OPERATED BY Leicestershire
County Council, Snibston Discovery
Museum contains a historic colliery railway,
interactive museum, country park and
nature reserve, all located on the site of
former Snibston Colliery. Created by Robert
Stephenson, the colliery produced coal
continuously from 1833 to 1983. The council
bought the site in 1986 and have turned the
derelict site into a major museum, which
opened its doors in 1992.

The colliery railway was built by Robert
Stephenson between 1833 and 1836 to
connect the colliery to the Leicester to
Swannington railway, which had been built
by his father, George. The section of railway

between the colliery and Coalville was
restored in 2001 and now carries passengers
on special events days through the year
(see website). At other times visitors travel
on a short trip from the mine into Coalville
and on to the old sidings complex. Motive
power is usually provided by Hunslet
0-6-0 diesel colliery shunting locomotive,
'Pitt', although steam also appears during
certain special events.

Statfold Barn Railway

The Grain Store, Ashby Road,
Tamworth, Staffordshire B79 0BU

TEL 01827 830871
WEBSITE www.statfoldbarnrailway.co.uk
ROUTE Within Statfold Barn Farm
LENGTH 3 miles | **GAUGES** 7¼in, 10¼in, 2ft,
  2ft 6in, 4ft 8½in (standard)
OPEN Only open to the public on Enthusiasts'
  Days by invitation (see website for details)

AN EXTENSIVE MULTI-GAUGE PRIVATE
railway that includes a large collection
of historic steam, diesel and electric
locomotives from around the world (in
particular, from Indonesia). The railway
is not open to the public but a number of
'Enthusiasts' Days' are held, for which railway
enthusiasts can apply for an invitation (see
website). Locomotives and rolling stock of
five different gauges run on different parts
of the railway; the Field Railway is 2ft
and 2ft 6in dual gauge and has an out-
and-back length of three miles. The line
features a two-platform station, extensive
engine sheds, turntable, carriage shed and
a midway halt. Locomotive restoration and
the building of new locos is also carried out
in the company's workshops. Also on site is
the Hunslet Museum, with its collection of
artefacts and ephemera from the Hunslet
Engine Company of Leeds. This famous loco
building company was bought by the owner
of the Statfold Barn Railway in 2005.

Steeple Grange Light Railway

Steeple Grange, Wirksworth,
Matlock, Derbyshire **DE4 4FS**

TEL 01246 235497
WEBSITE www.steeplegrange.co.uk
ROUTE Steeplehouse Junction to Recreation Ground
LENGTH ½ mile | **GAUGE** 18in
OPEN Sun and Bank Holidays, Apr to end Oct;
Sat, Jul to Sep; see website for special events

OPENED IN 1985, THE Steeple Grange Light
Railway operates trains along the trackbed
of a branch of the Cromford & High Peak
Railway. Featuring a steep 1 in 27 gradient,
the branch was built between Steeplehouse
and Middleton Quarry in 1883, closing
along with the rest of the C & HPR in 1967.
While the rest of the railway was opened as
the High Peak Trail footpath and cycleway,

Below Narrow gauge industrial diesel locos on
the 18in gauge Steeple Grange Light Railway.

the 'Killers' Branch', as it was known, was
relaid with 18in track using stock from
former mines and quarries. The railway owns
16 diesel, petrol and battery electric locos
from former industrial narrow gauge lines,
including diminutive 0-4-0 'Horwich', which
once worked at the BR locomotive works
of the same name. Passengers are carried
along this scenic route in former National
Coal Board 'Manrider' wagons. Future plans
include extending the line to link with the
National Stone Centre and the Ecclesbourne
Valley Railway (see page 100).

Telford Steam Railway

The **Old Loco Shed,**
Bridge Road, Horsehay,
Telford, Shropshire TF4 2NF

TEL 07816 762790
WEBSITE www.telfordsteamrailway.co.uk
ROUTE Horsehay and Dawley to Spring Village
(via mouth of Heath Hill Tunnel)
LENGTH ¾ mile | **GAUGE** Standard
OPEN Sun and Bank Holidays, Easter to Sep

THE TELFORD HORSEHAY STEAM Trust was
founded in 1976 to restore locomotives and
rolling stock. It is planned to operate these
on the Horsehay to Lightmoor branch, part
of the former GWR line from Wellington
to Buildwas, which closed in 1964. Services
along ½ mile of track started in 1984 and
a ¼-mile length of 2ft-gauge tramway
was opened in 1991. Trains are normally
operated by Peckett 1926-built 0-4-0ST
'Rocket', while former resident GWR
0-6-2T No. 5619 has been away visiting
other heritage railways. Future plans include
extensions northwards to Lawley Common
and southwards to Ironbridge. Work on
the northern extension has included
clearing spoil from Heath Hill Tunnel
and relaying track.

Above and below Ex-LMS 'Coronation' Class 4-6-2 No. 46235 'City of Birmingham' is the star railway exhibit at Birmingham's Thinktank Museum.

Thinktank Museum

Millennium Point, Curzon Street, Birmingham B4 7XG

TEL 0121 202 2222
WEBSITE www.thinktank.ac
OPEN Daily throughout the year

OPENED IN 2001, THIS new privately-funded museum houses some of the collection from the former Birmingham Museums & Art Gallery Science Museum, which originally opened in 1951. Exhibits include the world's oldest working steam pumping engine, built by James Watt in 1779, Richard Murdock's steam vehicle of 1784, and machine tools and transport sections. Standard gauge LMS 'Coronation' class 4-6-2 No. 46235 'City of Birmingham' (built 1939), and Birmingham Corporation Tramways tram No. 395 are also on display.

Twycross Zoo Miniature Railway

Twycross Zoo, Burton Road,
Atherstone, Warwickshire CV9 3PX

TEL 0844 474 1777
WEBSITE www.twycrosszoo.org
ROUTE Within zoo grounds
LENGTH 650yds | **GAUGE** 10¼in
OPEN Daily throughout the year

A MINIATURE LINE HAS been operating at
this zoo since 1969. Visitors are conveyed
on a circular trip through the zoo grounds
behind a North American-style, steam
outline 2-8-0 diesel hydraulic locomotive

Weston Park Railway

Brewood Lodge, Weston Bank,
Weston-under-Lizard, Shifnal,
Shropshire TF11 8NA

TEL 01952 850336
WEBSITE www.weston-park.com
ROUTE Within grounds of former stately home
LENGTH ¾ mile | **GAUGE** 7¼in
OPEN Contact Weston Park

OPENED IN 1980, THIS well constructed
miniature railway passes through woodland
and alongside lakes within the 1000-acre
landscaped grounds of Weston Park, a
17th century mansion now run as a hotel.
Employing three narrow gauge steam, and
two diesel, locomotives, the railway was built
for continual running using track and some
of the motive power from the former Hilton
Valley Miniature Railway, near Bridgnorth.
The line features ex-BR semaphore signalling
and an overall-roofed station

Right North American-style 2-8-0 'Michael
Charles Lloyd MBE', at the Weston Park Railway.

Winchcombe Railway Museum & Gardens

23 Gloucester Street, Winchcombe,
Gloucestershire GL54 5LX

TEL 01242 609305
WEBSITE www.winchcomberailwaymuseum.co.uk
OPEN Wed to Sun, Apr to Sep; daily during school
   holidays; see website for varying opening hours
STATION Heritage railway station Winchcombe

A HANDS-ON MUSEUM OF railway
life, situated near the Gloucestershire
Warwickshire Railway (see page 104),
featuring many visitor-operated exhibits,
including signals and bells. The collection
was established in 1962 and is now operated
by a voluntarily run Trust. The museum
and garden has one of the largest displays
of railway lineside notices in Britain. The
only surviving First World War London &
North Western Railway ambulance train
carriage body has been restored, and houses
a collection of equipment from railway first
aid teams and an extensive collection of
wagon plates. The carriage served during
the war in Italy and France.

MAIN-LINE STEAM

Rarely a week goes by without some form of main-line steam special somewhere on Britain's rail network. Here are some highlights from Central England.

Left Ex-LMS 'Princess Royal' Class 4-6-2 No. 6201 'Princess Elizabeth' makes a dramatic departure from Birmingham New Street with a Vintage Trains trip on 17 July 2010. This was the first time steam had been seen at New Street since the 1960s.

Below No. 6201 again, going fast through Holmes Chapel station in the early stages of its 'Scarborough Flyer' journey to York and Scarborough – one of a series of Friday excursions organised by the Railway Touring Company in summer 2011.

Above Ex-LMS 'Royal Scot' Class No. 46115 'Scots Guardsman' crosses the River Weaver, en route to Chester with a railtour organised by the Lune Rivers Trust on 4th September 2010.

Below Ex-GWR 'Hall' Class 4-6-0 No. 4965 'Rood Ashton Hall' and 'Castle' Class 4-6-0 No. 5043 'Earl of Mount Edgcumbe' haul the return journey of the 'Coronation Express' from Tyseley to Didcot, via Kidderminster and Cheltenham. The train is seen slowing for a caution signal at Standish Junction.

EASTERN ENGLAND

(18) V 20—20,000—4-13.   (W. & S. Ltd.)
Great Northern Railway.
TO
PETERBORO'

Right BR Standard Class '8P' 4-6-2 No. 71000
'Duke of Gloucester' on a visit to the Nene
Valley Railway at Peterborough.

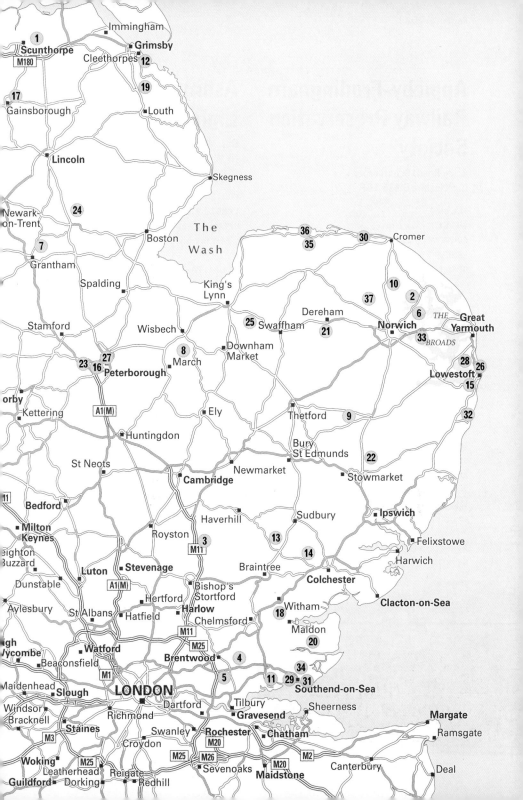

Appleby-Frodingham Railway Preservation Society

Brigg Road, Scunthorpe,
Lincolnshire DN16 1BP

TEL 01652 657053
WEBSITE www.afrps.co.uk
ROUTE Within Scunthorpe steelworks site
LENGTH 7 miles | **GAUGE** Standard
OPEN Most Sat, May to Sep; pre-booked enthusiasts
brakevan tours on selected days
in main season and in winter (see website)
STATION National rail network station Scunthorpe

FORMED IN 1990, THIS preservation
society is based at the TATA steelworks
in Scunthorpe and operates a variety of
railtours on the extensive internal railway
system on open days. The Society owns
and operates three industrial steam and
two diesel locomotives, although special
trains are occasionally hauled by one of the
steelworks diesel locomotives – some of these
are radio controlled. Tours can cover about
15 miles while in the winter enthusiasts are
taken to less accessible parts of the steelworks
in brakevans heated by coal stoves!

Below Lord Braybrooke on the 2-6-2 locomotive
named after him on his Audley End Railway.

Ashmanhaugh Light Railway

East View Farm, Stone Lane, Ashmanhaugh,
Nr Wroxham, Norfolk NR12 8YW

WEBSITE www.ashmanhaughlightrailway.co.uk
ROUTE Within landscaped farm site
LENGTH ½ mile | **GAUGE** 7¼in
OPEN First Sun afternoon of each month,
May to early Oct

LOCATED CLOSE TO THE Bure Valley Railway
(see page 134) and the Norwich to Cromer
'Bittern Line', this miniature railway was
built using equipment from the Little Melton
Light Railway that closed in 2002. Run by
a group of enthusiasts, the railway features
several highly interesting locomotives,
including petrol-engined 'Emmett-style'
'Thunderbox' and a Shay logging locomotive.

Audley End Miniature Railway

Audley End Estate Office, Bruncketts,
Wendens Ambo, Saffron Walden,
Essex CB11 4JL

TEL 01799 541354 or 01799 542134
WEBSITE www.audley-end-railway.co.uk
ROUTE Return loop in Audley End House grounds
LENGTH 1½ miles | **GAUGE** 10¼in
OPEN Daily during Easter week and summer
school holidays; see website for other selected
days in Mar, May, Jun, Oct and Dec

LORD BRAYBROOKE, OWNER OF Audley End
House, began building this miniature railway
in 1963 on a site within the grounds of his
country house. The first section of line was
opened by Stirling Moss in 1964, with trains
being operated by one steam and one diesel
locomotive. The line was extended to its

present layout, an extended return loop, in 1979. A journey on the line, which is fully signalled, takes passengers in covered coaches across bridges over the Rivers Fulfen and Cam, and through a tunnel before passing along the bank of the latter river. Steam locomotives on the roster include a one-third scale model (weighing three tons) of the Denver & Rio Grande Railroad 2-8-2 'Sara Lucy', a Great Northern Railway Ivatt 'Atlantic' 4-4-2, American-style 2-6-2 'Lord Braybrooke', GWR 4-6-0 'Polar Star' and LNWR 'George V' Class 4-6-0 'Loyalty'. Three diesel locos complete the line-up. A multi-gauge raised and ground-level miniature railway also operates during opening days.

Above Happy days on the 7¼in-gauge Barleylands Farm Museum Miniature Railway.

Barleylands Farm Park Miniature Railway

Barleylands Road, Billericay, Essex CM11 2UD

TEL 01268 290229
WEBSITE www.barleylands.co.uk
ROUTE Within farm park
LENGTH 900yds | GAUGE 7¼in
OPEN Daily, throughout the year, during opening times of Farm Park (weather permitting)

WITH THE EXCEPTION OF one locomotive, the whole railway came from the North Benfleet Miniature Railway in 1988. The entire railway was moved to Barleylands Farm and the first section opened in 1989. The line starts at the agricultural museum, where the engine shed is located. It runs for about 400yds, turning through 180° to Littlewood Junction where the engine runs round the train, and then runs for some 500yds mainly downhill to the exit from the boot fair field, where there is a small station and run-round loop. The four ex-North Benfleet locomotives are all one-eighth size

and include 4-6-2 'Britannia', 2-10-0 'Black Prince', 2-6-0 'Vulcan' and 4-4-2 tank 'Maid of Benfleet'. A further locomotive, narrow gauge 0-6-2 tank 'Gowrie' was added to the roster in 1994.

Barnards Farm Miniature Railway

Barnards Farm Gardens, Brentwood Road, West Horndon, Essex CM13 3LX

TEL 01277 811262
WEBSITE www.barnardsfarm.eu/railway.htm
ROUTE 1¼ mile (still under construction)
LENGTH 200yds | GAUGE 7¼in
OPEN Most Thu, Apr to Aug; selected Sun, when garden open (see website)

FEATURING TWO STATIONS, a bridge, engine shed and turntable, this new miniature railway partially opened in Barnards Farm Gardens in 2010. The gardens, part of the National Gardens Scheme, comprise landscaped walks, woodlands, a Japanese garden, formal gardens, a stream, ponds and sculpture. Motive power on this attractive line comprises one steam and one diesel locomotive.

Barton House Railway

Hartwell Road, The Avenue,
Wroxham, Norfolk NR12 8TL

TEL 01603 722858
WEBSITE www.bartonhouserailway.org.uk
ROUTE Within grounds of Barton House
GAUGES 3½in and 7¼in
OPEN Afternoons on third Sun each month,
   Apr to Oct; Easter Mon
STATION National rail network station Hoveton
   & Wroxham

Above Young drivers at work during a Junior Day
on the Barton House Railway near Wroxham.

THE ORIGINAL 3½IN-GAUGE MINIATURE
railway here was built in the early 1960s and
opened to the public in 1963. Since then a
7¼in line and a museum have been added.
The museum houses an extensive collection
of railway artefacts, mainly from the old
Midland & Great Northern Joint Railway.
The lines are fully signalled, using the
original M&GN signalbox from Honing East
which was re-erected on the Barton House
Railway in 1967. A fleet of three electric-
powered boats carry visitors to the railway
along the River Bure from Wroxham Bridge.

Belton Light Railway

Belton House, Belton, Grantham,
Lincolnshire NG32 2LS

TEL 01476 566116 (House)
WEBSITE www.nationaltrust.org.uk (House)
ROUTE Within grounds of Belton House
LENGTH 500yds | **GAUGE** 7¼in
OPEN Weekends and Bank Holidays, Apr to Oct

SET IN THE ATTRACTIVE grounds of the
National Trust's late 17th-century Belton
House, this end-to-end miniature railway
runs from a large adventure playground
through woodland and a tunnel to the far
end of the line, over ¼ mile away. Motive
power is provided by two Hymek-style
diesel hydraulic locomotives.

Bramley Line
Heritage Railway
Trust

Waldersea Depot, Long Drove, Friday Bridge,
Wisbech, Cambridgeshire PE14 0NP

TEL 0759 176 9180
WEBSITE www.bramleyline.org.uk
EVENTS A series of meetings and events are held
   throughout the year (see website)

THE BRAMLEY LINE HERITAGE Railway
Trust was established in 2010 to campaign
for the reinstatement of the Wisbech to
March railway line. Opened as a double-
track line in 1847, it was closed to passengers
in 1968 but retained for freight traffic to
Wisbech. The mothballed line is currently
owned by Network Rail and was last used
in 2001. Importantly, it is still physically
connected to the national rail network at
March and the Trust hopes to create a small
depot in the former goods shed at Waldersea.

Bressingham Steam Museum and Gardens

Low Road, Bressingham, Diss,
Norfolk IP22 2AA

TEL 01379 686900
WEBSITE www.bressingham.co.uk
ROUTE Within grounds of Bressingham Gardens
LENGTH Garden Line – 1,350yds; Waveney Valley
  Railway – 2½ miles; Nursery Line – 2½ miles |
  GAUGES 10¼in, 15in, 2ft, 4ft 8½in (standard)
OPEN Daily, all year; see website for special events

BRESSINGHAM IS NOT ONLY known for its extensive steam museum but also for its superb gardens and nurseries, totalling 480 acres. Created by Alan Bloom in 1973, the railway enthusiast is well catered for, with 10¼in, 15in and 2ft steam operating lines and a standard gauge museum. The 'Garden Line' opened in 1965. Originally 9¼in-gauge, but converted to 10¼in during 1995, it is the shortest, taking passengers on a 1,350yd ride through the house garden. The 15in-gauge 'Waveney Valley Railway', opened in 1973 and now 2½ miles in length, runs for part of its route alongside the River Waveney and is powered by two 1937 Krupp-built German 4-6-2s, 'Rosenkavalier' and 'Mannertrau', and 1976-built 4-6-2 'Flying Scotsman'. The 2ft-gauge 'Nursery Line', at 2½ miles in length, opened in 1966 and takes passengers through the nurseries, which are not normally accessible to the public. Four steam locos work this line, including two Hunslet 0-4-0 saddle tanks, 'Gwynedd' (built 1883) and 'George Sholto' (built 1909), both rescued from the Penrhyn Slate Quarries in North Wales. Passengers are carried in open toast-rack coaches, also from the Penrhyn Quarries. The large standard gauge museum houses royal coaches and main-line steam locomotives, including London, Tilbury & Southend Railway 4-4-2 tank 'Thundersley', GER Class T26 2-4-0 No. 490 and GNR 4-4-2 No. 251. A standard gauge demonstration line operates on Sundays and during special events. There is also a museum of props and vehicles from the *Dad's Army* TV series.

Below Built by Krupp in 1937, 4-6-2 'Mannertrau' operates on the 15in-gauge Waveney Valley Railway at Bressingham Steam Museum.

Above Indian Railways ZB style 2-6-2 N0. 7 'Spitfire' heads along the Bure Valley railway.

Bure Valley Railway

Aylsham Station, Norwich Road,
Aylsham, Norfolk NR11 6BW

TEL 01263 733858
WEBSITE www.bvrw.co.uk
ROUTE Aylsham to Wroxham
LENGTH 9 miles | GAUGE 15in
OPEN Weekends, Mar to Dec; daily, Apr to Oct and
    during school holidays;
STATION National rail network station Hoveton
    & Wroxham

THE BURE VALLEY RAILWAY runs along part of the trackbed of the branch line from Wroxham to Aylsham, opened by the East Norfolk Railway in 1878 and extended to County School in 1880. Although nominally independent, the railway was first operated by the Great Eastern Railway. Passenger services ceased in 1952 but freight continued until 1981. The track was lifted in 1984.

Running along the trackbed of this former branch line, the 15in-gauge Bure Valley Railway cost £2.5 million to build and was opened by author and broadcaster Miles Kington as a miniature passenger-carrying line in 1990. Since then it has had no fewer than five owners. The Bure Valley station at Wroxham is adjacent to that of the national rail network station, connected by a footbridge, and has a three-track layout with a turntable. As the line meanders along the valley of the River Bure, alongside the Bure Valley Walk, it passes through three other stations, at Coltishall, Brampton and Buxton, before arriving at Aylsham through a ¼-mile-long tunnel, where the railway has its overall-roofed terminus, engine sheds and workshops. Five steam locomotives and one diesel operate the line and visiting engines from the Romney Hythe & Dymchurch Railway and the Ravenglass & Eskdale Railway can occasionally be seen at work. Combined rail and Broads boat excursions are available in the summer.

Beyond Aylsham station, the trackbed survives as the Marriott's Way long distance footpath to the outskirts of Norwich.

Canvey Miniature Railway

Waterside Farm Sports Complex, Somnes
Avenue, Canvey Island, Essex SS8 9RA

TEL 07943 369896
WEBSITE www.cramec.org
ROUTE Within club grounds
LENGTHS 4,400ft (7½in-gauge railway); 1,440ft
    (elevated dual gauge railway) | GAUGES 3½in,
    5in and 7¼in
OPEN Sun, Apr to early Oct; Santa Specials in Dec
    (see website)

OWNED AND OPERATED BY the Canvey Railway & Model Engineering Club, this miniature railway comprises a dual gauge (3½in and 5in) elevated line, and a separate and extensive 7¼in ground-level line. The latter, around ¾ mile in length, features two linked, continuous circuits, a diamond crossing, loco and carriage sheds, turntables, bridge over a small river, covered station, level crossing and signalbox. A wide variety of members' locomotives can be seen in operation on open days.

Cleethorpes Coast Light Railway

Lakeside Station, Kings Road, Cleethorpes, Lincolnshire DN35 0AG

TEL 01472 604657
WEBSITE www.cleethorpescoastlightrailway.co.uk
ROUTE Kingsway to North Sea Lane
LENGTH 2 miles | **GAUGE** 15in
OPEN Daily during school hols, Easter to early Sep
STATION National rail network station Cleethorpes

OPENED IN 1948 AS a steam railway, this miniature line was subsequently converted to electric operation in 1954 and then to gas hydraulic in 1972. After a change of ownership in 1991 the line was rebuilt and steam returned in 1994. The railway passes alongside Lakeside Park, with fine panoramic views of the Humber Estuary and its excellent beaches, before turning inland through the park area. The line was extended to the Pleasure Island Family theme park in 2007. Steam locomotives operating on the line include 4-4-2 'Sutton Belle' (1933), and LNER 'O4' 2-8-0 No. 6284. The railway's pub, the Signal Box Inn at Lakeside, is reputedly the smallest pub in the world.

A new museum dedicated to seaside miniature railways is housed in the old locomotive shed of the now-closed Sutton Miniature Railway – pride of place goes to Basset-Lowke's 1909-built 4-4-2 'Little Atom'. Rare 15in-gauge vintage and veteran steam locomotives are part of one of the largest collections of seaside miniature railway equipment in the country.

Below Originally from the Sutton Miniature Railway in Warwickshire, 4-4-2 No. 2 'Sutton Flyer' heads a train across a level crossing on the Cleethorpes Coast Light Railway.

Colne Valley Railway

Castle Hedingham Station,
Yeldham Road, Castle Hedingham,
Halstead, Essex CO9 3DZ

TEL 01787 461174
WEBSITE www.colnevalleyrailway.co.uk
ROUTE Either side of Castle Hedingham station
LENGTH 1 mile | GAUGE Standard
OPEN Most weekends and Bank Holidays, Mar to
Oct; Wed & Thu, Aug; Steam with Santa in Dec

THE COLNE VALLEY & HALSTEAD Railway, completely opened in 1863 between Chappel & Wakes Colne and Haverhill, survived as an independent company until 1923, when it was absorbed into the LNER. Following a very busy period during the First World War, the line returned to its normal operation and after, a short experiment with diesel railcars, BR ceased passenger services in 1961 and closed the line in 1965.

In 1973 a preservation group moved into the site and started to clear the area of ten years of undergrowth. The first 'steam up' was held in 1975 and the first of many educational events was held in 1979. Castle Hedingham station has been recreated on a new site, using the original Colne Valley station building from Castle & Sible Hedingham, and a large quantity of steam and diesel locomotives and rolling stock is now preserved here. The railway specialises in educational visits and is well known for its excellent Pullman dining service. The latter is operated in three historic carriages, creating the luxurious atmosphere of the 'Orient Express'-style Pullman dining train. Castle Hedingham station has many other features for the railway enthusiast. Opened in 2010, the Tierney Model Railway Shed features an extensive '00'-gauge model railway (in operation on most open days) while two other model railways operated by Halstead Model Railway Club operate on special events days only. Opened in 2008, a 650yd-long, 7¼in miniature railway operates on most open days, weather permitting and the working signalbox is also open for visitors on most open days.

Below Steam operation at Castle Hedingham, on the Colne Valley Railway in Essex.

East Anglian Railway Museum

Chappel & Wakes Colne Station,
Wakes Colne, Essex CO6 2DS

TEL 01206 242524
WEBSITE www.earm.co.uk
OPEN Museum open daily throughout the year;
  see website for dates of special events and
  when trains are operating
STATION National rail network station Chappel
  & Wakes Colne

Above A diesel multiple unit at Chappel & Wakes
Colne on the East Anglia Railway Museum.

THIS WORKING MUSEUM CONTAINS
a comprehensive collection of railway
architecture, engineering and relics,
representing over 100 years of railways in
the Eastern Counties. It was formed in 1968
as the Stour Valley Railway Preservation
Society to preserve a section of the Stour
Valley Railway when closure was threatened.
When closure did not take place, the
museum, a registered charity, was formed
in 1986. Chappel & Wakes Colne station
is situated on the former GER branch line
from Marks Tey to Cambridge via Haverhill.
It opened in 1849 and is still open today
as far as Sudbury. Built in the 1890s, the
station building is a classic example of GER

architecture and is restored to its original
condition, with a heritage centre situated in
the storage arches underneath. Two restored
signalboxes include the original one (which
is no longer in operation) and one that was
moved from Mistley, near Manningtree, that
now controls train movements within the
site. A restored Victorian goods shed is now
used for functions. The museum is situated
near to Chappel Viaduct, which was opened
in 1849. It is the longest viaduct in East
Anglia and is reputed to be the largest brick
structure in Europe, containing over seven
million bricks, with each of the 32 arches
being 30ft wide. Running days, vintage train
events and a miniature railway day are held
at various weekends throughout the year.

East Anglia Transport Museum

Chapel Road, Carlton Colville, Lowestoft,
Suffolk NR33 8BL

TEL 01502 518459
WEBSITE www.eatm.org.uk
ROUTE Chapel Road to Woodside
LENGTH 300yds | GAUGE 2ft
OPEN Most weekends and Bank Holidays, Apr
  to Sep; Tue to Thu during school holidays;
  see website for special events

AN OPEN-AIR TRANSPORT museum which
includes working trams, trolley buses and
veteran road vehicles, operating in a 1930s
street scene. The 2ft-gauge railway, known as
the East Suffolk Railway, carries passengers
along a 300yd line between Chapel Road and
Woodside, within the site of the museum.
Opened in 1973 and based on light railway
operation, with track from a former sand
quarry, Canvey Island and the long-closed
Southwold Railway (see page 148), the line
is fully signalled, with a GER signalbox
from the Lowestoft area. The railway's two
industrial diesel locos date from the 1930s.

Ferry Meadows Miniature Railway

Nene Park, Peterborough, Cambridgeshire PE2 5UU

TEL 01933 398889
WEBSITE www.ferrymeadowsrailway.co.uk
ROUTE Within Nene Valley Park
LENGTH ½ mile | **GAUGE** 10¼in
OPEN Daily during school holidays, Feb to Oct;
    weekends, Mar to Oct

AN OUT-AND-BACK MINIATURE RAILWAY, opened in 1978, operates from a station adjacent to the café, to the children's play area within the Nene Valley Park. Power is provided by two steam outline locos; a Rio Grande 2-8-0 and a freelance 0-6-0.

Gainsborough Model Railway Museum

Florence Terrace, Gainsborough, Lincolnshire DN21 1BE

TEL 01427 613679
WEBSITE www.gainsboroughmodelrailway.co.uk
OPEN Selected open days (see website)
STATION National rail network station
    Gainsborough

OWNED AND OPERATED BY the Gainsborough Model Railway Society since 1946, this superb '0'-gauge model railway is based on the East Coast Main Line from King's Cross to Leeds. It covers an area of 2,500 square feet, with ½ mile of track, and requires ten operators. One of the largest '0'-gauge railways in Britain, it features a scale model of King's Cross terminus, 150 locos, 100 coaches, 200 wagons and vans, and nine stations. The railway is open to the public on selected days throughout the year.

Above The model of King's Cross station on the extensive '0'-gauge layout at Gainsborough.

Langford & Beeleigh Railway

Museum of Power, Hatfield Road, Langford, Maldon, Essex CM9 6QA

TEL 01621 843183
WEBSITE www.museumofpower.org.uk
ROUTE Within museum grounds
LENGTH ¼ mile | **GAUGE** 7¼in
OPEN Museum – Wed to Sun, Mar to Oct;
    weekends, Nov and Dec. Railway runs on special
    events days throughout the year (see website)

Above Motive power on the scenic 7¼in-gauge Langford & Beeleigh Railway, in Essex.

THE MUSEUM OF POWER is housed in a former pumping station and contains a collection of powered machines ranging from a working triple expansion steam pumping engine to a petrol powered iron. The surrounding seven acres, set each side of the River Blackwater, includes a model village, picnic area and the miniature Langford & Beeleigh Railway. The railway carries visitors on a journey through the museum's wooded grounds and meadows from Riverside Halt, near the car park, to the main station, Langford. Trains are normally steam hauled, from a pool of superb narrow gauge-style locomotives. The railway features colour aspect signalling, a three-road engine shed and a turntable, while Langford station boasts an overall roof, two platforms, coal stage and water tower. Future plans include extending the line via a bridge over the River Blackwater and building a branch line along the banks of the river to Beeleigh Falls, to enable visitors to visit Beeleigh Mill and its unique Wentworth Beam Engine.

Lincolnshire Wolds Railway

Ludborough Station, Station Road, Ludborough, Lincolnshire DN36 5SQ

TEL 01507 363881
WEBSITE www.lincolnshirewoldsrailway.co.uk
ROUTE Ludborogh to North Thoresby
LENGTH 1½ miles | **GAUGE** Standard
OPEN Selected steam operating days and special events (see website)

A SHORT STANDARD GAUGE railway is based at the rebuilt Ludborough station on the former Great Northern Railway's route between Grimsby Town and Louth, which opened in 1848 and closed to passengers in 1970. The line was kept open for freight until 1980, when it closed completely. A preservation society was set up in the same

year, with the aim of restoring part of the line. Since then the station, platforms and signalbox have been rebuilt and track relaid to North Thoresby. A collection of Lincolnshire railway artefacts and a model railway are housed in a small museum (open on operating days) on the site. Steam trains now operate between Ludborough and North Thoresby, making the railway the only standard gauge steam railway open to the public in Lincolnshire. Future plans feature extending the line northwards to Holton-le-Clay and southwards to Louth.

Above and below Visiting ex-GWR 0-6-0PT No. 6430 stops for a chat at Ludborough station and powers ahead with a goods train on the Lincolnshire Wolds Railway.

Mangapps Railway Museum

Southminster Road, Burnham-on-Crouch, Essex CM0 8QG

TEL 01621 784898
WEBSITE www.mangapps.co.uk
ROUTE Through farmland owned by the museum
LENGTH ¾ mile | **GAUGE** Standard
OPEN Weekends and Bank Holidays, Feb to Christmas (except Nov); daily in Aug

Above Ex-LNER Class 'N7' 0-6-2T No. 69621 visits the Mid-Norfolk Railway at Dereham.

Above A diesel multiple unit waits at the family-run Mangapps Railway Museum.

A FAMILY-RUN RAILWAY CENTRE which features the railway history of East Anglia and which opened on a greenfield site in 1989. A variety of steam and diesel locomotives, rolling stock and signalling are on display, in addition to an exhibition hall of railway artefacts. The museum has one of the largest collections of railway artefacts in Britain. Restored station buildings from the Great Eastern Railway, Mid-Suffolk Light Railway and the Midland & Great Northern Joint Railway are also on display. The museum also features a ¾-mile standard gauge passenger carrying line, with restored stations, signalboxes and artefacts from various locations around East Anglia. Trains are hauled by a variety of historic industrial steam and diesel locomotives.

Mid-Norfolk Railway

Dereham Station, Station Road, Dereham, Norfolk NR19 1DF

TEL 01362 690633
WEBSITE www.mnr.org.uk
ROUTE Wymondham Abbey to Dereham
LENGTH 11½ miles | **GAUGE** Standard
OPEN Weekends and Bank Holidays, Apr to Oct; more frequent services (excepting some Mon, Tue and Fri), Jun to Sep; Santa Specials in Dec; see website for numerous special events
STATION National rail network station Wymondham

THE MID-NORFOLK RAILWAY OPERATES along the route of the Wymondham to Wells-next-the-Sea branch line, which was opened as far as Dereham by the Norfolk Railway in 1847. A year later the railway was absorbed by the Eastern Counties Railway, which eventually built the remaining section to Wells, opening in 1857. In 1862, the line became part of the newly formed Great Eastern Railway, which doubled the track between Wymondham and Dereham in 1882. The line saw heavy use during the Second World War, serving many airfields, and was even protected by an armoured train.

Although diesel multiple units replaced steam passenger services as early as 1955, the branch from Dereham to Wells was listed for closure in the 1963 'Beeching Report' – although the Dereham to King's Lynn line was not. Passenger services ended between Dereham and Wells in 1964, between Dereham and King's Lynn in 1968 and from Wymondham to Dereham in 1969. However part of the line continued to be used for freight services.

The northerly section of line between Walsingham and Wells is now operated by the 10¼in-gauge Wells & Walsingham Light Railway (see page 150).

Opening as a tourist line in 1997, the Mid-Norfolk Railway today operates steam and diesel services between Wymondham and Dereham, with intermediate stations at Yaxham (where there is also a short 2ft-gauge line), Thuxton and Kimberley Park. Visiting locomotives are often seen and the railway also owns a further six miles of track northwards from Dereham, to the restored County School station. Once this opens the Mid-Norfolk will be the third longest heritage railway in England. Charter and excursion trains, along with commercial freight traffic and MOD military traffic, also use the line via the connection with the national rail network at Wymondham.

Above 'FD&Co. No 3' heads a train of vintage carriages on the Mid-Suffolk Light Railway.

Mid-Suffolk Light Railway

Brockford Station, Wetheringsett, Stowmarket, Suffolk IP14 5PW

TEL 01449 766899
WEBSITE www.mslr.org.uk
ROUTE within site at Brockford station
LENGTH ½ mile | **GAUGE** Standard
OPEN Museum – Sun and bank Holidays, Easter to end Sep; Wed, Aug; Railway runs on special events days throughout the year (see website)

THE MID-SUFFOLK LIGHT RAILWAY was an ambitious scheme to build lines from Haughley to Halesworth via Stradbroke and Laxfield, with a branch from Kenton to Westerfield. Work started in 1902, and 21 miles of the line was completed by 1904, as far as Cratfield, when goods traffic started. Severe financial difficulties prevented much work on the Kenton to Westerfield line, although it was partly constructed as far as Debenham. The line went into receivership, before opening to passengers in 1908 between Haughley and Laxfield. There were difficulties crossing the marshes near Halesworth, and before long the line beyond Laxfield and all of the Westerfield branch were both abandoned. The company remained independent of the Great Eastern Railway, and was taken over by the LNER in 1924. It survived the latter's proposal to turn it into a road in the 1930s, and closed to all traffic in 1952, being lifted the following year.

The present museum was established in 1991, and has brought a number of original MSLR buildings from Mendlesham, Brockford and Wolby on to the site. Steam trains run on selected dates. Visitors can use the Trackbed Walk of about one mile, as well as the waymarked Middy Light Railway Long Distance Path between Haughley and Brockford. Future plans include an extension of the running line to Blacksmith's Green.

Nene Valley Railway

**Wansford Station, Stibbington,
Peterborough, Cambridgeshire PE8 6LR**

TEL 01780 784444
WEBSITE www.nvr.org.uk
ROUTE Yarwell Junction to Peterborough
Nene Valley
LENGTH 7½ miles | **GAUGE** Standard
OPEN Weekends, Bank Holidays and most days
during school holidays, Mar to Oct; see website
for special events and Santa Specials
STATION National rail network station
Peterborough

ENGINEERED BY ROBERT STEPHENSON,
the Northampton & Peterborough Railway
opened in 1845 and the following year
became part of the newly formed London
& North Western Railway. One of the
line's features was the large number of
level crossings that had been used instead
of bridges during the building of the line.
These obviously saved money during the
construction but were expensive to operate.
This factor no doubt swayed Dr Beeching to
list the line for closure in his 1963 'Report'
(closure actually came about a year later).
However, the section from Yarwell Junction
to Peterborough was kept open for passenger
trains from Rugby and Market Harborough,
until that too closed in 1966. This last section
from Yarwell Junction to Peterborough is
now the Nene Valley Railway.

Nene Valley is well known for its
international flavour and location filming
for TV and cinema. Since 1974, with
assistance from Peterborough Development
Corporation, the Peterborough Railway
Society has had its headquarters at Wansford,
which has become the main centre for

foreign locomotives and rolling stock in
Britain. Trains started operating in 1977
and a new NVR station at Peterborough
(Nene Valley) was opened in 1986, adjacent
to a site which is being developed into
an international railway museum. From
Peterborough, the line runs through
Nene Park along the banks of the River
Nene, crossing the river twice, and into
open countryside, before passing through
Wansford and the 616yd Wansford Tunnel.
Current restored stock on the NVR consists
of examples from Germany, Denmark,
Sweden, France and Belgium, as well as
many from Britain (including the line's first
locomotive, former BR Class 5MT 4-6-0 No.
73050 'City of Peterborough'). Film makers
have taken advantage of the continental
flavour and the NVR stations have often
been cleverly disguised as foreign locations,
for films such as *Octopussy* and *Goldeneye*,
television dramas and commercials. A
Travelling Post Office demonstration train,
with mailbag exchange apparatus, can also
be seen in action. A new museum exhibiting
the railway's extensive collection of TPO
and Wagons-Lit rolling stock is being built
at Ferry Meadows.

Above The driver and fireman of BR Standard Class 5 4-6-0 No. 73050 rest between duties on the
Nene Valley Railway.

Opposite Ex-LMS Class '4F' 0-6-0 No. 44422 heads a light engine over the River Nene, near Wansford
on the Nene Valley Railway.

North Ings Farm Museum Railway

Fen Road, Dorrington, Lincolnshire LN4 3QB

TEL 01526 833100
WEBSITE www.northingsfarmmuseum.co.uk
ROUTE Circuit within museum site
LENGTH 600yds | **GAUGE** 2ft
OPEN First Sun of each month, Apr to Oct

Above Steam tram engine No. 9 'Swift' hauls a short train at North Ings Farm Museum Railway.

THIS SMALL MUSEUM OPENED to the public in 1990 and contains a selection of agricultural machinery and other items of interest. A 2ft narrow gauge railway started life in 1972, when the farm was being used for poultry rearing. During the very wet winter of 1971/72, the dumper trucks which were used to serve the 19 sheds became bogged down, and as a result the first items of railway equipment were purchased. The railway was an immediate success and several other items were purchased. In 1981 the poultry business closed, and the railway took on a new role conveying materials around the site. In 1988 the track to the lower lake was opened and since then the railway has proved a major attraction for visitors to the farm. Seven diesels and a steam tram are based on the railway, and passengers are carried in four coaches built on skip chassis. Future plans include new locomotive and carriage sheds.

North Norfolk Railway

See page 146

Pentney Park Railway

Pentney Park Caravan & Camping Site, Pentney, Kings Lynn, Norfolk PE32 1HU

TEL 01760 337479
WEBSITE www.pentney-park.co.uk
ROUTE Around perimeter of caravan site
LENGTH ¾ mile | **GAUGE** 7¼in
OPEN Telephone for details

THIS ATTRACTIVE MINIATURE LINE was started in 1986 and the 4,000ft of track gives an out-and-back ride with a return loop and several passing loops. It runs around the perimeter of this camping and caravan park, through woodland and open country, with a variety of gradients. A single-line token system is in use on special events weekends, when visiting steam locomotives can be seen in action.

Below A busy steam scene on the 7¼in-gauge Pentney Park Railway near Kings Lynn, Norfolk.

Pleasurewood Hills Theme Park

Leisure Way, Corton, Lowestoft,
Suffolk NR32 5DZ

TEL 01502 586000
WEBSITE www.pleasurewoodhills.com
ROUTE Within theme park
LENGTH 1,300yds and 800yds | GAUGES 7¼in
 and 2ft
OPEN Most weekends, Bank Holidays and school
 holidays, Apr to Oct; daily, July to Aug

TWO SEPARATE RAILWAYS, ONE narrow gauge
and the other a miniature line, are one of
the many attractions in this theme park.
The route, including tunnels, takes
passengers through woodland and at one
point the two lines cross each other. Basic
stations are provided on each line and
passenger journeys are included in the park
entrance fee. Motive power consists of two
diesel hydraulic locos on the 7¼in line, and
a petrol engine on the 2ft line.

Railworld Museum

Oundle Road, Peterborough,
Cambridgeshire PE2 9NR

TEL 01733 344240
WEBSITE www.railworld.net
OPEN See website for opening days

THIS SUSTAINABLE TRANSPORT CENTRE
features a model railway, a garden railway,
railway memorabilia, transport exhibition,
rail industry showcase, locomotives and
rolling stock. Unusual items at Railworld
Museum include an American Alco Bo-Bo
Switcher, a French 4-cylinder Compound
4-6-2, a Maglev train and a hover train. The
museum also has a café and holds special
events throughout the year.

Somerleyton Hall Miniature Railway

Somerleyton Hall, Lovingland,
Nr Lowestoft, Suffolk NR32 5QQ

TEL 01502 734901 (Hall)
WEBSITE www.somerleyton.co.uk
ROUTE Within grounds of Somerleyton Hall
LENGTH ¼ mile | GAUGE 7¼in
OPEN Telephone for details

A MINIATURE RAILWAY RUNS in the grounds
of this grand 17th-century country house.
It is famous for its 12 acres of formal
gardens, 19th-century yew hedge maze and
a greenhouse designed by Sir Joseph Paxton,
the architect of Crystal Palace. The miniature
railway offers good views of the house.

Southend Cliff Railway

Western Esplanade, Southend-on-Sea,
Essex SS1 1DT

WEBSITE www.southend.gov.uk
ROUTE Western Esplanade to Clifton Terrace
LENGTH 130ft | GAUGE 4ft 6in
OPEN Daily, Easter to Sep
STATION National rail network station
 Southend Central

OWNED AND OPERATED BY Southend-on-
Sea Borough Council, this is not only the
shortest funicular railway in Britain but
also the only one with a single track. It was
opened in 1912 to replace a novel wooden
moving walkway known as the Reno Inclined
Elevator and carries passengers a height
of 57ft on a gradient of 1 in 2.28. The line
was closed in 2003, but reopened in 2010
after a £3 million restoration. The fare is
currently 50p.

Above The driver of ex-GER Class 'J15' 0-6-0 No. 65462 passes the time of day.

North Norfolk Railway

Sheringham Station, Station Approach, Sheringham, Norfolk NR26 8RA

TEL 01263 820800
WEBSITE www.nnrailway.co.uk
ROUTE Sheringham to Holt
LENGTH 5¼ miles | **GAUGE** Standard
OPEN Weekends, Mar to Nov; daily, Apr to Oct and during school holidays; Santa Specials in Dec; see website for special events days
STATION National rail network station Sheringham

THE STEEPLY GRADED NORTH Norfolk Railway route was originally part of the meandering Midland & Great Northern Joint Railway, which linked the Midlands and Peterborough with Cromer, Great Yarmouth and Norwich. The joint railway was formed in 1893 from a number of independent railway companies, including the Eastern & Midlands Railway, and was run jointly by the Great Northern Railway and Midland Railway. The majority of this fascinating cross-country network was closed in 1959, apart from the Melton Constable to Cromer Beach branch (opened by the Eastern & Midlands Railway in 1887) which was closed in 1964. Part of this has since been preserved by the North Norfolk Railway.

After several rather optimistic preservation plans on other parts of the Midland & Great Northern system were rejected as being impractical, a preservation group moved in, initially at Weybourne, and now has its headquarters at Sheringham. In 1969, the year John Betjeman became the North Norfolk Railway's president, the railway became the first of the preservation societies in Britain to be floated as a public company, and by 1989 the present route had been fully reopened. The restored period stations, particularly at Weybourne, have often been used as TV and film locations. A journey along the line provides passengers with views of the Norfolk coastline and heathland, and a large collection of restored steam and diesel

locomotives and ex-LNER rolling stock operate the trains. The star of the railway is ex-LNER Class 'B12' 4-6-0 No. 8572, built in 1928, which was returned to traffic in early 1995 after a major 3½-year rebuild at Mansfeld locomotive works in Germany – it is currently undergoing a major overhaul at Weybourne. Other steam locomotives include Great Eastern Railway Class 'J15' 0-6-0 No. 65462, built in 1912, and several industrial examples built by Hunslet, Andrew Barclay and Bagnall. Several steam locomotives are also on extended loan to the railway, including David Shepherd's Class '9F' 2-10-0 No. 92203 'Black Prince' and ex-GWR 0-6-2T No. 5619 from the Telford Horsehay Steam trust (see page 123). The railway also operates several main-line diesel locomotives, a multiple unit and three four-wheeled railcars. A railway museum and museum signalbox are open to the public at Sheringham.

Above Great Northern Railway 0-6-2T No. 1744 hauls a fine rake of articulated teak coaches.
Below Ex-LMS Class '4' 2-6-0 No. 43106 ('The Flying Pig') revisits its old stamping grounds.

Southend Pier Railway

Shore End Station, Marine Parade, Southend-on-Sea, Essex SS1 1EE

TEL 01702 618747
WEBSITE www.southend.gov.uk
ROUTE Shore End Station to Pier Head Station
LENGTH 2,358yds | **GAUGE** 3ft
OPEN Daily throughout the year
STATION National rail network station
    Southend Central

Above 0-6-2T No. 4 'Wenhaston', on a plaque at the site of Wenhaston station, Southwold Railway.

OWNED AND OPERATED BY Southend-on-Sea Borough Council, Southend Pier is the longest pleasure pier in the world, extending nearly 1¼ miles into the Thames Estuary. The present iron pier was built to replace a worn out wooden pier and opened in stages between 1889 and 1929. The pier railway was an integral part of the pier's construction and was also extended in stages between 1890 and 1930. Built to a gauge of 3ft 6in, the single-track, third-rail electrified line was so popular that it was eventually doubled and at its peak carried over 50,000 passengers in a single day. New rolling stock replaced the Victorian toast-rack coaches in 1949 but by the 1970s the railway was in need of expensive repairs, following a fire at the pier head, and it closed in 1978.

Despite threats to close the pier, it was eventually repaired and the railway was rebuilt to a gauge of 3ft, and reopened as a single track with one passing loop in 1986. Trains are normally operated by two diesel multiple units, with a smaller battery powered car sufficing in winter. The pier and its railway has had its fair share of mishaps, culminating in the disastrous fire at the pier head in 2005, destroying the railway station and shops. A new station was only opened on the site in 2009. The Southend-on-Sea Pier Museum is located at the foot of the pier, close to the station.

Southwold Railway Trust

27 High Street, Southwold, Suffolk IP18 6AD

TEL 01502 725422
WEBSITE www.southwoldrailway.co.uk
OPEN Daily (except Wed) throughout the year; daily, late May Bank Holiday to end Aug

OPENED IN 1879, THE 3ft-gauge Southwold Railway operated along the 8¾ miles from Halesworth to Southwold. It was finally closed to all traffic in 1929, though the railway company itself was not finally wound up until 1989. The Southwold Railway Trust is dedicated to preserving the memory of this much-loved railway and reopening as much of the old route as possible. A working replica of 2-4-0 'Blyth' is currently under construction and it will eventually operate trains in the Southwold Railway Steam Park at the end of Blyth Road. The interior of the Trust's shop in Southwold is fitted out in the style of a Southwold Railway carriage.

The Southwold Museum in Victoria Street also includes many small relics and photographs of the railway. For more details visit the museum website (www.southwoldmuseum.org; tel 01509 272 6097).

Strumpshaw Steam Museum

Strumpshaw, Norwich, Norfolk NR13 4HR

TEL 01603 714535
WEBSITE www.strumpshawsteammuseum.co.uk
ROUTE Within grounds of Strumpshaw Hall
LENGTH ¾ mile | GAUGE 2ft
OPEN Sun and Wed, Apr to Sep; daily (except
Sat), Jul to Aug and during school holidays
(see website)

OPENED IN 1954, THIS museum contains
one of the largest private collections of
steam traction engines in Britain, many in
working order. The Spring Bank Holiday
steam rally, featuring around 50 traction
engines, attracts thousands of visitors to the
village. The narrow gauge railway operates
during open days.

Sutton Hall Railway

Tabors Farm, Sutton Hall, Shopland Road,
Nr Rochford, Essex SS4 1LQ

TEL 01702 334337
ROUTE Within Tabors Farm
LENGTH c.1,700yds | GAUGE 10¼in
OPEN Afternoons on fourth Sun of each month,
Easter to Sep

THIS 10¼IN-GAUGE, GROUND-LEVEL
miniature railway was formed in 1996
by members of the Shoeburyness Model
Railway Club. Motive power is normally
provided by powerful 2-10-0 'Evening Star'
along the route of almost one mile.

Below Steam outline 0-4-0 diesel 'Jimmy',
on the 2ft-gauge railway at Strumpshaw Hall.

Wells & Walsingham Light Railway

Wells-next-the-Sea, Norfolk NR23 1QB

TEL 01328 711630
WEBSITE www.wellswalsinghamrailway.co.uk
ROUTE Wells-next-the-Sea to Little Walsingham
LENGTH 4 miles | **GAUGE** 10¼in
OPEN Daily, early Apr to end Oct

Above Garratt 2-6-0+0-6-2 'Norfolk Hero', on the Wells & Walsingham Light Railway.

THE LONGEST 10¼IN-GAUGE RAILWAY in the world also operates the most powerful steam locomotive of that gauge; a 20ft-long 'Garratt' 2-6-0+0-6-2, 'Norfolk Hero', built in 1986. This unique little line, owned, built and operated by retired naval commander Roy Francis, opened in 1982. It runs on the trackbed of the old standard gauge Wells & Fakenham Railway, which opened in 1857 and was closed by BR in 1964. A 0-6-0 tank engine, 'Pilgrim', operated services from opening until 1986. This loco now operates on the Knebworth Park Railway (see page 59). Intermediate halts are provided at Warham St Mary and Wighton, and a former Great Eastern Railway signalbox, originally sited at Swainsthorpe, has been preserved at Wells station where it is used as a shop and tea room.

Wells Harbour Railway

Beach Road, Wells-next-the-Sea, Norfolk NR23 1DR

TEL 01328 878871
WEBSITE www.wellsharbourrailway.co.uk
ROUTE Wells Harbour to Pinewoods Holiday Park
LENGTH 1 mile | **GAUGE** 10¼in
OPEN Weekends and Bank Holidays, Easter to Oct; May to Sep and during school holidays; evening trains are also run during busy periods; see website for details

OPENED IN 1976, THIS seaside miniature railway operates a frequent scheduled service of trains between the Pinewood Holiday Park and harbour in the attractive seaside town of Wells. Motive power is provided by 0-4-2T steam locomotive, 'Edmund Hannay', petrol locomotive, 'Weasel', and steam outline diesel hydraulics, 'Densil' and 'Howard'.

Whitwell & Reepham Railway

Whitwell & Reepham Station, Whitwell
Road, Norwich, Norfolk NR10 4GA

TEL 01603 871694
WEBSITE www.whitwellstation.com
OPEN Weekends, all year; see website for details

Above Steam returns to Whitwell & Reepham
on the 50th anniversary of the line's closure.

LOCATED ON THE FORMER Midland & Great
Northern Joint Railway's line from Melton
Constable to Norwich City, Whitwell &
Reepham station opened in 1882 and closed
to passengers in 1959. Freight continued
along the line, via Themelthorpe Curve
to the Lenwade concrete factory, until
1985. From 1993 the Marriott's Way long
distance path was opened along the old
trackbed of the railway. The derelict station
was purchased in 2007 and since then the

Whitwell & Reepham Railway Preservation
Society has laid track, converted the old
goods shed into an engine shed, and
resurfaced the platform. The first steam
gala at the restored station was held on
28 February 2009 – exactly 50 years since
the M&GN closed to passengers.

Below Steam outline 0-6-0 diesel 'Densil' heads a train of holidaymakers along the Wells Harbour
Railway, in Norfolk.

MAIN-LINE STEAM

Rarely a week goes by without some form of main-line steam special somewhere on Britain's rail network. Here are some highlights from Eastern England.

Left BR Standard 'Britannia' Class 4-6-2 No. 70013 'Oliver Cromwell' emerges from Ipswich Tunnel with the Railway Touring Company's 'Broadsman', from Liverpool Street to Holt on 26 March 2011.

Below New-build 'A1' Class 4-6-2 No. 60163 'Tornado' heads over the crossing at Newark with the returning York to King's Cross Steam Dreams' 'Cathedrals Express', on 16 August 2010.

Above Ex-LNER 'A4' Class 4-6-2
No. 60019 'Bittern' approaches Thetford
with the Steam Dreams' 'Cathedrals
Express' from King's Cross to Norwich,
on 19 December 2009.

Right Ex-LNER 'V2' Class 2-6-2 No. 4771
'Green Arrow' heads a National Railway
Museum special from York to King's Cross
through Huntingdon, on 18 November 2006.

WALES

Below Ex-South African Railways NGG Class 16 Garratt 2-6-2+2-6-2 No. 87 threads through the Aberglaslyn Gorge with a train on the scenic Welsh Highland Railway.

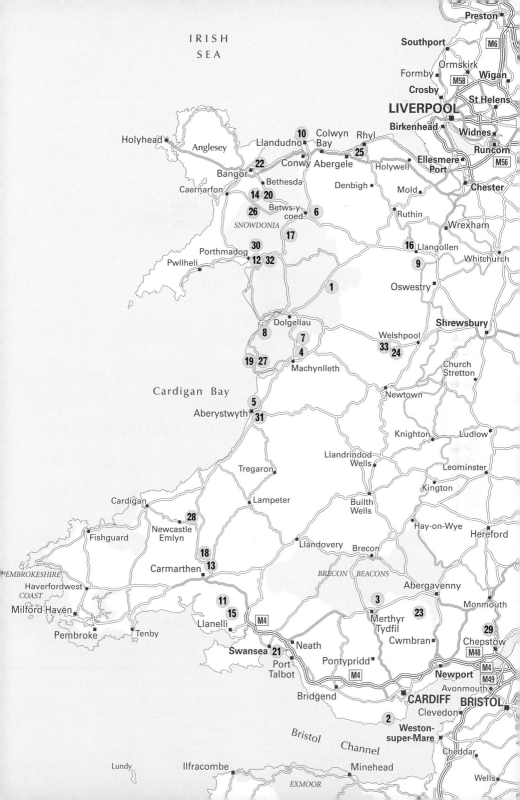

Bala Lake Railway

The Station, Llanuwchllyn,
Bala, Gwynedd LL23 7DD

TEL 01678 540666
WEBSITE www.bala-lake-railway.co.uk
ROUTE Llanuwchllyn to Bala (Penybont)
LENGTH 4½ miles | GAUGE 2ft
OPEN Daily (except Mon and Fri), early Apr to end
Jun and Sep; Bank Holidays, Apr to end Aug;
daily, Jul and Aug; see website for details

Above Hunslet 1902-built 0-4-0ST 'Holy War',
of the Dinorwic Slate Quarry, passes Lake Bala.

THE BALA & DOLGELLY RAILWAY opened in
1868, eventually becoming part of the mainly
single-track Great Western Railway route
from Ruabon to Barmouth. An important
through route for GWR trains to West
Wales, the line once saw heavy traffic on
summer Saturdays, with through carriages
to Barmouth or Pwllheli from Paddington,
Birkenhead, Birmingham and Manchester.
Listed for closure by Beeching, it lost its
freight traffic, which was diverted via the
Cambrian main line. Completely closed in
January 1965, the scheme for a narrow gauge
line along part of the trackbed alongside
Lake Bala was first proposed in 1971.

The present narrow gauge line skirts
the eastern shore of Lake Bala, the largest
natural lake in Wales, and was reopened in
stages between 1972 and 1976. Passenger
trains were initially diesel-hauled, but steam
services commenced in 1975. Trains are
normally operated by three Hunslet 0-4-0
saddle tanks; 'Holy War' and 'Alice' (both
built in 1902), and 'Maid Marion' (built in
1903), all originally from the Dinorwic Slate
Quarry (the latter having also worked on the
Bressingham and Llanberis Lake railways).
They also use two industrial narrow gauge
diesels. Passengers ride in purpose-built
covered carriages. Llanuwchllyn Station,
the headquarters of the railway, is a finely
preserved example of an original Bala
& Dolgelly Railway building. Also at
Llanuwchllyn are the railway's engine sheds
and an original GWR signalbox. Future
plans include extending the line half a mile
eastwards to a new terminus nearer Bala.

Barry Tourist Railway

The Station Buildings, Barry Island,
Vale of Glamorgan CF62 5TH

TEL 01446 748816 (weekdays only)
WEBSITE www.valeofglamorgan.gov.uk
ROUTE Barry Waterfront to Barry Island
LENGTH 1¼ miles | GAUGE Standard
OPEN Selected weekends and Bank Holidays,
Apr to Aug; Santa Specials in Dec
STATION National rail station Barry Island

OPERATED SINCE 2009 BY Cambrian
Transport, the Barry Tourist Railway has
a convoluted history dating back to 1979,
when the Butetown Historic Railway Society
first started running a train service along a
short piece of line near Butetown, Cardiff.
Displaced by the Cardiff Bay Development,
the Society then leased Barry Island station
from the Vale of Glamorgan Council in
1997, when it became the Vale of Glamorgan
Railway Company. Trains started running

from Barry Island to Gladstone Bridge in 2008 but the Council rescinded the lease agreement and chose Cambrian Transport to run it from the beginning of 2009.

Steam trains currently run from Barry Island station in two directions; southwards to Plymouth Road and northwards to the Docks Branch and Gladstone Bridge. Of interest to ageing steam enthusiasts, the running line passes close to the site of the famous locomotive graveyard of Dai Woodham, where several hundred locomotives were saved from the cutter's torch after withdrawal in the early 1960s.

Brecon Mountain Railway

Pant Station, Dowlais, Merthyr Tydfil, Mid-Glamorgan CF48 2UP

TEL 01685 722988
WEBSITE www.breconmountainrailway.co.uk
ROUTE Pant to Dolygaer
LENGTH 2 miles | GAUGE 1ft 11¾in
OPEN Weekends, Jan to Mar; frequent service Apr to Oct (daily, Jun to Aug); Santa Specials in Dec

THE BRECON & MERTHYR TYDFIL Junction Railway, opened throughout in 1868, was one of Britain's most scenic railways, involving tortuous gradients and the single-track Torpantau Tunnel. After passing into GWR ownership, the line was closed by BR in 1964. In 1972, a scheme to build a narrow gauge railway along part of the disused trackbed was put forward. Construction of the line from Pant to Pontsticill, in the Brecon Beacons National Park, began in 1978 and the first public train ran in 1980. A further ¼-mile extension along the side of Taf Fechan Reservoir, to the present terminus at Dolygaer, was opened in 1995. An extension of two miles through the 666yd-long Torpantau Tunnel, to a new terminus, is hopefully planned for the future.

Motive power is mainly steam and includes examples from Wales, Germany and South Africa, including the most powerful locomotive built for this gauge, a 2-6-2+2-6-2 Garratt No. 77. In recent years the mainstay has been 'Graf Schwerin-Löwitz', built by Am Jung of Germany in 1908 but this is now being overhauled. Trains are currently hauled by Baldwin 1930-built 4-6-2 No. 2, which spent its life in South Africa hauling limestone trains. Continental-style rolling stock, with end balconies, and a North American caboose have all been built in the company's well-equipped workshop at Pant, open for public viewing. A journey along the line starts at the grand purpose-built station at Pant and follows a 600yd new alignment before reaching the former B&M trackbed. Disused quarries can be glimpsed from the train before it enters the Brecon Beacons National Park near Taf Fechan Reservoir. At Pontsticill station the original signalbox can still be seen, although it is now a holiday cottage. The journey continues along the banks of the reservoir, with superb views of the Brecon Beacons, over rail obtained from various ammunition factory railways, until Dolygaer is reached. Passengers are not allowed to alight here and the train returns to Pontsticill, where a stop is made for refreshments in ex-British Railways covered wagons.

Below Built by Baldwin of Philadelphia in 1930, the Brecon Mountain Railway's 4-6-2 No. 2.

Centre for Alternative Technology

Llywyngwern Quarry, Pantperthog,
Machynlleth, Powys SY20 9AZ

TEL 01654 705989
WEBSITE www.cat.org.uk
ROUTE Lower car park to Centre
LENGTH 197ft | GAUGE 5ft 3in
OPEN Daily, throughout the year, except for
   selected days in Dec and Jan

LOCATED IN A FORMER slate mine, this
funicular railway (built to the Irish
'standard gauge') was opened to carry
visitors from a lower car park up to the
Centre for Alternative Technology in 1992.
It is operated by a water-balance system
and carries visitors a height of 109ft, on
a gradient of 1 in 1.81.

Constitution Hill Cliff Railway

Cliff Railway house, Cliff Terrace,
Aberystwyth, Ceredigion SY23 2DN

TEL 01970 617642
WEBSITE www.aberystwythcliffrailway.co.uk
ROUTE Marine Terrace to Constitution Hill
LENGTH 778ft | GAUGE 4ft 8½in
OPEN Daily, Easter to Oct
STATION National rail station Aberystwyth

THE LONGEST FUNICULAR CLIFF railway in
Britain, the Constitution Hill Cliff Railway
opened in 1896. Originally operated with
a water-balance system, it was electrified
in 1920 and carries passengers a height of
430ft on a gradient of 1 in 2. Visitors to the
summit are afforded views of up to 26 Welsh
mountain peaks (on a clear day!), and the
world's largest camera obscura.

Conwy Valley Railway Museum

The Old Goods Yard, Betws-y-Coed,
Conwy LL24 0AL

TEL 01690 710568
WEBSITE www.conwyrailwaymuseum.co.uk
ROUTE Within museum site
LENGTH 1 mile and ½ mile |
   GAUGES 7¼in and 15in
OPEN Daily throughout the year
STATION National rail station Betwys-y-Coed

LOCATED IN THE OLD goods yard at Betws-
y-Coed and adjacent to the station on the
Conwy Valley line from Llandudno Junction
to Blaenau Ffestiniog, this railway museum
dates back to the early 1970s, when a small
exhibition was opened in a British Railways
standard gauge coach. The present museum
building was later added and now houses
a fine collection of railway ephemera and
artefacts. Star of the show is a superb 15in-
gauge 'Britannia' 4-6-2. Outside there is a
7¼in miniature railway, on which visitors
are taken for a mile-long journey around the
museum site, hauled by one of the museum's
steam or diesel locomotives. A 15in-gauge
electric tramway also operates on the site,
with visitors being conveyed in a miniature
tramcar for a distance of ½ mile, parallel
to the standard gauge main line.

Above The Constitution Hill Cliff Railway is the
longest funicular cliff railway in Britain.

Corris Railway and Museum

Station Yard, Corris, Machynlleth,
Powys SY20 9SH

TEL 01654 761303
WEBSITE www.corris.co.uk
ROUTE Corris to Maespoeth
LENGTH 2 miles | **GAUGE** 2ft 3in
OPEN Sun, Bank Holidays and selected Sat, Easter
  to mid-Oct; Mon and Tue, mid-July to mid-Aug;
  Santa Specials in Dec (see website)

OPENED IN 1859 TO transport slate from the quarries around Corris to the main line at Machynlleth, this narrow gauge line was originally worked as a horse-tramway. Steam locomotives and passenger trains were introduced in 1879 and in 1930 the railway was taken over and worked by the GWR.

Passenger traffic ceased at the end of 1930 and goods traffic in 1948, when flooding severed the line north of Machynlleth only eight months after the railway had become part of British Railways.

Formed in 1996, the Corris Railway Society has reopened the line from Corris to Maespoeth and planning permission has been obtained for a further two miles southwards through the beautiful Esgairgeiliog Gorge. Future plans also include recreating the original overall-roofed station at Corris. The original engine shed at Maespoeth, built in 1878, has been restored and adapted to meet the present-day needs of the railway. Hauled by replica Corris Railway locomotive No. 7, steam-operated trains run on most weekends between May and September. Housed in the former Corris Railway buildings at Corris, the museum was opened in 1970 and is devoted to many exhibits and photographs from the railway.

Below Built from scratch by the Corris Railway Society, 0-4-2ST No. 7 waits to depart from Corris station, with a train for Maespoeth.

Above Half-size Lynton & Barnstaple 2-6-2T 'Yeo' on the 12¼in-gauge Fairbourne Railway.

Fairbourne Steam Railway

Beach Road, Fairbourne, Gwynedd LL38 2EX

TEL 01341 250362
WEBSITE www.fairbournerailway.com
ROUTE Fairbourne to Porth Penrhyn
   (for Barmouth Ferry)
LENGTH 2½ miles | GAUGE 12¼in
OPEN Daily, Easter to end Sep
STATION National rail station Fairbourne

THE FAIRBOURNE STEAM RAILWAY has had a very chequered history. Originally built as a 2ft-gauge horsedrawn construction tramway in 1896, the line was eventually rebuilt to 15in-gauge in 1916 by Narrow Gauge Railways, W J Bassett-Lowke's company. Using miniature steam locomotives passengers rode from Fairbourne, on the Cambrian Coast line, across sand dunes alongside the Mawddach estuary to Porth Penrhyn, where trains connected with a small ferry to Barmouth. After closure during the Second World War, following destruction by storms and military exercises, the line was reopened in 1947 and enjoyed considerable success during the late 1960s and early

1970s. The line faced closure in 1984 but was bought by a new owner, who regauged the line to 12¼in in the winter of 1985/86 using half-size replica narrow gauge locos, adding a tunnel, signalboxes, workshop and restaurant. The line currently uses two diesel and four steam locomotives, including a scale version of the Darjeeling Himalayan Railway 0-4-0ST 'Sherpa' and Lynton & Barnstaple 2-6-2T 'Yeo', with a total of 20 coaches. Another new owner took over the railway in 1995. In 2007 the railway company purchased the connecting ferry service across the Mawddach Estuary to Barmouth. The Rowen Centre at Fairbourne station contains a large 'G'-scale model railway.

Ffestiniog Railway Company

See page 162

Glyn Valley Tramway

Glyn Valley Historic Inn, Llanarmon Road, Glyn Ceiriog, Nr Llangollen, Clwyd LL20 7EU

TEL 01691 718896 (Hotel)
WEBSITE www.glynvalleyhotel.co.uk
OPEN During licensing hours

HOUSED IN THE EXCELLENT Glyn Valley Hotel in Glyn Ceiriog is a collection of photographs and ephemera of the Glyn Valley Tramway. Originally opened in 1873 as a horse-and-gravity worked slate tramway, this 2ft 4½in-gauge line was converted to steam haulage in 1888. The 8¾-mile route from Chirk along the picturesque valley of the River Ceiriog used tram-style steam locomotives until its closure in 1935. The roadside waiting room at nearby Pontfadog has been restored by the Glyn Valley Tramway Group and is open to the public.

Rather confusing to lovers of narrow gauge tramways, there are two separate organisations now dedicated to reviving the tramway in one form or another. They are the Glyn Valley Tramway Group (website www.glynvalleytramway.org.uk), which was founded in 1974 and is based at the Old Tramway Engine Shed in Glyn Ceiriog, and the Glyn Valley Tramway Trust (website www.glynvalleytramway.co.uk) formed in 2007. Readers are advised to visit both websites for more details.

which the line rises, firstly along the centre of the road, rising 400ft in 872yds. The upper section rises 150ft in 827yds along its own right of way. As the line is divided into two sections, passengers have to change cars at the halfway point, where there is a central winding house. The original steam-driven winding drums were replaced by electricity in 1958. Four original tramcars still survive, all 30ft-long with end balconies and seating 48 people, and are equipped with radio-telephone links to the winding house. Half Way station features interpretative material showing the history of the tramway.

Great Orme Tramway

Victoria Station, Church Walks,
Llandudno, Conwy LL30 2NB

TEL 01492 879306
WEBSITE www.greatormetramway.co.uk
ROUTE Victoria Station to Great Orme Summit
LENGTH 1 mile 8 chains | **GAUGE** 3ft 6in
OPEN Daily, late Mar to late Oct
STATION National rail network station Llandudno

Above The Great Orme Tramway at Llandudno is the only cable-operated tramway in Britain.

OPENED IN 1902, THE 3ft 6in-gauge Great Orme Tramway is the only cable-operated street tramway in Britain. Built to take passengers to the 679ft summit of the Great Orme, where there are magnificent views of Snowdonia, Anglesey and the Irish Sea, the line climbs gradients as steep as 1 in 4. The bottom terminus is at Victoria Station, from

Gwendraeth Railway Project

WEBSITE www.bpgv.co.uk

BUILT BY CONVERTING AN existing coal-carrying canal, the Burry Port & Gwendraeth Railway opened throughout in 1886. Transporting coal from collieries in the Gwendraeth Valleys to the harbour at Burry Port, the steeply graded line had a chequered career and was taken over by the Great Western Railway in 1922. Passenger trains ceased in 1953 but coal trains, hauled by specially modified diesel shunters working in multiple, continued until 1996 when the line closed. Despite closure, much of the track was left *in situ*, slowly disappearing beneath encroaching undergrowth.

Today, the Gwendraeth Railway Project aims to restore services along the old Burry Port and Gwendraeth Railway, firstly between Pontyates and Pontnewydd, and then northwards to the former terminus at Cwm Mawr and southwards to Burry Port Harbour. The site at Pontyates is currently being cleared, while the only surviving BP&GVR steam loco, 1900-built Avonside 0-6-0ST No. 2, is being restored at the Pontypool & Blaenavon Railway (page 170).

Above A Darjeeling-Himalaya train makes its way around the Dduallt spiral.

Ffestiniog Railway Company

Harbour Station, Porthmadog, Gwynedd LL49 9NF

TEL 01766 516000
WEBSITE www.festrail.co.uk
ROUTE Porthmadog Harbour to Blaenau Ffestiniog
LENGTH 13½ miles | **GAUGE** 1ft 11½in
OPEN Wed and Thu late Feb to mid-Dec; daily, end
    Mar to Oct; Santa Specials in Dec (see website)
STATION National rail network stations
    Porthmadog, Minffordd, Blaenau Ffestiniog

OPENED IN 1836 as a horsedrawn and gravity tramway to take slate from the quarries at Blaenau Ffestiniog down to the harbour at Porthmadog, the Ffestiniog Railway was converted to steam power in 1865. Always independent, the Ffestiniog managed to keep operating through to 1946 although passenger services ceased in 1939. In 1951, an early railway preservation group was formed and the first length of line across the Cob to Boston Lodge was reopened in 1955. In stages the line was reopened to Tan-y-Bwlch, Dduallt (where a spiral was built to take the railway at a higher level past the new hydro-electric reservoir) and finally to Blaenau Ffestiniog in May 1982. Here, FR trains now run into a newly built station adjacent to the national rail network Conwy Valley terminus, while at Minffordd passengers can make connection with the Cambrian Coast line. Original Victorian rolling stock and locomotives (dating from 1863), including the unique double Fairlies (introduced in 1872), have been beautifully restored at the company's Boston Lodge works. Carriages Nos 15 and 16, introduced in 1873, were the first true bogie coaches in Great Britain and were among the earliest iron-framed coaches in the world. A trip on the line affords the traveller wonderful views of Snowdonia as the train steadily climbs high above Porthmadog, hugging the contours, round sharp curves, through tunnels and along ledges cut into the mountainside. The Ffestiniog Railway Museum, at Porthmadog Harbour station,

depicts the history of the line and includes the 1863-built 0-4-0 saddle and tender tank locomotive, 'Princess', and the famous hearse wagon, as well as other artefacts and many other well known wagons.

Many historic steam locomotives currently operate on the railway, including Double Fairlies 'Merddin Emrys' (built 1879) and 'David Lloyd George' (built 1992), 0-4-0STT 'Palmerston' (built in 1864), Hunslet 2-4-0STT 'Blanche' and 0-4-0 tender 'Linda' (both built in 1893), and the recently built replica of a Lynton & Barnstaple Railway 2-6-2T, named 'Lyd'. The oldest surviving FR locomotive, 0-4-0STT 'Prince', is being returned to service in time for the railway's 150th anniversary of steam haulage, in 2013.

Since 2011, the Ffestiniog Railway has been physically connected to the newly opened Welsh Highland Railway (see page 180) at Porthmadog Harbour station, and it is now possible to travel once again by narrow gauge railway for the 38½ miles from Caernarfon to Blaenau Ffestiniog.

Above Lynton & Barnstaple 2-6-2T 'Lyd' waits to depart from Porthmadog Harbour Station.
Below Vintage narrow gauge steam and modern standard gauge diesel at Blaenau Ffestiniog.

Gwili Railway

**Bronwydd Arms Station,
Carmarthen SA33 6HT**

TEL 01267 238213
WEBSITE www.gwili-railway.co.uk
ROUTE Bronwydd Arms to Danycoed
LENGTH 2½ miles | **GAUGE** Standard
OPEN Daily (except Mon and Fri), Easter to Sep;
  selected days, Oct to Dec (see website)

THE FIRST SECTION OF the railway from Carmarthen to Aberystwyth was the broad gauge Carmarthen & Cardigan Railway (C&CR), which opened in 1864 as far as Pencader. The GWR branch to Newcastle Emlyn was not reached until 1895 (it never reached Cardigan!). Then along came an ambitious scheme to link the important docks at Milford Haven with the Midlands and the North of England – thus was the grandly titled Manchester & Milford Haven Railway born. It soon ran into financial difficulties and instead of striking across the mountains to Llanidloes on the Mid-Wales line, built an easier route from Aberystwyth to Pencader (where it met the existing C&CR) via Strata Florida and Lampeter. As a grand north-south route the railway failed miserably and became something of a pleasant rural backwater, being taken over by the Great Western Railway in 1911. Listed for closure in the 1963 'Beeching Report', the line was prematurely partially closed when flooding severed the northern part of the line in late 1964. While passenger services from Lampeter to Carmarthen struggled on for only a few more months, goods traffic continued to use the southern part of the line until 1973.

In 1978 a preservation group had starting running services over a short length of track at Bronwydd Arms station, three miles north of Carmarthen. By 1987 the line was extended to Llwyfan Cerrig, where there is a picnic site and the 7¼in-gauge Llwyfan

Above Ex-GWR 0-6-0PT No. 6430 takes on water at Bronwydd Arms on the Gwili Railway.

Cerrig Miniature Railway (see page 168). More recently the line has been extended to Danycoed, with plans to extend further northwards to Llanpumpsaint. Aided by material and equipment from the former Swansea Vale Railway, the railway is also being extended southwards from Bronwydd Arms to Abergwili Junction, on the northern outskirts of Carmarthen. The railway owns a large collection of mainly industrial steam and diesel locomotives, and a wide variety of passenger and goods rolling stock, including an award-winning Taff Vale Railway coach, dating from 1891, which was fully restored after being found in a field in Herefordshire. Bronwydd Arms signalbox originally stood at Llandybie on the Central Wales Line and was bought in 1985 for use on the Gwili Railway. Dating from 1885, the 21-lever box is now fully restored and operates signals in the station area.

Llanberis Lake Railway

Gilfach Ddu, Llanberis, Gwynedd LL55 4TY

TEL 01286 870549
WEBSITE www.lake-railway.co.uk
ROUTE Gilfach Ddu (Llanberis) to Penllyn
LENGTH 2½ miles | **GAUGE** 1ft 11½in
OPEN Selected days Feb to Nov; most days,
　　Apr to Oct; Santa Trains in Dec (see website)

THE 4FT-GAUGE PADARN RAILWAY was opened in 1843 to transport slate from the quarries at Llanberis to Port Dinorwic along the north shore of Llyn Padarn. Both the port and the railway were owned by the Dinorwic Quarry Company, who also operated a system of 1ft 10¾in lines within their quarries. Initially the line was a horse-worked tramway but steam power was soon introduced in 1848. The decline in the slate industry eventually caused the closure of the line in 1961 but in 1970 work began on building a narrow gauge tourist railway along part of the trackbed. By 1971, the route from Gilfach Ddu to Penllyn was complete and open to passengers. In 2003, the railway was extended from Gilfach Ddu to Llanberis,

Below Hunslet 0-4-0 No. 2 'Thomas Bach' heads a Llanberis Lake Railway train out of Llanberis.

with a new station across the road from the Snowdon Mountain Railway (see page 172). Trains are operated by three historic Hunslet 0-4-0 steam locomotives that originally worked in the nearby Dinorwic quarries, and passengers are carried in both open and closed carriages, all built in the railway's workshop. A journey along the line gives good views across the lake to Snowdon and the massive pumped storage hydro-electric plant that is inside the nearby mountain on the same side of the lake as the railway. The railway's workshops are located in the National Slate Museum (see page 169) at Gilfach Ddu.

Llanelli & Mynydd Mawr Railway

Cynheidre Colliery, Cynheidre, Llanelli, Carmarthenshire SA15

WEBSITE www.lmmrcoltd.com
OPEN Working parties on Sat at Cynheidre

OPENED IN 1803 AS a public railway, the horsedrawn Carmarthenshire Tramroad was built to transport coal, iron ore and limestone to Stradley Iron Works near Llanelli. Closed in 1844, the tramway reopened as the Llanelly & Mynydd Mawr Railway with steam haulage in 1883. It was absorbed by the Great Western Railway in 1922 and continued to transport coal from Cynheidre Colliery until 1989.

The current Llanelli & Mynydd Mawr Railway was founded in 1999 to reopen part of this historic railway. A new station platform, locomotive shed and stock shed has already been built at the Cynheidre colliery site near Llanelli, as the first phase towards relaying around ½ mile of track. Avonside 0-4-0ST No. 1498 'Desmond' is currently being restored at the Llangollen Railway. A 1965-built Sentinel 0-4-0 diesel hydraulic is operational at Cynheidre.

Llangollen Railway

Llangollen Station, Abbey Road, Llangollen, Denbighshire LL20 8SN

TEL 01978 860979
WEBSITE www.llangollen-railway.co.uk
ROUTE Llangollen to Carrog
LENGTH 7½ miles | **GAUGE** Standard
OPEN Most weekends and Bank Holidays, Feb to Oct; daily during school holidays, Feb to Dec; daily (except Fri), May to Jun; Santa Specials in Dec; see website for operating days and special events

OPENED IN 1865 AS the Llangollen & Corwen Railway, this line was a continuation of the Vale of Llangollen Railway which opened from Ruabon, on the Shrewsbury & Chester Railway, to Llangollen in 1862. Both lines were worked by the Great Western Railway, eventually forming the eastern section of that company's through route to Barmouth. Apart from the Ruabon to Llangollen section, which was double-track, the rest of this long line was single-track with trains passing at intermediate stations. Although

Opposite Ex-GWR 'Dukedog' 4-4-0 No. 9017 heads a vintage goods train along the Dee Valley.
Below The new-build GWR steam railmotor makes its maiden voyage at Berwyn.

once an important route for summer Saturday holiday trains from the Midlands and Merseyside to Barmouth and Pwllheli, the line was listed for closure in the 1963 'Beeching Report'. Closure came in early 1965 and the track was subsequently lifted.

Founded in 1972, the Flint & Deeside Railway Preservation Society moved into Llangollen, its station attractively situated on the north bank of the River Dee, in 1975, with the ultimate goal of reopening the line as far as Corwen. Since then much progress has been made, with Berwyn being reached in 1985, Deeside Halt in 1990, Glyndyfrdwy in 1992 and Carrog in 1996. Work is now progressing on the 2½ miles of track towards Corwen, where a new station will be built in the town centre. The two major engineering features of the line are the bridge over the River Dee to the west of Llangollen and the 689yd single-bore tunnel near Berwyn. A journey along the line, the only preserved standard gauge example in North Wales, gives passengers wonderful views of the Dee Valley as the train climbs high above the river and parallels the A5 trunk road. Berwyn station, now a holiday cottage, with its black and white timbered building and tea room is located in a magnificent position overlooking the River Dee. A large collection of steam (including many ex-GWR examples) and diesel locomotives maintain passenger services on the line, which is also a frequent host to visiting main-line engines from other heritage railways. A new locomotive shed was opened at Llangollen in November 1995, providing accommodation for up to ten locomotives and a carriage restoration section. The locomotive works at Llangollen is famous for its new-build steam locomotives, which include the GWR steam railmotor completed in 2011 and the two current projects, 'Grange' Class 4-6-0 'Betton Grange' and unrebuilt 'Patriot' Class 4-6-0 'The Unknown Warrior'. The 'Berwyn Belle' Wine & Dine train operates on some Saturday evenings and Sunday lunchtimes (see website for details).

Llechwedd Slate Caverns

Blaenau ffestiniog, Gwynedd LL41 3NB

TEL 01766 830306
WEBSITE www.llechwedd-slate-caverns.co.uk
ROUTE Within slate caverns
LENGTH 366ft | **GAUGE** 2ft and 3ft
OPEN Daily throughout the year

THIS SINGLE-LINE FUNICULAR railway opened in 1979 and carries visitors 131ft down into the underground slate caverns, on an average gradient of 1 in 2.79. A 2ft-gauge line, the Miners' Tramway, carries visitors on a ½-mile trip through the quarry workings.

Above Happy days on the 2ft-gauge Miners' Tramway in the Llechwedd Slate Caverns.
Below All aboard the 3ft-gauge funicular railway in the Llechwedd Slate Caverns.

Llwyfan Cerrig Miniature Railway

**Llwyfan Cerrig Station
(see Gwili Railway, page 164)**

TEL 01267 238213
WEBSITE www.gwili-railway.co.uk
ROUTE Within site of Llwyfan Cerrig station
   on Gwili Railway (see page 164)
LENGTH 200yd | **GAUGE** 7¼in
OPEN During operating days of Gwili Railway
STATION Heritage railway station Llwyfan Cerrig

THIS END-TO-END MINIATURE RAILWAY opened in 1993 as an added attraction for Gwili Railway passengers. The route takes trains through a wooded valley alongside the Gwili Railway trackbed. Trains are operated by two petrol hydraulic locomotives. There is no access to Llwyfan Cerrig station other than by travelling on the Gwili Railway.

Narrow Gauge Railway Museum

Wharf Station, Tywyn, Gwynedd LL36 9EY

TEL 01654 710472
WEBSITE www.ngrm.org.uk
OPEN Feb half-term; weekends in Mar; April
   to early Nov (hours vary)
STATION Heritage railway and national rail
   network stations Tywyn Wharf and Tywyn

A COMPREHENSIVE COLLECTION OF British narrow gauge locomotives, rolling stock and artefacts, mainly relating to the Welsh slate industry, covering a period spanning over 200 years. The museum is situated at the Talyllyn Railway's Wharf station in Tywyn. Both the station and museum were rebuilt with the aid of Heritage Lottery Funding and reopened by the Prince of Wales in 2005.

Above Diminutive Dundee Gas Works 0-4-0WT No. 2, on display at the Narrow Gauge Railway Museum in Tywyn.

Historic locomotives on display include 'Jubilee 1897', together with others from Welsh slate quarries, the Guinness Brewery Railway in Dublin, Dundee Gas Works and Manchester Locomotive Works. Of interest to lovers of 'Thomas the Tank Engine', the museum also houses a reconstruction of the Reverend W. Awdry's study in his last home in Gloucestershire.

National Slate Museum

Gilfach Ddu, Llanberis, Gwynedd LL55 4TY

TEL 01286 870630
WEBSITE www.museumwales.ac.uk/en/slate
OPEN Daily, Easter to end Oct; Sun to Fri, Nov to Easter

LOCATED IN THE FORMER 19th-century workshops of Dinorwic Quarry, the National Slate Museum is rail-connected to the nearby Llanberis Lake Railway (page 165), which uses part of the building as its own workshop. Originally opened in 1972, the recently refurbished museum features the largest working waterwheel in Britain and a terrace of four re-erected slateworkers' cottages. There is also much to interest lovers of narrow gauge slate railways, including the restored working quarry incline, engine shed and restored 0-4-0 narrow gauge steam locomotive, 'Una', built by Hunslet of Leeds in 1905. An extensive model railway show is held in the museum during a weekend in mid-February.

National Waterfront Museum

Oystermouth Road, Maritime Quarter, Swansea SAI 3RD

TEL 01792 638950
WEBSITE www.museumwales.ac.uk/en/swansea
OPEN Daily throughout the year

EXHIBITS FROM SWANSEA'S MARITIME, industrial and transport history are displayed in this new museum, which opened in 2005. On view is a Peckett 0-6-0T dating from 1916, a restored Swansea City tramcar and Mumbles Railway tramcar No. 15, the only surviving item from that railway. Of interest to railway historians is a working 4½ ton replica of Trevithick's first steam railway locomotive, 'Penydarren'. An extensive model railway and steam day is held during the first weekend in September each year.

Penrhyn Castle Industrial Railway Museum

Penrhyn Castle, Bangor,
Gwynedd LL57 4HN

TEL 01248 353084 (Castle)
WEBSITE www.nationaltrust.org.uk/penrhyn-castle
OPEN Daily (except Tues), mid-Mar to end Oct

SITUATED IN THE FORMER stables of this National Trust property is a large collection of industrial steam locomotives and rolling stock, both standard and narrow gauge, including exhibits from the Dinorwic Quarry and the Padarn and Penrhyn Railways. The oldest locomotive in the collection is the 4ft-gauge Padarn Railway 0-4-0 'Fire Queen', built in 1848. There is also a display of railway signs and a model railway collection.

Pontypool & Blaenavon Railway

Furnace Sidings Station, Garn Yr Erw,
Blaenavon, Gwent NP4

TEL 01495 792263
WEBSITE www.pontypool-and-blaenavon.co.uk
ROUTE Bleanavon High Level to Whistle Inn Halt
LENGTH 2 miles | **GAUGE** Standard
OPEN Most weekends, Apr to Oct

THE FORMER LONDON & NORTH Western Railway's branch between Pontypool and Blaenavon was fully opened in 1872 and closed to passengers in 1941. Coal traffic ceased in 1980 with the closure of the Big Pit Colliery and the line finally closed. Partial reopening by a preservation society in 1983, as the Pontypool & Blaenavon Railway (between Furnace Sidings and Whistle Inn), was centred around the Big Pit Mining

Below Visiting ex-GWR 0-6-0PT No. 6435 works a short goods train on the Pontypool & Blaenavon Railway, one of the highest standard gauge railways in Britain.

Museum. It was another 27 years before an extension was opened to Blaenavon High Level in 2010. The railway is set in the heart of a World Heritage Site and runs by a newly established country park that has been developed from ex-colliery waste sites – part of the line currently operated reaches 1,307ft above sea level at Whistle Inn Halt. A branch line to serve the Big Pit Mining Museum (website www.museumwales.ac.uk/en/bigpit) opened in late 2011. The main line is currently being extended in stages until it runs from Abersychan through to Brynmawr, a distance of eight miles. When the railway reaches Waunavon, it will reopen the station that, at 1,400ft above sea level, is the highest standard gauge station in England and Wales. The preservation society has acquired a station building from the site of Pontypool Crane Street station, deconstructing it for eventual reconstruction along the line. The railway is home to a wide variety of steam and diesel locomotives, many of them currently awaiting restoration.

 Above A busy scene on the Rhiw Valley Light Railway, with 0-6-2 'Powys' and 0-4-0 'Jack'.

longitudinal 'sofa' seats. A looped-shaped extension to the line, including bridging the River Rhiw, is planned for the future.

Rhiw Valley Light Railway

Lower House Farm, Manafon, Welshpool, Powys SY21 8BJ

WEBSITE www.rvlr.co.uk
ROUTE Within farm site
LENGTH ¾ mile | **GAUGE** 15in
OPEN See website for dates. Open Day in aid of charities is usually held during first week of Sep

A PRIVATE OUT-AND-BACK MINIATURE railway founded in 1970 that runs through fields with two gated crossings has been kept going by volunteers, and is open to the public only on selected days. Motive power is provided by two steam locomotives, 2-6-2T 'Powys', built by Severn Lamb, and 0-4-0 tender loco, 'Jack'. Passengers ride in four-wheeled and bogie carriages with

Rhyl Miniature Railway

Marine Lake, Rhyl, Clwyd LL18 1LN

TEL 01352 759109
WEBSITE www.rhylminiaturerailway.co.uk
ROUTE Around Marine Lake
LENGTH 1 mile | **GAUGE** 15in
OPEN Weekends and Bank Holidays, Easter to end Sep; daily during Whitsun Week and school summer holidays
STATION National rail network station Rhyl

OPENED IN 1911, THIS historic 15in-gauge seaside miniature railway takes passengers on a route around the perimeter of the Marine Lake at Rhyl, and on its southern shore parallels the North Wales Coast main line, where the locomotive shed is situated. Steam motive power includes three historic 4-4-2 'Atlantics' ('Joan', 'Railway Queen' and 'Michael'), built by Albert Barnes in the 1920s, and American 4-4-0 No. 44. A new Central station and museum was opened in 2007. Albert Barnes' 4-4-2 'Billy' is currently on display in the railway's museum.

Snowdon Mountain Railway

Llanberis, Nr Caernarfon,
Gwynedd LL55 4TY

TEL 0844 493 8120
WEBSITE www.snowdonrailway.co.uk
ROUTE Llanberis to Snowdon Summit
LENGTH 4¾ miles | **GAUGE** 2ft 7⅝in
OPEN To Clogwyn – daily, mid-Mar to May.
  To the Summit – daily May to end Oct
  (services can be restricted or cancelled by
  bad weather conditions. See website for
  further details)

Britain's only public rack and pinion steam mountain railway, with its unique gauge, takes passengers to the 3,560ft summit of the highest mountain in Wales from where, on clear days, there are spectacular views of Snowdonia and the Irish Sea. The line opened in 1896 but was closed on the same day after a fatal accident; the only one known on the line. It was reopened in April 1899 and until 1986 all trains were steam-hauled using the Swiss-built locomotives with their sloping boilers, some of which date back to the building of the railway. Carriages are positioned, uncoupled, on the uphill side of the locomotive and have independent braking systems. Trains are restricted to a speed limit of 5mph on the line, where gradients as severe as 1 in 5 can

Below Built at Winterthur in Switzerland in 1895, 0-4-2T No. 3 'Wyddfa' pushes its single coach up the Snowdon Mountain Railway.

be encountered. Four Hunslet-built diesel hydraulic locomotives were introduced in 1986 as an economy measure but many of the seven 0-4-2T (the continental nomenclature would be 0-2-1T) steam locos, four of which are now over 100 years old, are still in use. These are numbered 2 to 8 (No. 1 being involved in the accident on opening day) and are named 'Enid', 'Yr Wyddfa', 'Snowdon', 'Moel Siabod', 'Padarn', 'Ralph' and 'Eryri'. Three diesel electric railcars, capable of multiple unit working, were also tested on the line in 1995. To allow eight trains to operate on the line during busy periods, there are passing loops at Hebron, Halfway and Clogwyn. The spectacular new station and visitor centre on the summit were opened in 2009. Passengers are advised that train services can be restricted by bad weather conditions, especially at the beginning and end of the operating season.

Above A steam train departs from Snowdon Summit station with a train for Llanberis.

Below Two descending trains approach Clogwyn station on the Snowdon Mountain Railway, while in the distance is an ascending train.

Above Fletcher Jennings 0-4-2ST No. 1 'Talyllyn' heads a train of vintage coaches.

Talyllyn Railway Company

Wharf Station, Tywyn, Gwynedd LL36 9EY

TEL 01654 710472
WEBSITE www.talyllyn.co.uk
ROUTE Tywyn Wharf to Nant Gwernol
LENGTH 7½ miles | **GAUGE** 2ft 3in
OPEN Feb half-term and Sun, Mar; daily,
    Apr to end Oct; selected days, Nov and Dec;
    see website for details and special events
STATION National rail network station Tywyn

OPENED IN 1866 TO carry slate from the quarries above Nant Gwernol to Tywyn, this scenic 2ft 3in-gauge railway has never actually closed. When the slate quarry closed in 1946 the owner, Sir Henry Haydn Jones, managed to keep the railway running, but with little or no maintenance it was in a very run-down state by the time of his death in 1950. However, a group of volunteers led by the author Tom Rolt, amongst others, saved it from imminent closure by taking over the running of the line to Abergynolwyn, thus making it the world's first successful

railway preservation scheme. In 1976, the Preservation Society reopened the ¼-mile section of mineral line from Abergynolwyn to Nant Gwernol, at the foot of the first incline that led to the quarry. Trains are still hauled by some of the original and beautifully restored Talyllyn Railway and ex-Corris Railway (see page 159) locomotives. Four-wheeled coaches are used, as well as more recent additions; one from the Corris Railway. Locomotives, including three diesels, are numbered 1 to 9 and are named 'Talyllyn' (0-4-2 saddle tank, built 1865), 'Dolgoch' (0-4-0 well tank, built 1866), 'Sir Haydn' (0-4-2 saddle tank, built 1878 for the Corris Railway), 'Edward Thomas' (0-4-2 saddle tank, built 1921 for the Corris Railway), 'Midlander' (diesel mechanical, built 1940), 'Douglas' (0-4-0 well tank, built 1918), 'Tom Rolt' (0-4-2 tank, built 1949), 'Merseysider' (diesel hydraulic, built 1964) and 'Alf' (diesel mechanical, built 1950). A journey on the line today evokes all the atmosphere of a Victorian narrow gauge railway as the train slowly climbs along the wooded side of the valley of the Afon Fathew, affording panoramic views of Dolgoch Falls and the Welsh mountains. The fascinating Narrow Gauge Railway Museum (see page 168) is located at Tywyn Wharf station.

Below A view from 0-4-2T No. 7 'Tom Rolt', as it approaches the station and sheds at Pendre.

Above Suitably begrimed, former Corris Railway 0-4-2ST No. 4 'Edward Thomas' heads a short goods train on the Talyllyn Railway.

Below Fletcher Jennings 0-4-2ST No. 1 'Talyllyn' heads a train up the picturesque valley of the Afon Fathew on the Talyllyn Railway.

Teifi Valley Railway

Henllan Station, Nr Newcastle Emlyn,
Ceredigion SA44 5TD

TEL 01559 371077
WEBSITE www.teifivalleyrailway.org
ROUTE Henllan to Llandyfriog Riverside
LENGTH 2 miles | **GAUGE** 2ft
OPEN Easter to end Sep and Oct half-term;
Santa Specials in Dec (see website)

Above Built by Hunslet in 1894, 0-4-0ST 'Alan George' heads a train on the Teifi Valley Railway.

SITUATED ON THE TRACKBED of the former GWR branch line from Pencader to Newcastle Emlyn (opened in 1895, closed to passengers in 1952 and to goods in 1973), the narrow gauge Teifi Valley Railway began running trains in 1985. Based at Henllan, the line was extended to Llandyfriog in 1987 and further extended to Llandyfriog Riverside in 2006. Between Henllan and Llandyfriog the railway crosses eight bridges. The long-term aim of the railway is to extend westwards to Newcastle Emlyn and eastwards to Llandyssul, giving a total length of 6 miles. Trains are usually operated by steam locomotives, including Hunslet 0-4-0 saddle tank 'Alan George', built for the Penrhyn Slate Quarry in 1894, and 0-6-2 tank 'Sgt. Murphy', built for the Admiralty by Kerr Stuart in 1918, along with several industrial diesel locomotives that originally worked in the slate quarries of North Wales.

Tintern Old Station

Tintern, Nr Chepstow, Gwent NP16 7NX

TEL 01291 689566
WEBSITE www.tintern.org.uk/station.htm
OPEN Daily, Easter to end Oct; weekend
before Christmas

THIS STATION AND SIGNALBOX are situated on the former Chepstow to Monmouth branch line, opened in 1876 by the Wye Valley Railway, amalgamated with the GWR in 1905, closed to passengers in 1959 and closed completely in 1964. The beautifully restored station building and signalbox were reopened in 1975 as an information centre and café, with a display of local railway history. The signalbox is used to house arts and crafts exhibitions. Two restored railway coaches are also on site – a 1935 GWR corridor coach used as an information and sales area, and a 1955 BR example used as a lecture area for schools. A 5in-gauge miniature railway is laid along part of the old trackbed and operates on many weekends.

Above The former Wye Valley Railway station at Tintern is now a café and visitor centre.

Vale of Rheidol Railway

See page 178

Welsh Highland Railway

See page 180

Welsh Highland Heritage Railway

Tremadog Road, Porthmadog, Gwynedd LL49 9DY

TEL 01766 513402
WEBSITE www.whr.co.uk
ROUTE Porthmadog to Pen-y-Mount
LENGTH ¾ mile | **GAUGE** 1ft 11½in
OPEN Daily, end Mar to end Sep; daily
  (except Mon) in Oct
STATION National rail network station
  Porthmadog

WHAT IS NOW KNOWN as the Welsh Highland Heritage Railway has been operating passenger services over a short length of track from their own station at Porthmadog, just across the road from the national rail network station, since 1980. Their initial aim was to reopen the entire Welsh Highland Railway but a High Court action in 1995 decided that the Ffestiniog Railway could rebuild and operate it from Porthmadog Harbour to Caernarfon (see page 180). The heritage railway currently owns and operates several steam locos, notably 2-6-2T 'Russell', built by Hunslet in 1906 for the North Wales Narrow Gauge Railway, which are all housed in the railway's workshop at Gelert's Farm. Special trains occasionally venture onto the Welsh Highland Railway's main line, via a connection at Pen-y-Mount. On normal operating days visitors are given a ride on the railway and treated to a visit to Gelert's Farm Works, where there is also the 7¼in-gauge Porthmadog Woodland Railway.

Below The Cambrian main line runs past the terminus of the Welsh Highland Heritage Railway at Porthmadog.

Vale of Rheidol Railway

Park Avenue, Aberystwyth,
Ceredigion SY23 1PG

TEL 01970 625819
WEBSITE www.rheidolrailway.co.uk
ROUTE Aberystwyth to Devil's Bridge
LENGTH 11¾ miles | **GAUGE** 1ft 11¾in
OPEN Daily (except selected Mon, Fri and Sun)
and Bank Holiday weekends, Apr to Oct; daily,
Jun to early Sept
STATION National rail network station
Aberystwyth

THE VALE OF RHEIDOL Light Railway was opened in 1902 as a narrow gauge line to serve leadmines, the timber industry and tourism. In 1913 the railway was amalgamated with its bigger neighbour, Cambrian Railways, which in turn was taken into the Great Western Railway empire in 1922. The GWR then virtually rebuilt the line, scrapped two of its original locomotives and built three new replacements. These three 2-6-2T locomotives, No. 7 'Owain Glyndwr', No. 8 'Llywelyn' and No. 9 'Prince of Wales' are still working on the line. Goods traffic ceased in 1920, winter passenger services in 1931, and from then on the railway had to earn its living purely from tourism. Following temporary closure during the Second World War, the railway

was nationalised in 1948, unlike its near neighbour the Talyllyn Railway (see page 174), eventually becoming the only steam-operated line on British Railways in 1968. The railway was privatised in 1989, when it was sold to the Brecon Mountain Railway (see page 157). They, in turn, sold it to the Phyllis Rampton Narrow Gauge Railway Trust in 1996, which recently invested in a new loco and carriage works at Aberystwyth.

Trains run from part of the main-line terminus at Aberystwyth, passing the former GWR standard gauge engine shed which houses VOR locomotives and rolling stock. The Afon Rheidol is soon crossed on a newly reconstructed bridge and the railway begins to climb, gradually at first, up the southern side of the valley before taking water at the intermediate station of Nantyronen. The gradients soon become steeper, with the line winding its way up a ledge cut into the hillside, and after pausing at the crossing point at Aberffrwd passengers are treated to magnificent views of the river far below. The final approach to the terminus at Devil's Bridge is a continuous 1 in 50 gradient with numerous sharp curves, and the entrance to the station, 639ft above sea level, is through a deep rock cutting. Near the station are the famous beauty spots of Mynach Falls, Devil's Punchbowl and Jacob's Ladder.

Below left 2-6-2T No. 9 'Prince of Wales' heads a train through Aberffwrd.
Below 2-6-2T No. 7 'Owain Glyndwr' leaves Rheidol Falls during British Rail days.

Above A Ffestiniog Railway Double Fairlie 0-4-4-0T heads through the Aberglaslyn Pass.

Below Headed by Beyer–Garratt No. 87, a WHR train crosses the main street in Porthmadog.

Welsh Highland Railway

Harbour Station, Porthmadog, Gwynedd LL49 9NF

TEL 01766 516000
WEBSITE www.festrail.co.uk
ROUTE Porthmadog (Harbour) to Caernarfon
LENGTH 25 miles | **GAUGE** 1ft 11½in
OPEN Weekends and school holidays, Feb half-term to mid-Dec; most days Apr to Oct; daily, July to Sep; Santa Specials in Dec
STATION National rail network station Porthmadog

Above Superpower of four locomotives hauling a long mixed train on the Welsh Highland Railway.

THE WELSH HIGHLAND RAILWAY originated as the North Wales Narrow Gauge Railway Company in 1877 and was acquired by the Welsh Highland Railway in 1923. In 1934 the WHR was leased to its neighbour, the Ffestiniog Railway (see page 162). The line, the longest narrow gauge railway in Wales (22 miles), ran from Porthmadog to Dinas Junction, via the Pass of Aberglaslyn and Beddgelert, through the heart of Snowdonia but was not a success and finally closed in 1937. Track was lifted in 1941 and in 1964 a preservation group, Welsh Highland Railway (1964) Ltd, was formed to reopen the line (see page 177).

Because the trackbed was still in the hands of the official receiver, plans to reopen the line involved lengthy litigation and argument between the WHR Ltd and the neighbouring Ffestiniog Railway, who also wanted to take over the project. However, in 1995 the Ffestiniog Railway was given permission to rebuild the railway and an award of £4.3 million from the National Lottery Millennium Fund helped to speed up the process.

Opened in stages from 1997, the ambitious 1ft 11½in-gauge Welsh Highland Railway is the longest heritage railway in Britain. Its route runs firstly along the trackbed of the closed Carnaerfon to Afonwen standard gauge line to Dinas, then strikes off in an easterly direction along the route of the old Welsh Highland Railway into the Snowdonia National Park (to Rhyd Ddu, Beddgelert, Aberglaslyn Pass and Porthmadog). The steam locomotives hauling the trains are massive (by narrow gauge standards) Beyer-Garratt articulated locos, rehabilitated from South Africa. At Porthmadog the line crosses the standard gauge Cambrian Coast line over a level diamond crossing, ending its journey through the street for a short distance, before reaching Porthmadog Harbour station. Here it connects with the Ffestiniog Railway to Blaenau Ffestiniog. It is now possible to travel once again by narrow gauge steam railway for all of the 38½ miles from Caernarfon to Blaenau Ffestiniog; a truly awesome scenic ride through Snowdonia.

Welshpool & Llanfair Light Railway

The Station, Llanfair Caereinion,
Welshpool, Powys SY21 0SF

TEL 01938 810441
WEBSITE www.wllr.org.uk
ROUTE Welshpool (Raven Square) to Llanfair
  Caereinion station
LENGTH 8 miles | **GAUGE** 2ft 6in
OPEN Weekend, Bank Holidays and school holidays,
  Apr to early Nov; daily (except some Mon and
  Fri), late May to Sep; daily, late Jul to Aug; Santa
  Specials in Dec; see website for details
STATION National rail network station Welshpool

OPENED IN 1903, THE Welshpool & Llanfair
Light Railway was one of the first railways
built under the Light Railways Act of 1896.
It has some of the steepest gradients (max
1 in 24) on any adhesion railway in Britain,
and was built to carry general merchandise,
coal, timber and livestock between farms in
the Banwy Valley and the local market town
of Welshpool. Until closure, W&L trains
ran through the back streets of the town to
an interchange at the Cambrian Railways
standard gauge station. From the beginning
the railway was run by the Cambrian until
it was absorbed into the GWR in 1922.
The last passenger train ran in 1931 but
goods traffic continued, and in 1948 the
line became part of the nationalised British
Railways. BR closed the line in 1956 but a
preservation group stepped in and reopened
the first section to passengers in 1963. The
line, following the delightful Banwy valley
from Llanfair Caereinion, now ends at the
new Raven Square station on the west side
of Welshpool, using buildings from the
1863 Eardisley station. The two original
'Swindonised' Beyer Peacock locomotives,
'The Earl' and 'Countess', still work on the
line alongside steam engines from Austria,
Finland, Sierra Leone and Antigua, and
continental-style balcony carriages from
Austria and bogie coaches from Sierra Leone.

Below and opposite Hunslet 2-6-2T No. 14 takes on water at Llanfair Caereinion and heads
a passenger train across the River Banwy, on the Welshpool & Llanfair Light Railway.

MAIN-LINE STEAM

Rarely a week goes by without some form of main-line steam special somewhere on Britain's rail network. Here are some highlights from Wales.

Left Steam returned to the Central Wales Line on 15 July 2006, in the form of LMS '5MT' Class 4-6-0 No. 45407 and BR Standard '4MT' Class 2-6-0 76079, seen here at Llandeilo with the Railway Touring Company's 'Central Wales Explorer'.

Above Organised by West Coast Railways, BR Standard '4MT' Class 2-6-0 No. 76079 hauls its train along the scenic Cambrian Coast line near Tonfanau, on 23 August 2007.

Left Painted in war-time black, LMS 'Princess Coronation' Class 4-6-2 Pacific No. 6233 'Duchess of Sutherland' leaves Conwy through the old city walls, with the returning 'Welsh Dragon' from Holyhead to Crewe on 24 April 2010. The train was organised by Princess Margaret Rose Trust (PMRT) Railtours.

Right Ex-GWR 'Manor' Class 4-6-0 No. 7802 'Bradley Manor' storms up Talerddig Bank with Past-Time Rail's 'Cambrian Coast Express', returning from Aberystwyth to Shrewsbury on 16 September 2006.

NORTHERN ENGLAND & ISLE OF MAN

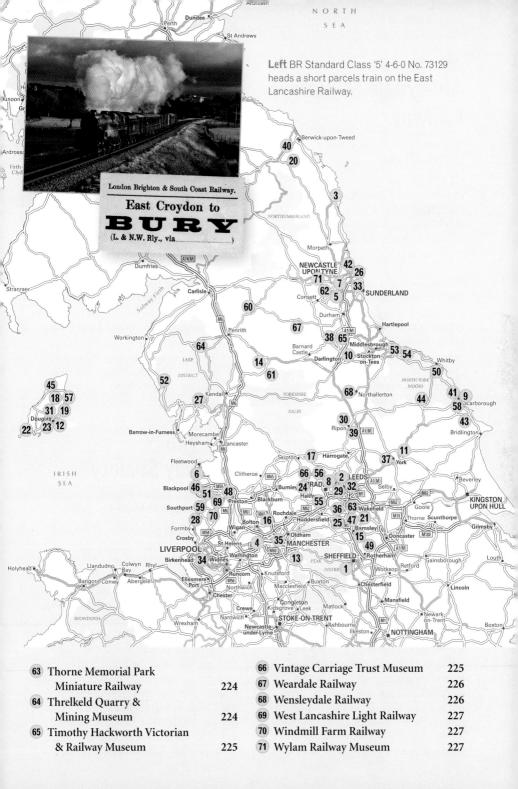

Left BR Standard Class '5' 4-6-0 No. 73129 heads a short parcels train on the East Lancashire Railway.

London Brighton & South Coast Railway.

East Croydon to

BURY

(L. & N.W. Rly., via_____)

Abbeydale Miniature Railway

Abbeydale Road South, Dore,
Sheffield S17 1LA

TEL 0114 221 1900
WEBSITE www.loco.talktalk.net/smee06
ROUTE Within Ecclesall Woods
LENGTH c.¼ mile | GAUGES 5in and 7¼in
OPEN Bank Holidays and alternate Sun,
    mid-Mar to early Oct

Above The extensive dual gauge Abbeydale Miniature Railway near Sheffield.

OWNED AND OPERATED BY the Sheffield & District Society of Model & Experimental Engineers, this dual gauge, ground-level miniature railway has been located on its present site in Ecclesall Woods since 1978. Fully signalled, the line features two stations, level crossings, footbridges, challenging gradients, locomotive and carriage sheds, and a turntable. Also on site is an elevated multi-gauge track for gauges '0' to 7¼in and a dual gauge (32mm and 45mm) garden railway.

either being used or restored, including examples dating back to 1917 and the 1920s. Rolling stock includes 'V' skips, ammunition wagons and air-braked coaches. The journey takes passengers from Bridge Road, through a landscaped area, over a mill race and up to a wooded area in a cutting to Kirkstall Abbey. Future plans include an extension to Leeds Industrial Museum (see page 206).

Abbey Light Railway

Bridge Road, Kirkstall, Leeds LS5 3BW

WEBSITE www.abbeylightrailway.webs.com
ROUTE Kirkstall Abbey to Bridge Road
LENGTH ¼ mile | GAUGE 2ft
OPEN Sun and Bank Holiday afternoons
    throughout the year, weather permitting

FOUNDED IN 1976 AS a family railway and supported by volunteers to restore vintage narrow gauge railway locomotives and rolling stock, the Abbey Light Railway opened for passengers in 1986. A well equipped machine shop is able to carry out heavy repairs and construction of new equipment from 10¼in to 2ft gauges. A collection of seven petrol and diesel industrial narrow gauge locomotives are

Aln Valley Railway Society

Barter Books, Alnwick Station,
Northumberland NE66 2NP

TEL 01665 604888 (bookshop)
WEBSITE www.alnvalleyrailway.co.uk
    and www.barterbooks.co.uk

PRESENTLY BASED AT LONGHOUGHTON Goods Yard north of Alnmouth and also at Wooler, the society is dedicated to reopening the branch line from Alnmouth to Alnwick. The three-mile branch line was opened in 1850 and was closed by British Railways in 1968. Northumberland County Council have recently approved the scheme, although it will be some years before steam is again seen in Alnwick. With its overall roof still intact, Alnwick station is currently home to a superb secondhand book shop.

Astley Green Colliery Museum

Higher Green Lane, Astley Green,
Tyldesley, Manchester M29 7JB

WEBSITE www.agcm.org.uk
OPEN Sun, Tue and Thu afternoons, all year

SET ON A FORMER colliery site close to the
Bridgewater Canal, this 15-acre museum
includes a twin tandem compound steam
winding engine and a collection of 28
colliery locomotives. Demonstration freight
trains are run on a 1,250yd stretch of line
within the site.

Beamish Open Air Museum

Beamish, Co Durham DH9 0RG

TEL 0191 370 4000
WEBSITE www.beamish.org.uk
OPEN Daily throughout the year; closed
    most Mon and Fri, Nov to Mar

OPENED IN 1970, BEAMISH is a very large,
200-acre, open-air, award-winning museum
of late-19th century life in Northern
England. Exhibits include re-created houses,
shops, school, farm and colliery. There is
much of railway interest, including a range of
typical North Eastern Railway buildings, such
as the 1867 Rowley station (reconstructed at
Beamish after being moved from its site near
Newcastle), a goods shed and signalbox, and
a short length of line. Locomotives on display
include a full-size replica of the famous
Stockton & Darlington Railway 'Locomotion
No. 1', NER Class 'Cl' 0-6-0 No. 876, built in
1889, and several ancient industrial steam
examples. A 1½-mile electric tramway runs
through the site.

Left and below At Beamish, (left) the full-size
working replica of the Stockton & Darlington
Railway's 'Locomotion No. 1' and, (below) built
in 1863, Furness Railway 0-4-0 No. 20 halts at the
reconstructed Rowley station (below).

Blackpool & Fleetwood Tramway

Blackpool Transport Services, Rigby Road, Blackpool, Lancashire FY1 5DD

TEL 01253 473001
WEBSITE www.blackpooltransport.com
ROUTE Starr Gate to Fleetwood Ferry
LENGTH 11 miles | **GAUGE** Standard
OPEN Daily throughout the year
STATION National rail network stations Blackpool North and Blackpool South

ONE OF BLACKPOOL'S BIGGEST tourist attractions, this street tramway along the Fylde Coast is the only survivor of systems that were once widespread in the towns and cities of Britain. It is also only one of three non-heritage tramways to use double-deck trams in the world (the others are in Hong Kong and Alexandria, Egypt) and was the only remaining tram system in Britain until the opening of the Manchester Metrolink in 1992. The tramway was originally opened in 1885, with electric power taken from a conduit system. This was replaced by overhead wires in 1899 and the tramway was extended further in the first years of the 20th century. The present owners, Blackpool Corporation, took over the Blackpool & Fleetwood Tramway in 1920 and further extended the route to Starr Gate in 1926. Over 80 electric trams once operated an intensive service along the sea front. Examples include 1930s single and double-deck tramcars. During Blackpool Illuminations each autumn, the trams are decorated with coloured lights and over six million passengers are carried each year. A major investment of £100 million to upgrade the entire track and introduce 16 new Bombardier trams is well underway. As from 2012, these will operate from the new depot at Starr Gate while the older trams will be based at the old Rigby Road Depot – this heritage fleet will then only operate on selected days during the year along the central section of the route.

Below Built in 1934, double-deck Balloon tram No. 717 on the Blackpool & Fleetwood Tramway.

Above A line-up of industrial steam locomotives on the Bowes Railway at Springwell.

Bowes Railway Centre

**Springwell Village, Nr Gateshead,
Tyne & Wear NE9 7QJ**

TEL 0191 416 1847
WEBSITE www.bowesrailway.co.uk
ROUTE Within railway centre
LENGTH 1 mile | **GAUGE** Standard
OPEN Mon to Sat throughout the year. Trains
   operate on selected Sun and special events
   days (see website)

THE BOWES RAILWAY was designed by
George Stephenson as a colliery line and
opened in 1826. It was built to carry coal
from collieries along its length to Jarrow on
the River Tyne for shipment. The line passed
into the ownership of the Bowes family in
1850, which operated it until the collieries
were nationalised in 1947. It used a mixture
of rope-worked inclines and locomotive-
hauled sections, and operated virtually
unchanged until 1974. It is now a scheduled
Ancient Monument and the centre at
Springwell includes the only working rope-
hauled standard gauge incline in the world.

Preservation began in 1975 and visitors
can now travel in steam-hauled brakevans
along a short length of track from the
engineering centre and up the east incline
to Blackham's Hill, where they alight to
visit the rope haulage buildings and watch
demonstrations. An extension was opened
in 1996, from Blackham's Hill to Wrekenton
along the line's old Pelaw main railway
branch. The centre also houses the largest
collection of colliery rolling stock in the
country, several steam and diesel industrial
locomotives, and the restored 19th-century
railway workshops. The Bowes Railway
Path links Routes 7 and 14 of the National
Cycle Network.

Bradford Industrial Museum

Moorside Mills, Moorside Road,
Eccleshill, Bradford,
West Yorkshire BD2 3HP

TEL 01274 435900
WEBSITE www.bradfordmuseums.org/venues/
    industrialmuseum
OPEN Tue to Sun throughout the year

THIS INDUSTRIAL MUSEUM, SITUATED in
a former wool-spinning mill built in 1875,
houses a large collection of stationary steam
and gas engines, and a transport section
which includes road vehicles, a Hudswell-
Clarke 0-4-0 saddle tank locomotive built
in 1922, and the last surviving Bradford
tramcar and trolley bus. Visitors can take
rides on a horsedrawn tramway and there
are regular exhibitions throughout the year.

Central Tramway

16 St Nicholas Cliff, Scarborough,
North Yorkshire YO11 2ES

TEL 01723 501754
ROUTE Foreshore Road to St Nicholas Gardens
LENGTH 254ft | GAUGE 4ft 8½in
OPEN Daily, Apr to Sep
STATION National rail network station
    Scarborough

THERE WERE ONCE FIVE funicular railways
in Scarborough but only two, the Central
Tramway and the older South Cliff Lift
(see page 221) remain open. The Central
Tramway opened in 1881 and, uniquely,
was originally operated by a steam engine
that powered the winding drum. It was
converted to electric power in 1920 and
today carries passengers on a gradient
of 1 in 2.82.

Above Built in 1922, Hudswell Clark 0-4-0ST
'Nellie' at the Bradford Industrial Museum.

Darlington Railway Centre and Museum ('Head of Steam')

North Road Station, Darlington,
Co Durham DL3 6ST

TEL 01325 460532
WEBSITE www.darlington.gov.uk/headofsteam
OPEN Tue to Sun, Apr to Sep; Wed to Sun, Oct
    to March
STATION National rail network station Darlington
    North Road

NORTH ROAD STATION WAS built in 1842
for the Stockton & Darlington Railway.
Refurbished in 2008 and now known as
'Head of Steam', the railway museum and
restoration centre is housed in the restored
station building, goods shed and historic
Hopetown Carriage Works. Exhibits include
the original SDR 'Locomotion No. 1' (built
in 1825) and 0-6-0 'Derwent' (built in 1845),
as well as historic rolling stock that includes
a SDR coach (built in 1846) and a NER

example (built in 1860). The Centre also houses the Ken Hoole Study Centre, with its large collection of railway photographs, archive material and the library collection of the North Eastern Railway Association. North Road station, with its overall roof, is still used by Regional Railways trains operating on the Darlington to Bishop Auckland service.

Derwent Valley Light Railway

The Yorkshire Museum of Farming, Murton Park, Murton Lane, Murton, York YO19 5UF

TEL 01904 489966
WEBSITE www.dvlr.org.uk
ROUTE Within station site
LENGTH ½ mile | **GAUGE** Standard
OPEN Sun and Bank Holidays, Easter to end Sep

THE ORIGINAL DERWENT VALLEY Light Railway, an independent company, opened in 1913 and ran for 16 miles from Layerthorpe in York to Cliffe Common, just outside Selby. Services were originally mixed traffic but passenger services ceased in 1926. Closure

of the line to goods traffic was in stages – to Elvington in 1968, to Dunnington in 1973, and final closure of the remainder in 1982. During the Second World War the railway was heavily used by the War Department as a supply route to the airfields at Elvington, Skipwith and the depot at Wheldrake. The ½-mile section that remains runs from Murton Lane to the Osbaldwick road.

The railway (also known as the 'Blackberry Line') has been run since 1993 by the Great Yorkshire Railway Preservation Society and is based on a site at the former DVLR station at Murton Lane, which also houses the Yorkshire Museum of Farming and a reconstructed Viking village. Locomotives working and on display include an Andrew Barclay 0-4-0 industrial saddle tank and nine small diesels, together with a small collection of rolling stock. An award-winning restored former North Eastern Railway signalbox is also open to visitors. Wheldrake station is one of three surviving original DVR timber station buildings and was dismantled piece by piece from its former site and reconstructed at Murton. A run-round loop and engine shed are currently being constructed. To the west, the trackbed of the line from Osbaldwick to Layerthorpe has been converted to a footpath and cycleway.

Below Built in 1929, Hudswell Clark 0-6-0T No. 65 in action at Murton, on the Derwent Valley Light Railway near York.

Douglas Horse Tramway

Tramway Stables, Queen's Promenade, Douglas, Isle of Man IM2 4NR

TEL 01624 696420
WEBSITE www.douglas.gov.im
ROUTE Derby Castle to Victoria Pier
LENGTH 1½ miles | **GAUGE** 3ft
OPEN Daily, mid-May to mid-Sep

Above The 3ft-gauge horse tramway runs along the seafront at Douglas, on the Isle of Man.

OPENED IN 1876 BY Thomas Lightfoot, this horsedrawn tramway has been in continuous operation, apart from temporary closure during the Second World War, ever since. It was sold in 1882 to The Isle of Man Tramways Ltd and then again to the Isle of Man Tramways & Electric Power Co Ltd in 1894. As a result of the failure of Dumbell's Bank in 1900 the Douglas Corporation bought the tramway from the liquidator for £50,000, and the Corporation continues to run the system to this day. A total of 23 tramcars, dating from 1883 to 1913, are used on this service on the double-track road tramway along Douglas Promenade. Stables for the 45 working horses are situated at Derby Castle and are open to visitors. In winter the horses are put to grazing at various parts of the island.

Dragon Miniature Railway

Marple Garden Centre, Dooley Lane, Marple, Stockport, Cheshire SK6 7HE

WEBSITE www.freewebs.com/dragonrailway
ROUTE Within grounds of garden centre
LENGTH ½ mile | **GAUGE** 7¼in
OPEN Weekends and school holidays all year

OPENED ON ITS PRESENT site in 1999, this family-run miniature railway is laid out in a dumb-bell shaped circuit through a landscaped and wooded area in the Marple Garden Centre, and features a station, waiting room, shop bridge, tunnel and engine sheds. Motive power consists of five coal-fired steam locomotives and five petrol-powered diesel outline locos.

East Lancashire Railway

See page 196

Eden Valley Railway

Warcop Station, Warcop, Appleby, Cumbria CA16 6PR

WEBSITE www.evr-cumbria.org.uk
ROUTE Warcop to Sandford
LENGTH 1 mile | **GAUGE** Standard
OPEN Bank Holidays and most Sun, Apr to Sep

THE EDEN VALLEY RAILWAY opened between Kirkby Stephen and Clifton, south of Penrith, in 1862. Passenger services were withdrawn in 1962 but the Appleby to Warcop section was left open for military trains to an army training centre. These ceased in 1989, when

Above Warcop station is the headquarters of the Eden Valley Railway, in Cumbria.

the track was mothballed. The Eden Valley Railway Society was formed in 1995, with the aim of restoring the 6-mile line between Appleby and Flitholme, near Warcop. In 2004, the Eden Valley Railway Trust was given permission to reopen the railway. Since 2006, trains have been running again but only along the short section between Warcop and Sandford. A large collection of mainly industrial diesel locos, along with diesel and electric multiple units, is based at Warcop.

Elsecar Heritage Railway

Wath Road, Elsecar, Barnsley, South Yorkshire S74 8HJ

TEL 01226 746746
WEBSITE www.elsecarrailway.co.uk
ROUTE Rockingham station to Hemingfield Basin
LENGTH 1 mile | **GAUGE** Standard
OPEN Bank Holidays and most Sun, Apr
   to Oct; Santa Specials in Dec

THE ELSECAR RAILWAY IS situated in a large open-air industrial archaeology museum, which incorporates the old Elsecar Ironworks. The Elsecar workshops were once the hub of industrial activity on the Wentworth Estate for the mining and engineering enterprises of the Earl Fitzwilliam of Wentworth Woodhouse. The workshops were built between 1850 and 1860 and were taken over by the National Coal Board in 1947, before finally closing in the early 1980s. The Elsecar branch of the South Yorkshire Railway opened in 1850 and the single-track line ran through Mexborough, across the Dearne & Dove Canal via a lifting bridge. The line carried mineral traffic serving the collieries and ironworks, and when Cortonwood Colliery closed in 1984 the track was lifted. The present railway employs two industrial steam locomotives and two diesels. Passengers are carried in four ex-BR Mark 1 coaches from the former workshop site at Rockingham, through an attractive conservation area beside a branch of the Dearne & Dove Canal, to Hemingfield. A run-round loop is being installed at Hemingfield, while long-term plans include extending the line a further mile to Cortonwood.

Below Built in 1954, Peckett 0-6-0ST No. 2150 'Mardy Monster', on the Elsecar Railway.

East Lancashire Railway

Bury Station, Bolton Street, Bury, Lancashire BL9 0EY

TEL 0161 764 7790
WEBSITE www.east-lancs-rly.co.uk
ROUTE Heywood to Rawtenstall
LENGTH 12 miles | **GAUGE** Standard
OPEN Weekends, Jan to Nov; Wed to Sun and
    Bank Holidays, Apr to Sep; Santa Specials
    in Dec (see website)
STATION National rail network station Bury
    Interchange (Manchester Metrolink)

THE ORIGINAL EAST LANCASHIRE Railway
came into being as early as 1846, to serve
cotton mills in the Irwell Valley north of
Bury. The line was extended to Bacup in
1852 and the railway was absorbed by the
Lancashire & Yorkshire Railway in 1859, and
then the London & North Western Railway
in 1922, before becoming part of the LMS
in 1923. The line was closed to passengers
between Bury and Rawtenstall in 1972, and
to freight in 1980.

Below British Railways Standard Class '5'
4-6-0 No. 73129 takes on water.

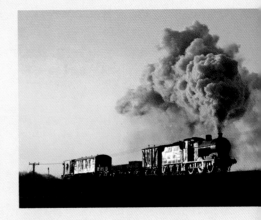

Above Ex-LMS Class '4F' 0-6-0 No. 44422 heads
a short goods train.

Prior to closure, a preservation
group had already moved in to Bury and
subsequently opened a transport museum
in 1969. After financial assistance exceeding
£1 million from the local councils and
county council, the first public trains started
running between Bury and Ramsbottom
in 1987, with Rawtenstall being reached in
1991. Opened in 2003, the steeply graded
eastward link from Bury to Heywood
connects with the national rail system. Trains
are operated along the picturesque Irwell
Valley, with its several viaducts, by a variety
of preserved main-line steam and diesel
locomotives. Steam locomotives include
LMS Class '3F' 0-6-0 No. 47324, LMS 'Black
Five' 4-6-0 No. 5337 and BR Standard Class
'8' 4-6-2 No. 71000, 'Duke of Gloucester'.
Visiting locomotives from other railways
can frequently be seen in action and the
ELR has built up a reputation for its varied
collection of preserved diesels, which can be
seen in action on several diesel weekends (see
website). Preserved main-line diesels include
examples from Classes 01, 05, 08, 20, 24, 33,
37, 40, 50 and 55.

Close to the ELR Bury Bolton Street
station is the Bury Transport Museum
(www.burytransportmuseum.org.uk; tel
0161 763 7949). The museum houses historic
road and railway vehicles.

Above Ex-LNER Class 'K4' 2-6-0 No. 61994 'The Great Marquess', at work amid a wintry scene on the East Lancashire Railway.

Below Ex-LNER Class 'A4' 4-6-2 No. 60007 'Sir Nigel Gresley' crosses the river at Summerseat on the East Lancashire Railway.

Embsay & Bolton Abbey Steam Railway

Bolton Abbey Station, Bolton Abbey, Skipton, North Yorkshire BD23 6AF

TEL 01756 710614
WEBSITE www.embsayboltonabbeyrailway.org.uk
ROUTE Embsay to Bolton Abbey
LENGTH 4 miles | **GAUGE** Standard
OPEN Sun and Bank Holidays, all year; Tue and weekends, Apr to Oct; daily, late July to end Aug; Santa Specials in Dec; see website for special events

Above Ex-LNER Class 'D49' 4-4-0 'Morayshire', on the Embsay & Bolton Abbey Railway.

THE BRANCH LINE FROM Skipton to Ilkley via Bolton Abbey was opened by the Midland Railway in 1888. Bolton Abbey station was often frequented by royalty visiting the nearby Bolton Hall. The line was listed for closure in the 1963 'Beeching Report' and was closed completely between Embsay Junction and Ilkley in March 1965.

In 1979, the Yorkshire Dales Railway obtained a Light Railway Order for part of the line and since then has reopened 4 miles from Embsay, with its original Midland Railway buildings, to a new award-winning terminus at Bolton Abbey. The railway owns and operates a very large collection of finely restored industrial steam locomotives, vintage carriages and diesels. Future plans

include a physical link at Embsay Junction with the main railway network to Skipton station via the freight only line from Swinden Quarry on the former Grassington branch.

Above A steam-hauled train on the curiously gauged railway at Great Laxey Mine.

Great Laxey Mine Railway

Laxey Station, Laxey, Isle of Man IM4 7NH

TEL 01624 860186
WEBSITE www.laxeyminerailway.im
ROUTE Within old lead mine site
LENGTH ¼ mile | **GAUGE** 1ft 7in
OPEN Sat and Bank Holidays, Easter to late Sep; Sun in Aug; for special events see website

OPENED IN 1877, THIS unusually gauged railway once carried lead and zinc ores from the Great Laxey Mine. Part of its route passes through a tunnel under the Manx Electric Railway (see page 207). The railway was abandoned in 1929 but reopened in 2004 as a tourist attraction and features two working replicas of the original 19th-century 0-4-0 locomotives, 'Ant' and 'Bee'.

Groudle Glen Railway

Groudle Glen, Onchan, Isle of Man

WEBSITE www.ggr.org.uk
ROUTE Lhen Coan to Sea Lion Rocks
LENGTH ¾ mile | **GAUGE** 2ft
OPEN Easter weekend; Sun early May to end Sep;
evening trains on Wed, late Jul to late Aug; see
website for special events

OPENED BY R. M. BROADBENT in 1896
to take visitors from picturesque Groudle
Glen to a rocky headland, where sea lions
and polar bears were kept in a dammed
sea inlet, this narrow gauge railway was an
immediate success. Trains were operated by
2-4-0 steam locomotive 'Sea Lion', built by
Bagnall in 1896, and in 1905 a second engine,
'Polar Bear', arrived. After the First World
War, battery locomotives operated the trains
but six years later the steam locos returned.
After closure during the Second World War,
services ran from 1950 until closure in 1962.
    Restoration of the line began in 1982 by
the Isle of Man Steam Railway Supporters'
Association (website www.iomrsa.com)
and in 1986 the line partly reopened, with
trains being hauled by two Hunslet diesel
locomotives. 'Sea Lion' was rescued in a
semi-derelict condition from Loughborough,
and fully restored by instructors and
apprentices of the BNFL Training Centre
at Sellafield, before returning to service in

Below Built in 1896, Bagnall 2-4-0 'Sea Lion'
heads for Sea Lion Rocks station.

1987. Sister engine 'Polar Bear' also survived
and has been restored to working order at
the Amberley Working Museum (see page
40), occasionally visiting its old home for
special events. A second steam locomotive,
'Annie', was completed in 1998 and a replica
of 'Polar Bear' in 2003. Complete restoration
of passenger services to Sea Lion Rocks was
completed in 1992. Lhen Coan terminus
station has an attractive Swiss-style overall
roof, while at Sea Lion Rocks the new station
and tea rooms were opened in 2003.

Heatherslaw Light Railway

Ford Forge, Heatherslaw, Cornhill-on-Tweed,
Northumberland TD12 4TJ

TEL 01890 820317
WEBSITE www.heatherslawlightrailway.co.uk
ROUTE Heatherslaw to Etal village
LENGTH 2 miles | **GAUGE** 15in
OPEN Daily, Apr to Oct

Above Newly introduced steam locomotive
'Bunty', on the Heatherslaw Light Railway.

SITUATED ON THE HEATHERSLAW Estate,
with its restored water mill and blacksmith's
forge, this 15in-gauge miniature railway was
built from scratch in 1989. It follows the
picturesque River Till, with trains operated
by steam locomotives 'Lady Augusta', built
in 1989, and 'Bunty'. Passengers are carried in
a variety of disc-braked coaches, all built in
the railway's workshops.

Hemsworth Water Park Miniature Railway

Hoyle Mill Road, Kinsley, Pontefract, West Yorkshire WF9 5JB

TEL 01977 617617
WEBSITE www.hemsworthcouncil.co.uk/waterpark
ROUTE Within grounds of water park
LENGTH 300yds | GAUGE 7¼in
OPEN Daily, Easter to Sep

SITUATED IN THE PLAYWORLD section of the large Hemsworth Water Park, this miniature railway was built in 1993 with help from members of the Wakefield Model Engineers Society. The total circuit, which includes level crossings, engine shed and turntable, includes a 1 in 80 gradient. Operating the trains are two simply designed battery locomotives.

Isle of Man Railway Museum

Station Road, Port Erin, Isle of Man

OPEN Daily, Apr to Oct

OPENED IN 1975, THE museum of the Isle of Man Railways is situated in the old carriage shed adjacent to the station at Port Erin (and is also known as the Port Erin Railway Museum). Exhibits include Beyer Peacock 2-4-0 steam locomotives 'Peveril' (built in 1875) and 'Mannin' (built in 1926), and a unique six-wheeled Manx Northern Railway carriage, the 'Royal Saloon', (the Duke of Sutherland's carriage), as well as other Isle of Man Railway artefacts and ephemera.

Isle of Man Steam Railway

Strathallan Crescent, Douglas, Isle of Man IM2 4NR

TEL 01624 662525 (timetable enquiries)
WEBSITE www.iomsrsa.com
ROUTE Douglas to Port Erin
LENGTH 15½ miles | GAUGE 3ft
OPEN Daily, mid-Mar to early Nov

PART OF THE ONCE extensive Isle of Man Railway's narrow gauge system, this line was opened in 1874 and has been in more or less continuous use since then. While the rest of the island's steam railway system had all closed by 1968, nationalisation by the Manx Government in 1977 saved the Douglas to Port Erin section from a similar fate. The Victorian atmosphere still

pervades the whole line, from the beautifully maintained station buildings to the vintage locomotives and carriages. A journey along the line, with its rolling Manx scenery and glimpses of the Irish Sea, is akin to taking a trip back in time to a period 100 years ago, when the pace of life was less frenetic. The majority of the original Beyer-Peacock 2-4-0 steam locomotives still survive – the oldest locomotive on the books is Beyer Peacock 2-4-0T No. 4 'Loch', built in 1874 – and the railway is also home to two diesel railcars from the former Donegal Railway Company in Ireland, currently awaiting restoration in the carriage shed at Douglas Station. Locomotive No. 15 'Caledonia', an 0-6-0T built by Dubs in 1885, was fully restored to working order to celebrate the centenary of the opening of the Snaefell Mountain Railway in 1995 (see page 221).

Strangely, the nationalised railway does not have its own website, so visitors to the line should visit the website of the Isle of Man Steam Railway Supporters Association (see left). Current timetables can also be viewed on www.iombusandrail.info/railtimetables.html

Above Two vintage modes of transport on the Isle of Man.

Below The Steam Railway runs close to the coast near Port Soderick.

Keighley & Worth Valley Railway

The Railway Station, Haworth, West Yorkshire BD22 8NJ

TEL 01535 645214
WEBSITE www.kwvr.co.uk
ROUTE Keighley to Oxenhope
LENGTH 5 miles | **GAUGE** Standard
OPEN Weekends, Bank Holidays and school holidays, Feb to Dec; daily, Jun to mid-Sep; Santa Specials in Dec; see website for special events
STATION National rail network station Keighley

THIS WAS ONE OF the earliest preserved standard gauge railways in Britain, reopened by a preservation society in 1967. The railway still serves the community of the Worth Valley as originally intended. The former Midland Railway branch from Keighley, on the main Leeds to Skipton line, to Oxenhope opened in 1867 to serve the large number of local mills along the valley, and was closed by British Railways in 1962. The line, although short, offers much to the visitor together with its associations with the Brontës at Haworth and the filming of E. Nesbit's *The Railway Children* at Oakworth. A large collection of nearly 40 steam and diesel locomotives has been built up over the years and the railway is also home to two museums, The Vintage Carriage Trust at Ingrow (see page 225) and the Railway Museum at Oxenhope, as well as extensive workshop facilities. Locomotives range from Lancashire & Yorkshire Railway 0-6-0 No. 957, built in 1887, former BR Standard Class '4MT' 2-6-2 tank No. 80002, National Trust-owned

Below Built in 1887, Lancashire & Yorkshire Railway 0-6-0 No. 957 heads a train of vintage carriages on the Keighley & Worth Valley Railway.

LNWR 0-6-2 'Coal Tank' No. 1054, and LMS '4F' 0-6-0 No. 43924. Other locos awaiting restoration include LMS 'Jubilee' Class 4-6-0 No. 45596 'Bahamas', built in 1935, which is on display at Oxenhope Exhibition Shed. Steam trains operate most of the services along this picturesque route, calling at carefully restored, award-winning gas-lit stations. Early morning services at weekends are usually operated by a diesel multiple unit or railbus. The tiny station at Damems is reputedly the smallest in Britain.

Above Ex-LMS Class '4F' 0-6-0 No. 43924 heads a passenger train on the scenic Keighley & Worth Valley Railway.

Below Repatriated from Sweden in 1973, WD 2-8-0 No. 90733 heads a goods train very close to a pot of gold on the heritage line.

Kirklees Light Railway

The Railway Station, Park Mill Way,
Clayton West, Nr Huddersfield,
West Yorkshire HD8 9XJ

TEL 01484 865727
WEBSITE www.kirkleeslightrailway.com
ROUTE Clayton West to Shelley (via 511yd Shelley
   Woodhouse Tunnel)
LENGTH 3¾ miles | **GAUGE** 15in
OPEN Weekends and Bank Holidays, all year; daily
   during school holidays; Santa Specials in Dec
   (see website)

THIS 15IN GAUGE MINIATURE railway
operates every weekend along part of
the trackbed of the former Lancashire &
Yorkshire Railway's branch from Clayton
West Junction to Clayton West, opened in
1879 and finally closed by British Rail in

Below An impressive steam line-up at Clayton
West engine shed, on the Kirklees Light Railway.

1983. The Kirklees Light Railway was the
brainchild of Brian Taylor, who was also
involved in the building of a 10¼in-gauge
miniature steam railway at Shibden Park,
Halifax (see page 220). After several years of
searching for a suitable site, work started on
the present line in 1990. The first train ran to
Cuckoo's Nest in 1991 and to Skelmanthorpe
in late 1992. Locomotives operating on
the line include Hunslet-type 2-6-2 tank
'Fox', articulated 0-4+4-0s 'Hawk' and 'Owl',
and 0-6-4 saddle tank 'Badger'. Rolling
stock consists of nine 20-seat carriages, the
fully enclosed examples being heated. All
locomotives and rolling stock were built for
the railway by Brian Taylor, who has built
and continues to supply equipment for other
railways. Special events run throughout the
year, including a Santa Express and driver
experience courses. Clayton West is also
home to the Barnsley Society of Model
Engineers, who operate a passenger-carrying
miniature railway on most weekends.

Lakeshore Railroad

South Marine Park, South Shields,
Tyne & Wear NE33 2LD

ROUTE Around lake within park
LENGTH 555yds | **GAUGE** 9½in
OPEN Weekends and school holidays, Easter
   to Nov; daily mid-May to mid-Sep

OPENED IN 1972, THIS miniature railway
runs around the perimeter of a boating
lake and passes through woodland.
Developments have included construction
of a station and water tower, and a two-train
service is in operation on Bank Holidays
and some Sundays in July and August.
Steam locomotives operating are a ⅙-scale
Atcheson, Topeka & Santa Fe 4-6-2 No.
3440, and a ¼-scale Ferrocarril National
del Magdalena Columbia 2-6-2 No. 27.
Passengers are carried on a total of nine
toast-rack coaches.

Above LMS Fairburn 2-6-4T No. 42085 speeds along the Lakeside & Haverthwaite Railway in Cumbria.

Lakeside & Haverthwaite Railway

Haverthwaite Station, Nr Ulverston, Cumbria LA12 8AL

TEL 015395 31594
WEBSITE www.lakesiderailway.co.uk
ROUTE Haverthwaite to Lakeside
LENGTH 3½ miles
OPEN Daily, Apr to Oct; weekends, Nov; Santa Specials in Dec; see website for special events

THE FORMER FURNESS RAILWAY branch line from Ulverston to Newby Bridge opened in 1869 and was extended to Lakeside station in 1872. At the same time, the Furness Railway also took over the steamers on Lake Windermere, connecting with their trains at Lakeside station. The line was particularly popular with holidaymakers in the summer months, when special trains would travel to Lakeside from destinations in northwest England. Closure of the line came in 1965, when British Railways also sold the Windermere steamers.

A preservation group took over the steeply graded section from Haverthwaite and steam trains started running again in 1973, when the line was opened by the then Bishop of Wakefield and famous railway photographer, the Rt Rev Eric Treacy. The short but highly scenic journey can be taken in conjunction with a 10½-mile trip along Lake Windermere, as trains connect with steamers at Lakeside terminus. A collection of restored industrial and ex-BR steam and diesel locomotives are used on the line. The main motive power is supplied by two LMS-designed and BR-built 2-6-4 tank engines, Nos 42073 and 42085, dating from 1950 and 1951 respectively. Steam locomotive driving experiences are also available.

Lakeside Miniature Railway

Pleasureland Station, Esplanade, Southport, Merseyside PR8 1RX

TEL 01772 745511
WEBSITE www.lakesideminiaturerailway.co.uk
ROUTE Within Marine Park
LENGTH ½ mile | **GAUGE** 15in
OPEN Weekends, Easter to Jun; daily, Jul to Oct
STATION National rail network station Southport

THIS SEASIDE MINIATURE RAILWAY opened in 1911, using two Bassett-Lowke locos which now reside in the USA. Extended to the beach in 1948, most of the route runs alongside the Marine Lake from Pleasureland to the pier and beach. Motive power consists of three diesel electric steam outline locos ('Prince Charles', 'Duke of Edinburgh' and 'Golden Jubilee'), and two diesel hydraulics ('Princess Anne' and steam outline, 'Jenny'). Three sets of carriages provide seating for 72 passengers. The railway is also home to an exhibition and film show of Rowland Emmet's famous Far Tottering & Oyster Creek Railway, originally created for the Festival of Britain in 1951.

Leeds Industrial Museum

Armley Mills, Canal Road, Armley, Leeds LS12 2QF

TEL 0113 263 7861
WEBSITE www.leeds.gov.uk/armleymills
OPEN Tue to Sat, Bank Holidays and Sun afternoons, all year

OPENED IN 1982, THIS industrial museum is housed in a restored 19th-century water-powered textile mill. A large collection

Above Hunslet 18in-gauge 'Jack', on the mixed gauge demo track at Leeds Industrial Museum.

of railway items includes a display of steam, diesel and mine locomotives, and an operating narrow gauge railway. On display are restored Hunslet 0-4-0WT 'Jack', Hudswell Clarke 0-4-0ST 'Lord Granby' and Hudswell Clarke 2-6-2DM 'Junin' – the world's first commercially built diesel locomotive. Demonstration trains are run on a mixed gauge (18in and 2ft) narrow gauge line for about 300yd from the gallery and through the museum grounds to the weir on the River Aire.

Lightwater Express

Lightwater Valley Theme Park, North Stainley, Ripon, North Yorkshire HG4 3HT

TEL 0871 720 0011
WEBSITE www.lightwatervalley.co.uk
ROUTE Continuous loop within Theme Park
LENGTH 1 mile | **GAUGE** 15 in
OPEN During School and Bank Holidays, early April to early Sep; weekends, May, Sep and Oct

THIS MINIATURE RAILWAY LINKS many of the attractions in a large theme park. Marketed as the Lightwater Express, the line features three stations, a Victorian-style loco shed, two bridges and a tunnel. Motive power consists of a steam-outline diesel, 'Rio Grande' built in 1979. Passengers travel in open and closed stock furnished with transverse seating. The engine shed at Lightwater houses an interesting collection. The railway was once home to three historic miniature steam locos that have since moved elsewhere 'Yvette' (a 4-4-0 built in 1946), 'Little Giant' (an 'Atlantic' 4-4-2 built in 1905 by Bassett-Lowke) and 'John' (an 'Atlantic' 4-4-2, built in 1920 by Albert Barnes).

Manx Electric Railway

Derby Castle Station, Douglas, Isle of Man

TEL 01624 663366
WEBSITE www.manxelectricrailway.co.uk
ROUTE Douglas to Ramsey
LENGTH 17¾ miles | **GAUGE** 3ft
OPEN Daily, mid-Mar to early Nov

THE MANX ELECTRIC RAILWAY opened between Douglas and Laxey in 1893 and was extended to Ramsey in 1899. In operation ever since, it was nationalised by the Manx government in 1957, and still employs some of the original Victorian motor and trailer cars. The line is double-track throughout, much of it running along the roadside with many small tram stops, and electric power is taken from overhead lines. The journey from Douglas, where it connects with a sea-front horsedrawn tramway (see page 194), to Ramsey, is fascinating. Firstly it passes the Groudle Glen Railway (see page 199), before reaching the sylvan station at Laxey where it connects with the Snaefell Mountain Railway (see page 221). The section of line northwards entails a very steep climb from Laxey to the 550ft-high summit above Bulgham Bay, and skirts some breathtaking coastline, with fine views of the Irish Sea. For a timetable visit www.iombusandrail.info

Above The Snaefell Mountain Railway and the Manx Electric Railway meet at Laxey.
Below Vintage tramcar No. 2 and trailer, on the roadside section north of Douglas.

railway to successfully employ steam locomotives. Designed by John Blenkinsop, four two-cylinder steam locomotives were built using a rack and pinion system, with cogs on the driving wheels meshing with an outer toothed rail. The railway was converted to standard gauge in 1881.

In 1960, the Middleton became the first standard gauge line to be run by volunteers and continued to operate freight services until 1983. Home to preserved steam and diesel locomotives built in Leeds, the railway also owns an interesting collection of rolling stock which is used on the line or exhibited in the museum. Operating steam locomotives include North Eastern Railway Class 'Y7' 0-4-0T No. 1310, built in 1891, and Manning Wardle 0-6-0ST 'Sir Berkeley'.

Above A steam-hauled goods train makes its way along the Middleton Railway near Leeds.

Middleton Railway Trust

Moor Road, Hunslet, Leeds LS10 2JQ

TEL 0845 680 1758
WEBSITE www.middletonrailway.org.uk
ROUTE Moor Road to Park Halt
LENGTH 1¼ miles | GAUGE Standard
OPEN Weekends and Bank Holidays, Apr to Dec; Wed in Aug; Santa Trains in Dec (see website)

FOUNDED BY ACT OF Parliament in 1758, the Middleton Railway is the world's oldest continuously working railway. It was originally built as a wooden waggonway to a gauge of 4ft 1in, to carry coal from collieries on Charles Branding's Middleton Estate to the city of Leeds. Initially using horse power, in 1812 it became the first commercial

Monkwearmouth Station Museum

North Bridge Street, Sunderland, Tyne & Wear SR5 1AP

TEL 0191 567 7075
WEBSITE www.twmuseums.org.uk/ monkwearmouth
OPEN Daily (Mon to Sat and Sun afternoons) throughout the year
STATION National rail network station St Peter's (Tyne & Wear Metro)

MONKWEARMOUTH STATION IS ONE of Britain's finest stations, built in an impressive neo-classical style in 1848 to mark the election of George Hudson (the infamous 'Railway King') as the MP for Sunderland. The station was closed to passengers in 1967, although Tyne & Wear Metro trains still pass beside the platform. Restored features include the booking office, unchanged since 1866, waiting shelter on the west platform and the siding area, housing restored rolling stock. The museum has a yearly series of changing exhibitions on transport themes, with a programme of holiday activities.

Above The impressive Monkwearmouth station was built in 1848.

Museum of Liverpool

Pier Head, Liverpool L3 1DG

TEL 0151 478 4545
WEBSITE www.liverpoolmuseums.org.uk
OPEN Daily throughout the year
STATION National rail station Liverpool Lime St

ONE OF THE HIGHLIGHTS of the brand new Museum of Liverpool, which opened in 2011, is electric motor coach No. 3 from the Liverpool Overhead Railway, which closed in 1956. Also on display in the Great Port Gallery is 0-4-2 'Lion', built in 1838 by Todd, Kitson & Laird of Leeds for the Liverpool & Manchester Railway. In 1859, 'Lion' was sold to the Mersey Docks & Harbour Board, where she was used as a stationary engine until 1928. After some years displayed on a plinth at Lime Street station, the loco starred in the 1952 film *The Titfield Thunderbolt*, before being acquired by the museum in 1965. Restored to full working order in 1979, the loco worked under her own steam at the 150th anniversary of the Rainhill Trials.

Right A replica of Robert Stephenson's 'Planet' and 1879-built 0-4-0ST, in Manchester.

Museum of Science & Industry

Liverpool Road, Manchester M3 4FP

TEL 0161 832 2244
WEBSITE www.mosi.org.uk
OPEN Daily throughout the year

THIS MUSEUM IS LOCATED in the original station buildings of the Liverpool & Manchester Railway, which opened in 1830. In addition to the many and varied railway exhibits there is much to interest everyone, with displays on cotton mills, aviation, gas, electricity, space, water supply and sewage disposal. Railway exhibits, all built in Manchester, include sectioned Isle of Man Railway 2-4-0 tank No. 3, 'Pender', built by Beyer Peacock in 1873, a working replica (with some original parts) of the 1829 'Novelty', South African Railways Class GL 3ft 6in-gauge Garratt 4-8-2+2-8-4 No. 2352 and ex-BR Class EM2 electric Co-Co No. 1505, 'Ariadne', built in 1954. Steam train rides hauled by a replica of Robert Stephenson's 'Planet' loco are given at weekends along nearly 1 mile of track within the museum complex and run past the original booking halls, waiting room and warehouse. The latter is the oldest railway building in the world and houses various displays on Manchester's industrial and social history.

National Coal Mining Museum for England

Caphouse Colliery, New Road, Overton, Wakefield, West Yorkshire WF4 4RH

TEL 01924 848806
WEBSITE www.ncm.org.uk
ROUTE Within museum site
LENGTH 2,000yds | GAUGE 2ft 3in
OPEN Daily throughout the year

OPENED AS THE YORKSHIRE Mining Museum in 1988, this heritage museum is located at the former Caphouse Colliery and features a single line funicular railway, known as the 'Paddy Train', that carries visitors through the site to a mine adit.

National Railway Museum

Leeman Road, York YO26 4XJ

TEL 08448 153139
WEBSITE www.nrm.org.uk
OPEN Daily throughout the year
STATION National rail network station York

THE NATIONAL COLLECTION, FORMED from the Clapham Collection and the North Eastern Railway Museum collection at York, opened in 1975 and is housed in two large halls (formerly York locomotive sheds), with the Great Hall opening in 1992. Railway technology is displayed around a central turntable in the Great Hall and exhibits range from the very early days of rail transport to the present, with over 60 restored British-built locomotives (steam, diesel and electric) on view. Pride of place must go to the recently re-streamlined LMS 4-6-2, 'Duchess of Hamilton'. The South Hall contains 130 exhibits that illustrate travel

Above Streamlined LMS 'Coronation' Class 4-6-2 No. 6229 'Duchess of Hamilton', at the NRM.

by train with both passenger and goods trains lined up at platforms. These range from Queen Adelaide's royal saloon, built in 1842, a Lynton & Barnstaple Railway coach, built in 1897, and a Wagons-Lits Night Ferry sleeping car, built in 1936, to numerous goods vehicles dating from 1815 to 1970. In addition there is a hands-on children's centre, a superb model railway and an extensive library with poster, photograph and drawing collections. Numerous other locomotives, some in full working order, and rolling stock are on loan to other museums and heritage railways throughout Britain. The museum's conservation workshops now have a public viewing area where ongoing restoration work can be seen in action. See website for special events, such as the steam and diesel shuttle weekends to the 'Locomotion' Museum at Shildon (see opposite).

The 7¼in-gauge South Garden Miniature Railway operates on a 200yd track in the South Yard of the museum. Trains are normally hauled by a petrol hydraulic locomotive and operate during weekends and school holidays.

National Railway Museum 'Locomotion'

Shildon, Co Durham DL4 1PQ

TEL 01388 777999
WEBSITE www.nrm.org.uk
OPEN Daily throughout the year
STATION National rail network station Shildon

AN OFFSHOOT OF THE National Railway Museum at York, Shildon has a rotating display of historic locos and rolling stock. The site includes the Welcome Building containing Timothy Hackworth's 'Sans Pareil', the Timothy Hackworth Museum (see page 225), the Collection Building with its conservation workshop, a display of more than 70 railway heritage vehicles, the prototype 'Deltic' and the LNER 'V2' 2-6-2 'Green Arrow', record-breaking 'A4' 4-6-2 'Mallard' and the historic Soho railway workshop. Shildon includes a site railway that links all of these attractions and offers steam train rides on special event days.

Above A working replica of Timothy Hackworth's 'Sans Pareil' at Shildon.

Below 'Deltic' main-line diesel, LNER Class 'A4' 4-6-2 'Mallard' and GNR 'Stirling Single'.

Newby Hall Miniature Railway

Newby Hall & Gardens, Ripon,
North Yorkshire HG4 5AE

TEL 0845 450 4068
WEBSITE www.newbyhallandgardens.com
ROUTE Within gardens of Newby Hall
LENGTH 1 mile return | **GAUGE** 10¼in
OPEN Tue to Sun and Bank Holidays, Apr to Sep;
    daily, July and Aug

OPENED BY EARL MOUNTBATTEN of Burma
in 1971, this scenic miniature railway runs
through the grounds of late 17th-century
Newby Hall. The line runs for nearly 1
mile from a picturesque miniature station
alongside the River Ure, giving good views
of the house, gardens and orchards. From
Newby Hall station the railway crosses a
lifting steel bridge, two box-girder bridges
and passes through a curving tunnel. Train
services are operated by two 'Western' class
diesels, 'Countess de Grey' and 'Lady Mary
Vyner', built by Severn Lamb, and a fine one-
fifth scale model of an unrebuilt 'Royal Scot'
class 4-6-0, built in 1950 by J. Battinson.

Norham Station Museum

Station House, Norham,
Northumberland TD15 2LW

TEL 01289 382217
WEBSITE www.forgottenrelics.co.uk/stations/
    norham.html
OPEN Bank Holiday afternoons (tel for details)

THIS PRIVATELY-OWNED MUSEUM on the
former North Eastern Railway branch from
Tweedmouth to Kelso, features the original
signalbox, booking office and porter's room.

The Grade II listed station, opened in 1849
and closed in 1965, now houses a museum,
cared for by the widow of the last man to
work at the station.

North Bay Railway

Burniston Road, Scarborough,
North Yorkshire YO12 6PF

TEL 01723 368791
WEBSITE www.nbr.org.uk
ROUTE Peasholm Park to Scalby Mills
LENGTH ¾ mile | **GAUGE** 20in
OPEN Weekends all year; daily, Apr to Oct
STATION National rail network station
    Scarborough

Above Built in 1932, 4-6-2 steam outline diesel
'Triton' heads a train on the North Bay Railway.

OPERATING SINCE 1931 AND originally
owned by Scarborough Borough Council,
this famous miniature railway takes visitors
along the coast, offering fine views of
Scarborough Bay. All four locomotives are
steam outline diesels – 4-6-2 'Neptune' was
built in 1931 for the opening of the line,
while the others, 'Triton', 'Poseidon' (both
4-6-2s) and 4-6-4T 'Robin Hood' were built
in 1932 and 1933 respectively. Passengers are
carried in 10 of the original bogie coaches
built for the line in 1931.

North Tyneside Steam Railway & Stephenson Railway Museum

Middle Engine Lane, West Chirton, North Shields, Tyne & Wear NE29 8DX

TEL 0191 200 7146
WEBSITE www.ntsra.org.uk
ROUTE Percy Main to Middle Engine Lane
LENGTH 1¾ miles | **GAUGE** Standard
OPEN Weekends and Bank Holidays, mid-Apr to end Oct; Santa Specials in Dec
STATION National rail network station Percy Main (Tyne & Wear Metro)

Below Trains to the Railway Museum are hauled by Peckett 1939-built 0-6-0ST, 'Ashington No. 5'.

BOTH THE MUSEUM AND the railway share the same buildings, originally used as the Tyne & Wear Metro Test Centre. The museum displays the progress of railways with a collection of vintage and more modern steam, diesel and electric locomotives. Exhibits include Killingworth Colliery 0-4-0 'Billy', dating back to the early 19th century, and Bo-Bo electric locomotive No. E4, built by Siemens in 1909. The 1¾-mile standard gauge steam railway connects the Tyne & Wear Metro station at Percy Main with the site on Sundays and Bank Holiday Mondays. Steam trains are normally hauled by 1939-built Peckett 0-6-0ST 'Ashington No. 5', which once worked at Ashington Colliery in County Durham.

North Yorkshire Moors Railway

See page 214

Orchard Farm Lakeside Railway

Orchard Farm Holiday Village, Hunmanby, Filey, North Yorkshire YO14 0PU

TEL 01723 891582
WEBSITE www.orchardfarmholidayvillage.co.uk
ROUTE Within Orchard Farm Holiday Village
LENGTH 600yds | **GAUGE** 10¼in
OPEN Weekends and school holidays Mar to Oct

OPENED IN 1995, THIS miniature railway runs around a lake within the grounds of a holiday village. The line features a covered two-platform station, tunnel and footbridge. Trains are operated by a North American-style diesel, with passengers carried in open bogie coaches.

Above BR Standard Class '4' 4-6-0 No. 75029, 'The Green Knight', enters Pickering station.

North Yorkshire Moors Railway

Pickering Station, Pickering, North Yorkshire YO18 7AJ

TEL 01751 472508 and 01751 473535 (talking timetable)
WEBSITE www.nymr.co.uk
ROUTE Grosmont to Pickering
LENGTH 18 miles | **GAUGE** Standard
OPEN Daily, end Mar to end Oct; Santa Specials in Dec; see website for special events
STATION National rail network stations Grosmont and Whitby

WHAT IS NOW KNOWN as the North Yorkshire Moors Railway was one of the earliest railways built in Britain. Engineered by George Stephenson, it opened in 1836 as the Whitby & Pickering Railway, along the route of an old turnpike road, and initially featured horsedrawn trains and a rope-hauled inclined plane. In 1845, it was taken over by George Hudson's York & North Midland Railway and was rebuilt and enlarged for steam operation. The North Eastern Railway bought the line in 1854, and in 1865 a new route was opened to bypass the 1,500yd 1 in 15 Beck Hole Incline, which was replaced by the 1 in 49 gradient between Grosmont and Goathland. Absorbed into the LNER in 1923, the line was eventually closed by British Railways as a through route to Malton and York in 1965.

The North Yorkshire Moors Railway Preservation Society took over part of the line in 1967 and in 1973 trains started running again on what is now the second-longest preserved standard gauge railway in the country. A workshop and engine sheds have been established at Grosmont and trains are operated by a large collection of powerful main-line steam and diesel locomotives. Locomotives include NER Class 'T3' 0-8-0 No. 63395, SR 'Schools' class 4-4-0 No. 30926 'Repton', two LMS Class '5' 4-6-0s, SR Class 'S15' 4-6-0 No. 30825, LNER Class 'A4' No.

60007 'Sir Nigel Gresley' and ex-S&DJR 2-8-0 No. 53809, as well as several ex-BR diesels. A large and varied collection of rolling stock includes a Pullman set. NYMR trains connect with the main network at Grosmont, on the scenic Whitby to Middlesbrough Esk Valley Line. Certain NYMR steam-hauled trains continue their journey along the Esk Valley from Grosmont to the historic harbour town of Whitby. A journey on the railway, one of the most visited in Britain, across the wild grandeur of the North Yorkshire Moors National Park to Pickering involves a steep climb to Goathland, known to TV addicts as Aidensfield in *Heartbeat*, before entering the picturesque Newtondale Gorge. The railway is frequently host to visiting locomotives from other preserved railways.

Above Ex-Southern Railway Class 'S15' 4-6-0 No. 825 leaves snowy Goathland station.

Below Through Newtondale Gorge behind SDJR 2-8-0 No. 53809 and a Stanier 'Black Five' 4-6-0.

Orchid Line Miniature Railway

Curraghs Wildlife Park, Ballaugh,
Isle of Man IM7 5EA

TEL 01624 897323 (wildlife park)
WEBSITE www.mers.org.im/orchidline.htm
ROUTE Within wildlife park
LENGTH ½ mile | **GAUGES** 3½in, 5in and 7¼in
OPEN Afternoons on Sun and Bank Holidays,
early Apr to late Oct

OWNED AND OPERATED BY the Manx Steam & Model Engineering Club, this multi-gauge miniature railway opened in 1992 and features a station, engine shed, signalling, five substantial steel girder bridges, level crossings, steep gradients and a tunnel. Up to five locomotives take visitors half a mile across swampland and through woods.

Pleasure Beach Express

Ocean Boulevard, Blackpool,
Lancashire FY4 1EZ

TEL 0871 222 1234 (theme park)
WEBSITE www.blackpoolpleasurebeach.com
ROUTE Within Pleasure Beach complex
LENGTH not known | **GAUGE** 1ft 9in
OPEN Late Feb to Mar; Thu to Mon, mid-Apr to
May; daily, Jun to mid-Nov and school holidays

THIS UNUSUALLY GAUGED MINIATURE railway was built in 1933 at Blackpool's Pleasure Beach. There are two stations and trains are operated by three one-third scale steam outline diesel locomotives, built by Hudswell Clarke of Leeds in the 1930s. Two of them, 4-6-2 'Mary Louise' and 4-6-4T 'Carol Jean', are similar to those on the North Bay Railway in Scarborough (see page 212).

Pugneys Light Railway

Pugneys Country Park, Asdale Road, Durkar,
Wakefield, West Yorkshire WF2 7EQ

TEL 01924 302360
WEBSITE www.wakefield.gov.uk/pugneys.htm
ROUTE Within country park
LENGTH 750yds | **GAUGE** 7¼in
OPEN Weekends, Bank and school hols all year

SET IN A COUNTRY PARK that features a modern watersport centre and two lakes, this miniature railway carries visitors from Lakeside station to a nature reserve. Passengers ride on sit-astride open bogie carriages hauled by a petrol hydraulic loco.

Ravenglass & Eskdale Railway

See page 218

Ribble Steam Railway

Chain Caul Road, Preston,
Lancashire PR2 2PD

TEL 01772 728800
WEBSITE www.ribblesteam.org.uk
ROUTE Preston Riverside Strand Road Crossing
LENGTH 1½ miles | **GAUGE** Standard
OPEN Most weekends and Bank Holidays,
Apr to Oct; Santa Specials in Dec; see website
for selected Wed dates

HOME TO THE RAILWAY collection from the now-closed Southport Railway Museum, the Ribble Steam Railway opened in 2005. During the summer months it runs steam-hauled trains along part of the standard

Above and below Visiting GWR 0-6-2T No. 5643 crosses the swingbridge in Preston Docks and, below, heads a passenger train along the Ribble Steam Railway.

Rosehill Victoria Park Railway

Rosehill Park, off Park Grove, Rawmarsh, Rotherham, South Yorkshire S62 7JS

TEL 01709 543788 (Secretary)
WEBSITE www.rdmes.co.uk
ROUTE Within Rosehill Park (aka Victoria Park)
LENGTH ¼ mile | **GAUGES** 3½in, 5in and 7¼in
OPEN Sun afternoons, Easter to Oct

gauge Preston Docks line, crossing Preston Marina on a swing bridge. The adjoining museum includes nearly 50 industrial steam and diesel locomotives. It is one of a handful of heritage railways to operate regular revenue-earning freight trains – bitumen trains once again operate between Immingham Docks and a bitumen plant served by the railway.

LOCATED IN THE GROUNDS of Rosehill Hall, Victoria Park became a public amenity in 1901 for Queen Victoria's Diamond Jubilee. Opened as a miniature railway in 1997, this railway is operated in a walled garden by the Rotherham & District Model Engineers Society. The multi-gauge raised track caters for all three gauges, while a ¼-mile ground-level track is built to 7¼in gauge.

Ruswarp Miniature Railway

The Carrs, Ruswarp,
Nr Whitby, North Yorkshire
YO21 1RL

TEL 01947 600109
WEBSITE www.chainbridgeriverside.com
ROUTE Alongside River Esk
LENGTH ½ mile | **GAUGE** 7¼in
OPEN Weekends, Easter to Oct; daily during
  school holidays, all year
STATION National rail network station Ruswarp

SET IN A PICTURESQUE setting alongside
the River Esk, near Whitby, this circular
miniature railway first opened in 1990 and
operates three locomotives; steam 2-4-2
'Danny', steam 2-4-2T 'Emily' and petrol
hydraulic Class 20-style, 'Shan'. The site also
includes a picnic area.

St Annes Miniature Railway

Seafront (south of the pier),
Lytham St Annes, Lancashire

TEL 01772 864875
ROUTE Through sand dunes near seafront
LENGTH 700yds | **GAUGE** 10¼in
OPEN Daily, Easter to Sep
STATION National rail network station
  St Annes-on-Sea

A MINIATURE RAILWAY HAS operated at
Lytham St Annes since the 1950s, but the
current line originated in the early 1970s.
Today, brightly decorated trains are hauled
on this 700yd circuit around a miniature golf
course and through sand dunes by a diesel
hydraulic 'Western' Class lookalike or a steam
outline diesel locomotive.

Ravenglass & Eskdale Railway

Ravenglass, Cumbria CA18 1SW

TEL 01229 717171
WEBSITE www.ravenglass-railway.co.uk
ROUTE Ravenglass to Dalegarth
LENGTH 7 miles | **GAUGE** 15in
OPEN Weekends, Feb to early Nov; daily,
  school holidays and mid-Mar to end Oct;
  Santa Express in Dec; see website for
  special events, including some evenings
STATION National rail network station Ravenglass

THE RAVENGLASS & ESKDALE RAILWAY
opened in 1875 as a 3ft-gauge line to carry
haematite iron ore from mines in Eskdale
to the Furness Railway at Ravenglass. The
first locomotive was Manning Wardle
0-6-0 'Devon'. Passenger services started in
1876 but the company became bankrupt
and was managed by a receiver. Passenger
trains stopped in 1908 and freight services
ceased in 1913. However, W. J. Bassett-
Lowke, the famous manufacturer of model
and miniature railways, came to the rescue
and regauged the line to 15in. The first
locomotive was 'Atlantic' 4-4-2 'Sans Pareil'
and in 1915 trains ran again on what was
then billed as the 'World's Smallest Public
Railway'. A daily train service operated
and an additional locomotive, 0-8-0
'Muriel' (later to become 'River Irt' and
converted to 0-8-2), was purchased from
Sir Arthur Heywood. The line flourished
with the growth of granite traffic and a
new locomotive, 2-8-2 'River Esk', was
built. In 1925 the line was purchased by
Sir Aubrey Brocklebank (Director of the
Cunard Steamship Company, the Suez Canal
Company and the Great Western Railway),
who enlarged the quarries and stone
crushing plant. Following the end of the
Second World War, the RER was purchased
by the Keswick Granite Company in 1948,

who closed the quarries in 1960 and put the line up for sale by auction.

However, an eleventh-hour rescue operation was mounted by railway enthusiasts and the line was saved again. In 1967, another locomotive, 2-8-2 'River Mite', entered service and with improved revenues the railway has been progressively restored. The railway workshops constructed 2-6-2 'Northern Rock' in 1976 and have also built new diesel and steam locomotives for Blackpool Pleasure Beach (see page 216)

and a Japanese leisure park. The RER also pioneered the use of radio for operation of their trains, a system that is now widely used by the main-line railways. The headquarters of the line at Ravenglass, also home to the railway-owned Ratty Arms public house and an interesting railway museum, is situated adjacent to the main-line railway station on the Cumbrian Coast Line. Six steam and six diesel locomotives operate on the line, and coaching stock consists of a mixture of open, semi-open and closed saloons.

Below Built in 1894, 0-8-2 'River Irt' is turned at Ravenglass station, after arriving from Dalegarth on the Ravenglass & Eskdale Railway.

Saltburn Inclined Tramway

Marine Parade, Saltburn-by-the-Sea, Tees Valley TS12 1DP

ROUTE Marine Parade to Saltburn Pier
LENGTH 207ft | **GAUGE** 4ft 2½in
OPEN Weekends, mid-Mar to Oct;
   daily, summer season
STATION National rail network station Saltburn

OPENED IN 1883, THIS funicular cliff railway replaced an earlier vertical lift that had become unsafe. Owned by Redcar & Cleveland Borough Council, it has always operated with a water-balance system (the oldest still operating in Britain) and carries passengers a height of 120ft on a gradient of 1 in 1.73. The water for the system originates from a spring at the cliff base.

Saltburn Miniature Railway

bottom of Saltburn Bank, Saltburn-by-the-Sea, Cleveland TS12 1HH

TEL 07813 153975 and 07977 384724
WEBSITE www.saltburn-miniature-railway.org.uk
ROUTE Cat Nab station to Forest Halt
LENGTH ½ mile | **GAUGE** 15in
OPEN Weekends and Bank Holidays, Easter to end
   Sep; Tue to Sun in Aug

OPENED IN 1947, THIS seaside miniature railway is run by a group of volunteers, close to the beach at Saltburn. The railway has two resident locomotives, streamlined steam outline diesel electric 4-6-2 'Prince Charles' (built in the 1950s) and steam outline diesel hydraulic 0-4-0T 'George Outhwaite', built in 1994. It runs from Cat Nab station to Forest Halt further inland.

Above An 0-6-0 steam loco at work on the 10¼in-gauge miniature railway at Shibden Park.

Shibden Park Railway

Shibden Park, Listers Road, Halifax, West Yorkshire HX3 6XG

TEL 07854 658635
ROUTE Within Shibden Park
LENGTH ½ mile | **GAUGE** 10¼in
OPEN Weekends, Bank Holidays and school
   holidays, all year
STATION National rail network station Halifax

THIS MINIATURE RAILWAY WAS built in the early 1980s and acquired by the present owner in 1991. It is situated in a park that contains Shibden Hall, a museum house of the 18th century. The line operates in the lower part of the park, passing the picnic area and boating lake, and gives a scenic ride which includes a tunnel, two bridges and a cutting. One 0-6-0 narrow gauge steam locomotive and a Bo-Bo diesel electric provide the motive power.

Above 4-6-2 diesel electric 'Prince Charles' gets ready to leave Cat Nab station at Saltburn.

Shipley Glen Tramway

Prod Lane, Baildon, Shipley,
West Yorkshire BD17 5BN

TEL 01274 589010
WEBSITE www.glentramway.co.uk
ROUTE Within Walker Wood, Shipley Glen
LENGTH ¼ mile | GAUGE 1ft 8in
OPEN Sun afternoons throughout the year

THIS UNIQUE VICTORIAN CABLE-OPERATED
tramway was opened in 1895 and was
originally powered by a gas engine, until
converted to electricity in 1928. The original
winding equipment is still in use. Two
pairs of toast-rack coaches operate on
two independent tracks, which run uphill
through woodland on a maximum gradient
of 1 in 7. The tramway serves the Glen's
visitor attractions, including a children's
funfair, countryside centre, tea garden and
the nearby historic village of Saltaire.

Snaefell Mountain Railway

Laxey Station, Laxey, Isle of Man IM4 7NH

TEL 01624 662525
WEBSITE www.iomguide.com/mountainrailway.php
ROUTE Laxey to Snaefell Summit
LENGTH 5 miles | GAUGE 3ft 6in
OPEN Daily, mid-Apr to early Oct
STATION Heritage station Laxey (see page 207)

OPENED IN 1895 THIS mountain railway
climbs to the 2,036ft summit of Snaefell, the
highest point in the Isle of Man, from which
(on a clear day) there are magnificent views
of Wales, England, Scotland and Ireland. The
electric tram vehicles collect their current
through overhead wires, and climb gradients
as steep as l in 12. Five of the six operating
trams date back to the original opening of

the railway and are similar in style to those
used on the neighbouring Manx Electric
Railway (see page 207). The gauge, at 3ft 6in,
is 6in wider than that of the MER, and dual
gauge track is provided at Laxey, where the
two lines interchange. For timetable visit
www.iombusandrail.info.

South Cliff Tramway

Esplanade, Scarborough,
North Yorkshire YO11 2AF

TEL 0172 336 1459
ROUTE Esplanade to South Sands
LENGTH 284ft | GAUGE 4ft 8½in
OPEN Daily, Apr to Oct
STATION National rail station Scarborough

NOW OWNED AND OPERATED by
Scarborough Borough Council, the South
Cliff Tramway is the oldest funicular cliff
railway in Britain. Opened in 1875 with a
gradient of 1 in 1.75, the railway operated
with a water-balance system until 1935, when
it was converted to electric power. Following
a serious incident in 1998 the line was closed
for remedial work, reopening a year later.

Below Car No. 2 nears the summit of the
mountain on the Snaefell Mountain Railway.

Above A battery electric tramcar on the 3ft 6in-gauge Southport Pier Tramway.

Southport Pier Tramway

Southport Pier, Promenade, Southport, Merseyside PR8 1QX

TEL 01704 539701
WEBSITE www.visitsouthport.com
ROUTE Pier Forecourt to Pier Head
LENGTH 1,200yds | GAUGE 3ft 6in
OPEN Daily, throughout the year
STATION National rail network station Southport

SOUTHPORT PIER, THE SECOND longest pleasure pier in Britain, opened in 1860. A 3ft 6in-gauge horsedrawn tramway was opened in 1863 to carry steam boat passengers' baggage. It later converted to cable haulage and then steam haulage. The line was electrified in 1905 and taken over by Southport Corporation in 1936, closing for the duration of the Second World War. Following relaying of the line to 1ft 11½in-gauge, the line reopened in 1950 with passengers carried in a diesel train.

A serious fire in 1990 nearly led to the pier's demolition but it has since been rebuilt and is now a Grade II Listed Structure. Built to a gauge of 3ft 6in, a new tramway opened in 2005, with services being handled by a 100-seater, two-car, articulated battery-powered tram car.

South Tynedale Railway

Railway Station, Alston, Cumbria CA9 3JB

TEL 01434 381696
WEBSITE www.strps.org.uk
ROUTE Alston to Kirkhaugh (no road access)
LENGTH 2¼ miles | GAUGE 2ft
OPEN Weekends and Bank Holidays, Easter to end Oct; selected weekdays, Apr to Oct and Dec; daily, mid-Jul to Aug

THE FORMER NORTH EASTERN Railway branch line along the South Tyne valley was opened from Haltwhistle, on the Carlisle to Newcastle route, to Alston in 1852 and closed by British Railways in 1976. Initially, preservation of this scenic branch in its standard gauge form was planned but this scheme failed. A new proposal for a 2ft-gauge line was put forward and in 1983 a short length of narrow gauge track was opened from Alston. Gilderdale Halt was opened in 1987 and Kirkhaugh in 1996. Future plans include extending the line still further to Slaggyford, giving a total distance of 5 miles. It is possible that one day in the future the railway may extend even further northwards towards Lambley, but in the meantime a footpath follows the route and crosses Knar Burn on a high railway viaduct.

Many of the steam and diesel locomotives used on the railway have been obtained from a wide variety of sources, both in the UK and abroad. Much of the equipment is second-hand, and many items have been rebuilt before being used on the railway. Included are 0-6-0 well tank No. 3 'Sao Domingos', built in Germany in 1928, 0-4-0 tank No. 6 'Thomas Edmondson', built in Germany in 1918, 0-6-0 tender engine No. 10 'Naklo', built in Poland in 1957, 0-4-2 tanks No. 12 'Chaka's Kraal' and No. 6, built by Hunslet in 1940 for a South African railway, as well as many industrial diesel locomotives. Many of the coaches were newly constructed at Alston in 1991 to a continental design. Comprehensive signalling equipment and a former North Eastern Railway signalbox from Ainderby have been re-erected at Alston and all train movements are controlled from here. As there is no car access to Gilderdale or Kirkhaugh, all journeys must start at Alston, which stands 875ft above sea level and makes this England's highest narrow gauge railway. A journey along the line gives passengers views of the beautiful South Tyne valley, crossing the river on a three-arch viaduct north of Alston, and a viaduct between Gilderdale and the present terminus at

Kirkhaugh – once the site of a Roman fort which guarded the ancient Maiden Way to Hadrian's Wall.

Stainmore Railway

Kirkby Stephen East Station, South Road, Kirkby Stephen, Cumbria CA17 4LA

TEL 01768 371700
WEBSITE www.kirkbystepheneast.co.uk
ROUTE Within station site
LENGTH n/a | **GAUGE** Standard
OPEN Weekends, all year; selected special events
STATION National rail station Kirkby Stephen

BUILT TO CARRY COKE to blast furnaces in Workington and Barrow-in-Furness, the South Durham & Lancashire Union Railway opened between Barnard Castle and Tebay in 1861. It was soon taken over by the Stockton & Darlington Railway, before becoming part of the newly-formed North Eastern Railway in 1863. Trains were usually double-headed over the line's Stainmore Summit and across the iconic Belah Viaduct but this ended in 1962 when the line was closed. The line through Appleby East to the army depot at Warcop remained open until 1989 but by then the station had taken on a new lease of life as a mill. By 1992 the mill had closed and the site had become derelict. However, the 6½-acre site was bought for use as the eastern terminus of a proposed preserved railway by the Stainmore Railway Company. Since then, a band of enthusiastic volunteers have been restoring the station and laying track with the aim of opening a heritage centre and railway. First reopened to the public in 2009, the station saw working steam locos once again in August 2011, for the 150th anniversary of the Stainmore line.

Left, above A wintry scene near Kirkhaugh on the narrow gauge South Tynedale Railway.

Left After nearly 50 years, steam returned to Kirkby Stephen East station at Stainmore.

Tanfield Railway

Marley Hill Engine Shed, Old Marley Hill, Gateshead, Tyne & Wear NE16 5ET

TEL 0845 463 4938
WEBSITE www.tanfieldrailway.co.uk
ROUTE Sunniside to East Tanfield
LENGTH 3 miles | **GAUGE** Standard
OPEN Sun and Bank Holidays all year; Wed to Thu, late Jul to Aug; North Pole Express in Dec

SITUATED ON THE SITE of one of the oldest railways in the world, the wooden-railed Tanfield Waggonway (opened in 1725), the Tanfield Railway also boasts an early 18th-century railway bridge and an engine shed dating from 1854. The colliery line was eventually closed by British Railways in 1968, and by 1977 a group of preservationists had reopened the first section to the public. The line was extended to Sunniside in 1981 and East Tanfield in 1982. Beautifully restored vintage four-wheeled coaches are hauled by a very large collection of small, mainly steam, industrial locomotives. Causey station is the start of a woodland walk where the famous Causey railway arch, the world's first railway bridge, built in 1727, can be seen.

Below 0-6-0ST 'Renishaw Ironworks No. 6' with vintage carriages on the Tanfield Railway.

Thorne Memorial Park Miniature Railway

Thorne Park, South Parade, Thorne, Doncaster, West Yorkshire DN8 5DZ

WEBSITE www.thornerailway.org.uk
ROUTE Within Thorne Park
LENGTH ½ mile | **GAUGES** 5in and 7¼in
OPEN Every 1st and 3rd Sun, Easter to Sep

OPERATED BY DONCASTER & DISTRICT Model Engineering Society, this dual gauge miniature railway has been on its present site for over 50 years. The route consists of an inner and outer circle with diamond crossover, providing a continuous run through the grassed park area next to an athletic stadium. The Society owns two steam (both from the now-closed Sandtoft Miniature Railway), one petrol and one battery electric locomotive – although other visiting steam locos are a regular sight. A vintage diesel is used during quiet periods.

Threlkeld Quarry & Mining Museum

Threlkeld, Nr Keswick, Cumbria CA12 4TT

TEL 01768 779747
WEBSITE www.threlkeldquarry.co.uk
ROUTE Within quarry site
LENGTH ½ mile | **GAUGE** 2ft
OPEN Daily, Mar to Oct

THRELKELD QUARRY WAS OPENED in the 1870s to supply granite ballast for the Penrith to Keswick railway. It first closed in 1937 but was reopened after modernisation in 1949, before being finally closed by Amey Roadstone in 1982. Located in the quarry site, this quarrying and mining museum incorporates the former Caldbeck Mining Museum and the Threlkeld Quarry Project. A 2ft-gauge railway operates within the site and star of the show is the 1926-built Bagnall 0-4-0 saddle tank, 'Sir Tom', which hauls trains daily in the summer holidays.

Timothy Hackworth Victorian & Railway Museum

Soho Cottages, Hackworth Close, Shildon, Co Durham DL4 1PQ

TEL 01388 777999 (NRM 'Locomotion')
WEBSITE www.railcentre.co.uk/museum/museum. htm
OPEN Daily throughout the year
STATION National rail network station Shildon

Now PART OF THE National Railway Museum at Shildon (see page 211), this museum is devoted to the pioneer steam locomotive engineer, Timothy Hackworth (1786–1850), and situated in the former Hackworth family home. Set in 15 acres, it includes period Victorian rooms, and some remaining buildings from Soho Works and the Stockton & Darlington Railway. Hackworth was responsible for building the first Stephenson locomotives and worked on the Stockton & Darlington Railway as an engineer. He built the first six-coupled engine, 'Royal George', for the S&DR in 1827 and 0-4-0 'Sans Pareil', which competed in the famous 1829 Rainhill Trials on the Liverpool & Manchester Railway. A working replica of this locomotive can be seen operating along 400yds of track on events days. The track runs from an 1850s goods shed via 1840s coal drops towards the present Bishop Auckland to Darlington railway line. Rolling stock is represented by a Fawcett coach, a dandy cart and chaldron wagons.

Vintage Carriage Trust Museum

Ingrow Railway Centre, South Street, Ingrow, Keighley, West Yorkshire BD21 5AX

TEL 01535 680425
WEBSITE www.vintagecarriagestrust.org
OPEN Daily throughout the year
STATION Heritage railway station Ingrow

A PURPOSE-BUILT MUSEUM opened in 1990, which currently houses approximately half of the Trust's collection, where sound and video presentations bring the collection to life. The Trust has won several awards and its exhibits have often been used in films and television programmes. The Trust owns nine historic railway carriages built between 1876 and 1950, which have appeared on screen in *The Secret Agent* (1995) and *The Feast of July* (1994). Included are examples from the Manchester, Sheffield & Lincolnshire Railway, Midland Railway, East Coast Joint Stock, Great Northern Railway and the Metropolitan Railway. Locos owned by the Trust include 'Bellerophon', built in 1874 by Haydock Foundry, and 'Lord Mayor', built in 1893 by Hudswell-Clarke. Both locomotives and coaches also operate on the nearby Keighley & Worth Valley Railway (page 202).

Below Fascinating artefacts at the Vintage Carriage Trust Museum at Ingrow.

Weardale Railway

Stanhope Station, Station Road, Stanhope,
Bishop Auckland, Co Durham DL13 2YS

TEL 01388 526203
WEBSITE www.weardale-railway.org.uk
ROUTE Wolsingham to Stanhope
LENGTH 18 miles | GAUGE Standard
OPEN See website for details
STATION National rail station Bishop Auckland

Above Built in 1954, Robert Stephenson &
Hawthorn NCB 0-6-0ST No. 49, at Weardale.

THE WEARDALE RAILWAY PRESERVATION
Society was formed in 1993 to assist with the
campaign to reopen the mothballed railway
line from Bishop Auckland to Eastgate in
the scenic Wear Valley. Originally opened
in stages between 1843 and 1895 to serve
the local limestone quarries, the passenger
service ceased in 1953, with freight lingering
on until 1961 when the line was cut back to
St John's Chapel. The present terminus is
at Eastgate where, until 1993, bulk cement
trains operated to serve the Lafarge factory.
Now owned by the Weardale Railway
Trust, heritage train services on the line are
normally operated by a Class 141 railbus,
with heritage steam or diesel traction
running at weekends and on special events
days. There's a main-line connection at
Bishop Auckland and revenue-earning
coal traffic was recently introduced.

Wensleydale Railway

Leeming Bar Station, Leases Road, Leeming
Bar, Northallerton, North Yorkshire DL7 9AR

TEL 08454 505474
WEBSITE www.wensleydalerailway.com
ROUTE Leeming Bar to Redmire
LENGTH 16 miles | GAUGE Standard
OPEN Tue, Fri, weekends and Bank Holidays,
    Apr to Nov; daily, mid-Jun to Sep
STATION National rail network station
    Northallerton (bus link)

THIS DELIGHTFUL RURAL LINE through the
Yorkshire Dales was opened by the North
Eastern Railway between Northallerton
and Hawes in 1878. The line westward
from Hawes to Garsdale was opened by the
Midland Railway in 1878. Passenger traffic
between Northallerton and Hawes ceased
in 1954 and from Garsdale to Hawes (along
with freight traffic) in 1959. The remaining
branch from Northallerton was cut back to
Redmire in 1964 and the line remained open
for stone trains to Redmire Quarry until
1992. Since then the Wensleydale Railway
Association, with financial help from the
MOD who use the line to transport military
vehicles, have reintroduced passenger trains
between Leeming Bar and Redmire. A bus
service links Northallerton station on the

Below A Class 110 diesel multiple unit calls at
Bedale station on the Wensleydale Railway.

East Coast Main Line with Leeming Bar station. Trains are operated by diesel multiple units but steam can also be seen in action on certain weekends during the summer.

West Lancashire Light Railway

Becconsall Station, Alty's Brickworks, Station Road, Hesketh Bank, Nr Preston, Lancashire PR4 6SP

TEL 01772 815881
WEBSITE www.wllr.net
ROUTE Delph to Becconsall
LENGTH ¼ mile | **GAUGE** 2ft
OPEN Sun and Bank Holidays, Apr to end Oct

FOUNDED IN 1967 BY six schoolboys, this narrow gauge line, situated round two sides of a flooded clay pit, obtained its first steam engine in 1969, with steam trains operating in 1980. All passenger services are normally operated by steam locomotives 'Irish Mail' (ex-Dinorwic Quarry and built by Hunslet in 1903), 'Montalban' (built by Orenstein & Koppel in 1913), 'Stanhope' (built by Kerr Stuart in 1917) and 'Utrillas' (built by O&K in 1907). A large collection of non-operational narrow gauge steam and internal combustion engine locomotives are also on

Below Hunslet 1903-built 0-4-0ST 'Irish Mail', at work on the West Lancashire Light Railway.

view. The terminus at Becconsall features the carriage and locomotive sheds, station and storage sidings, while at Delph there is a simple run-round loop.

Windmill Farm Railway

Red Cat Lane, Burscough, Lancashire L40 1UQ

TEL 01704 892282
WEBSITE www.windmillanimalfarm.co.uk
ROUTE Windmill Farm to Lakeview
LENGTH 1 mile | **GAUGE** 15in
OPEN Daily, Easter to Sep

FIRST OPENED IN 1997, this miniature railway was built by one man, Austin Moss, and runs from Windmill Farm station to Lakeview station, where there is a picnic site and lake. The railway has a very large collection of locos, including three steam and eight steam outline diesel and electric.

Wylam Railway Museum

Falcon Centre, Falcon Terrace, Wylam, Northumberland NE41 8EE

TEL 01661 852174
WEBSITE www.tynedaleheritage.org
OPEN All visits must be booked in advance. The museum is currently closed for refurbishment.
STATION National rail network station Wylam

THIS ATTRACTIVE SMALL MUSEUM illustrates Wylam's unique place in railway history through a series of exhibits about the work and achievements of the local pioneers and local railway projects. It opened in 1981 to celebrate the 200th anniversary of the birth of George Stephenson, born in Wylam.

MAIN-LINE STEAM

Rarely a week goes by without some form of main-line steam special somewhere on Britain's rail network. Here are some highlights from Northern England.

Left Ex-LMS 'Royal Scot' Class 4-6-0 No. 46115 'Scots Guardsman' heads the southbound run of 'The Waverley', from Carlisle to York on 29 August 2010. These trains ran most Sundays from July until early September in 2010, and were organised by the Railway Touring Company.

Below Ex-LMS 'Royal Scot' Class 4-6-0 No. 46115 'Scots Guardsman' heads past Mossley, en route from Manchester to Huddersfield with a train organised by West Coast Railways, on 14 July 2009.

Above Stanier Class '5' 4-6-0 No. 45428 leaves Whitby with a train for Grosmont and Pickering via the North Yorkshire Moors Railway, on 4 July 2011.

Above Stanier Class '5' 4-6-0 No. 45231 heads 'The Fellsman' just south of Hellifield, on 14 September 2011. Running between Lancaster and Carlisle via Blackburn and the Settle & Carlisle line, the 'Fellsman' is operated by Statesman Rail during the summer season.

Below The Railway Touring Company's multi-day rail tour of Great Britain, hauled by ex-LNER 'A4' Class 4-6-2 No. 60007 'Sir Nigel Gresley', crosses the Royal Border Bridge at Berwick-upon-Tweed.

SCOTLAND

Above Ex-LMS 'Black 5' 4-6-0 No. 45407 heads across the lonely Rannoch Moor near Corrour with a charter train from Fort William.

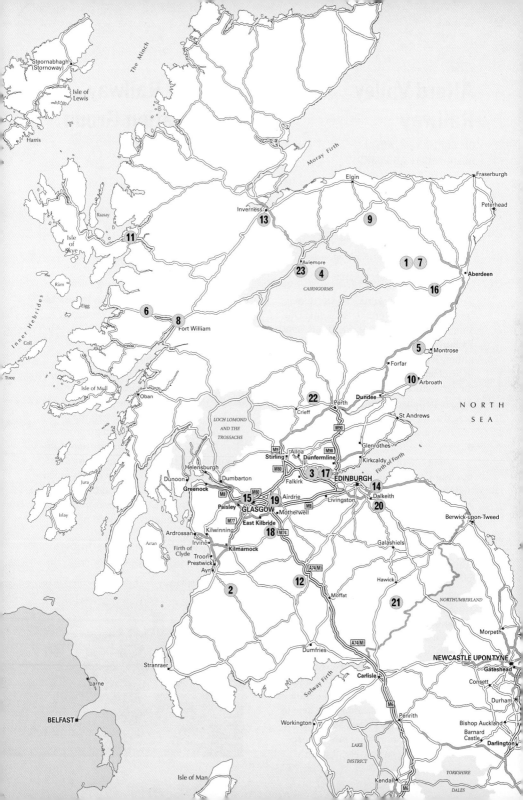

Alford Valley Railway

Old Station Yard, Alford,
Aberdeenshire AB33 8FD

TEL 019755 63942 or 07879 293934
WEBSITE www.alfordvalleyrailway.org.uk
ROUTE Alford Station to Haughton Country Park
LENGTH ½ mile | **GAUGE** 2ft
OPEN Weekends and Bank Holidays, Apr to
   Oct; daily, Jul and Aug; Santa Specials in Dec
   (see website)

THE MEANDERING RURAL BRANCH line
from Kintore to Alford, in the scenic Don
Valley, opened in 1859 as the Alford Valley
Railway. Never a great financial success, the
railway was taken over by the Great North
of Scotland Railway in 1866, its importance
for agricultural traffic far outweighing its
meagre passenger receipts. Passenger services
ceased at the beginning of 1950 and the line
was completely closed by British Railways
in 1966.

Using equipment salvaged from a closed
peat railway at New Pitsligo, work began
on building a narrow gauge railway at the
Alford terminus in 1979 and now trains
are operated by a narrow gauge Simplex
industrial diesel and two steam outline
diesels, 'James Gordon' and 'The Bra' Lass'. At
Alford the original GNoSR engine shed and
platform have survived. The former has been
recently restored and is used for stabling
stock. The former turntable pit is now a
flower bed. A new wooden station building
has been built on the platform by volunteers
and this now houses a small museum and
tourist information centre. The railway is a
tourist line operating from Alford station
and through a golf course to Haughton Park,
although an original section from here to
Murray Park is now closed. Nearby is the
Grampian Transport Museum (see page
235), with a display of GNoSR items.

Ayrshire Railway Preservation Group

Dunaskin Heritage Centre,
Waterside, Ayr KA6 7JF

TEL 01292 313579 (evenings and weekends)
WEBSITE www.arpg.org.uk
ROUTE Within site of heritage centre
LENGTH 600yds | **GAUGE** Standard
OPEN Selected Sun, end May to end Sep
   (see website)

OPERATED BY THE AYRSHIRE Railway
Preservation Group, the Scottish Industrial
Railway Centre was originally located at
the site of Minnivey Colliery, itself once
part of the industrial railway system of
the Dalmellington Iron Company. This
commenced operations in 1845 at Dunaskin
(Waterside), and as the ironworks grew so
did the railway system. The period after
the First World War brought a slump in
demand for iron and coal, and the ironworks
closed in 1922, although coal continued to
be mined and the colliery was nationalised
in 1947. Production at Minnivey continued
until 1976 and the last mine to close was at
Pennyvenie in 1978. The railway line from
Dunaskin to Minnivey was lifted in 1980

Below Former NCB Andrew Barclay 0-4-0ST
No.10 gives rides at Dunaskin in Ayrshire.

but it remained *in situ* up to Pennyvenie. In 1988 Chalmerston opencast mine was opened and the railway from Dunaskin was relaid by British Coal. The Ayrshire Railway Preservation Society took the lease of the derelict site at Minnivey in 1980, until 2002. Then, the centre was closed and all stock moved further down the line to Dunaskin, where the group now runs steam open days on selected Sundays in the summer. Future developments are hoped to include increasing the length of brakevan rides, using the former NCB locomotive shed at Dunaskin to display various items including the group's large collection of steam and diesel industrial locomotives, and restoration of the former station building at Waterside.

Above Ex-Caledonian Railway Class '2P' 0-4-4T No. 55189, on the Bo'ness & Kinneil Railway.
Below Ex-LNER Class 'D49' 4-4-0 'Morayshire', at work on the Bo'ness & Kinneil Railway.

Bo'ness & Kinneil Railway

Bo'ness Station, Union Street, Bo'ness, West Lothian EH51 9AQ

TEL 01506 822298
WEBSITE www.srps.org.uk
ROUTE Bo'ness to Manuel
LENGTH 5 miles | **GAUGE** Standard
OPEN Weekends and Bank Holidays, Apr to Oct; daily, Easter, July (except Mon) and Aug; Santa Specials in Dec; see website for special events

THIS FORMER COLLIERY LINE along the foreshore of the Firth of Forth was originally built in 1851 as the Slamannan Railway, being later absorbed by the North British Railway, and finally closed to all traffic by British Rail in 1980. By then, the Scottish Railway Preservation Society had already set up a base on the line and reopened it in stages, from Bo'ness to Kinneil in 1984, to Birkhill in 1989 and to Manuel (with a physical link to the Edinburgh to Glasgow main line) in 2010. The SRPS collection of locomotives and rolling stock, formerly based at Falkirk, were moved to Bo'ness in 1988. Visitors to the railway can also visit the clay mine near Birkhill station. A large collection of finely restored steam and diesel locomotives are based at Bo'ness, including such historic items as LNER Class D49 4-4-0 No. 246 'Morayshire', built in 1928, and North British Railway Class J36 0-6-0 'Maude', built in 1891. The Scottish Railway Exhibition museum (see page 240) is situated adjacent to Bo'ness station.

Above Popular with skiers, the funicular railway to Cairngorm is the highest railway in Britain.

Cairngorm Mountain Railway

Cairngorm Ski Area, Aviemore PH22 1RB

TEL 01479 861261
WEBSITE www.cairngormmountain.com
ROUTE Base Station – Ptarmigan Station
LENGTH 2,153yds | GAUGE 6ft 6¾in
OPEN Daily, throughout the year (weather permitting)
STATION National rail network station Aviemore (bus link)

THE CAIRNGORM MOUNTAIN RAILWAY is now the highest railway in Britain, since it opened in 2001. This broad gauge single-track (with passing loop) funicular railway was built to replace an existing chair lift and operates in virtually any weather. The railway has proved exceptionally popular, especially with skiers during the winter months. The majority of the line is built on concrete stilts, apart from the final 250yds near the summit which is in an artificial tunnel. Each with a capacity of 120 passengers, the single carriages are raised or lowered by a cable attached to an electric-powered winding drum at the summit – a vertical distance of 1,485ft, on an average gradient of 1 in 4.2. On a clear day, the views from the 3,600ft summit and Ptarmigan Visitor Centre are simply stunning.

Caledonian Railway

The Station, Park Road, Brechin DD9 7AF

TEL 01356 622992
WEBSITE www.caledonianrailway.com
ROUTE Brechin to Bridge of Dun
LENGTH 4 miles | GAUGE Standard
OPEN Sun, Jun to Aug; most Sat Jul and Aug; Santa Specials in Dec; see website for special events

THE FORMER CALEDONIAN RAILWAY line from Montrose to Brechin via Bridge of Dun opened in 1848 and was built as a branch line, with its terminus at Brechin. From here another line left for Edzell and the Brechin to Forfar railway. Passenger services on the Brechin to Bridge of Dun section lasted until 1952, when many of the other lines in the county of Angus also lost their services. However, the main line through Bridge of Dun continued with a passenger service until 1967, when all Aberdeen to Glasgow trains were re-routed via Dundee. A single line from Kinnaber Junction was retained for local freight and in 1979 the Brechin Railway Preservation Society took over the shed at Brechin. British Railways finally closed the freight-only line in 1981. The trackbed to Bridge of Dun was purchased with the

Below A Birmingham Railway Carriage & Wagon Works diesel with the station master at Brechin.

Above The restored booking office at Glenfinnan Station Museum

assistance of Angus District Council, Tayside Region and the Scottish Tourist Board. First trains ran to Bridge of Dun in 1992 and stock from the closed Lochty Railway in Fife also augmented the line's potential. Locomotive stock consists of ex-BR diesels (including examples of Classes 20, 26 and 27) owned by the Caledonian Railway Diesel Group, and industrial steam and diesel locomotives.

Glenfinnan Station Museum

Station Cottage, Glenfinnan, Inverness-Shire PH37 4LT

TEL 01397 722295
WEBSITE www.glenfinnanstationmuseum.co.uk
OPEN Daily, June to mid Oct
STATION National rail network station Glenfinnan

THIS SMALL RAILWAY MUSEUM was set up in 1991 to save the redundant station buildings on the down platform of Glenfinnan station from being demolished. The restored booking office contains railway memorabilia

illustrating the history of the Mallaig Extension Railway, which opened in 1901 between Fort William and Mallaig. A dining car set in a BR Mk 1 coach offers meals and a self-catering sleeping car which sleeps up to 10 people is available for hire.

Grampian Transport Museum

Grampian Transport Museum, Alford, Aberdeenshire AB33 8AE

TEL 019755 62292
WEBSITE www.gtm.org.uk
OPEN Daily, Apr to Oct

A LARGE MUSEUM CONTAINING historic Scottish transport exhibits, ranging from the beautifully restored tram of the Cruden Bay electric railway to a Sentinel steam wagon and a steam-powered tricycle. A history of the region's railway is displayed in the recreated Great North of Scotland Railway station, at the adjacent Alford Valley Railway (see page 232).

'The Jacobite'

Postal address: West Coast Railways, Jesson Way, Crag Bank, Carnforth, Lancashire LA5 9UR

TEL 0845 128 4681
WEBSITE www.westcoastrailways.co.uk
ROUTE Fort William to Mallaig
LENGTH 42 miles | **GAUGE** Standard
OPEN Mon to Fri, mid May to end Oct; weekends, Jul and Aug; advance booking is essential
STATION National rail network station Fort William

'THE JACOBITE' IS A very popular, regular steam-operated tourist train that runs on the national rail network between Fort William and Mallaig, between mid-May and the end of October each year. It was originally introduced by British Rail in 1984, when it

was called the 'West Highlander', and later named 'The Lochaber'. Since privatisation of British Rail in 1995, the train, (now named 'The Jacobite'), has been operated by West Coast Railways (see page 249). Motive power usually consists of preserved LNER Class K4 2-6-0 No. 61994 'The Great Marquess', LNER Peppercorn Class 2-6-0 No. 62005 'Lord of the Isles', or an LMS Stanier 'Black Five' 4-6-0, of which many have been preserved around the UK.

Recently described as one of the great railway journeys in the world, 'The Jacobite' passes through magical Highland scenery, taking in Glenfinnan Viaduct (made famous in 'Harry Potter' films), the village of Arisaig, the silver sands of Morar (made famous in the film *Local Hero*) and the fishing port of Mallaig. Some of the carriages used in 'The Jacobite' were also used for the filming of the 'Hogwarts Express' in the 'Harry Potter' series of films.

Below Ex-LNER Class 'B1' 4-6-0 No. 61264 leaves Glenfinnan with a westbound 'The Jacobite', headed for Mallaig.

Keith & Dufftown Heritage Railway

Dufftown Station, Dufftown, Banffshire AB55 4BA

TEL 01340 821181
WEBSITE www.keith-dufftown-railway.co.uk
ROUTE Keith to Dufftown
LENGTH 11 miles | GAUGE Standard
OPEN Weekends and Bank Holidays, Easter to early Oct; Fri, Jun to Aug; Santa Specials in Dec
STATION National rail network station Keith

MARKETED AS 'THE WHISKY LINE', the Keith & Dufftown Railway is a fairly recent newcomer to Britain's heritage railways. Originally opened in 1862, the original Keith & Dufftown Railway was taken over by the Great North of Scotland Railway in 1866. The line served numerous whisky distilleries in the Spey Valley and was listed for closure in the 'Beeching Report' of 1963. Passenger services ceased in 1968, although goods traffic to distilleries at Dufftown continued until 1985. Despite this, the line remained in use for occasional luxury charter passenger trains visiting the Glenfiddich Distillery in Dufftown, until it was taken over by a group of volunteers in 2000. Diesel railcar services now operate along the scenic line between the beautifully restored station at Keith Town and Dufftown, with an intermediate station at Drummuir. Sadly, the connection with the national network at Keith has been severed.

Below A diesel multiple unit waits to depart from Keith Town station with a train for Dufftown.

Kerr's Miniature Railway

West Links Park, Arbroath, Angus DD11 2PT

TEL 01241 874074
WEBSITE www.kerrsminiaturerailway.co.uk
ROUTE Adjacent to the Aberdeen to Edinburgh railway line at Arbroath
LENGTH ½ mile | GAUGE 10¼in
OPEN Weekends, Apr to end Sep; daily during Easter and summer school holidays
STATION National rail network station Arbroath

THIS HISTORIC FAMILY-RUN MINIATURE railway began operations in 1935 as a 7¼in-gauge line, being converted to 10¼in during 1938. En route, the line passes through a 40ft-long tunnel before reaching a run-round loop at Hospitalfield Halt. Six locos operate on the line, including a steam 4-6-2, steam 0-6-0, two internal combustion Bo-Bo diesel outlines and two internal combustion steam outlines, including the historic 1936-built 4-4-2 'Auld Reekie'.

Friends of The Kyle Line

Kyle Station, Kyle of Lochalsh IV40 8AQ

TEL 01599 534824
WEBSITE www.kylerailway.co.uk
OPEN During station opening times
STATION National rail station Kyle of Lochalsh

THE 'FRIENDS' OPERATE A shop and a museum containing railway memorabilia related to the Kyle line, and photography depicting day-to-day scenes from the Lochalsh and Skye areas. They are also hoping to restore Kyle of Lochalsh signalbox to its former glory. Kyle station occasionally sees the arrival of chartered steam trains.

Leadhills & Wanlockhead Railway

Station Road, Leadhills, Biggar,
South Lanarkshire ML12 6XP

TEL 01555 820778
WEBSITE www.leadhillsrailway.co.uk
ROUTE Leadhills to Glengonnar Halt
LENGTH 1½ miles | **GAUGE** 2ft
OPEN Weekends and Bank Holidays,
    Easter and May to Sep

THE FORMER CALEDONIAN RAILWAY branch
from Elvanfoot (on the Glasgow to Carlisle
main line) to Wanlockhead was built in
1900 as a light railway to serve the local lead
mining industry. Gradients as steep as 1 in
35 were encountered and as a light railway
the trains were restricted to a maximum
speed of 20mph. At 1,405ft above sea level,
Wanlockhead was the highest standard gauge
railway station in Britain and the summit
of the line, at 1,498ft, was also the highest
of any standard gauge line in Britain. In the
1930s, a Sunday service operated using a

Below Leadhills station on the Leadhills &
Wanlockhead Railway in South Lanarkshire.

Sentinel steam railcar but trains were usually
operated by a CR 0-4-4 tank engine, based
at the tiny Leadhills engine shed. Following
closure of the lead mines, the railway was
eventually closed to all traffic in 1938. Rispin
Cleuch Viaduct, built by 'Concrete Bob'
McAlpine, was demolished in 1991.

A preservation group was formed in
1983 to reopen part of the route as a narrow
gauge railway and work commenced in 1986.
A limited diesel service was in operation in
1988/89 and in 1990 the railway borrowed
a steam engine. An 0-4-0 Orenstein &
Koppel, built in Berlin in 1913 and acquired
from a Belgian museum, is currently being
restored at Leadhills. Passengers are carried
in fully air-braked coaches with sprung
axles. Although the line stops less than a
mile short of the former terminus at
Wanlockhead, it is hoped that it will be
extended for about one mile to the east
of Leadhills in the near future.

Ness Islands Railway

Whin Park, Bught, Inverness IV3 5SS

TEL 01463 235533
WEBSITE www.nessislandsrailway.co.uk
ROUTE Within Whin Park
LENGTH ½ mile | **GAUGE** 7¼in
OPEN Weekends, Easter to end Oct; daily during
    school holidays
STATION National rail network station Inverness

THE UK'S MOST NORTHERLY public
miniature railway, the Ness Islands Railway,
opened in 1983 and was relaid in 1989 along
the bank of a river, incorporating a 140ft-
span iron bridge that was first built in 1837.
Motive power consists of diesel hydraulic,
'Uncle Frank', and steam 0-4-2 'Uncle
John' – both built by Mardyke Miniature
Railways. The latter engine is normally used
at weekends only.

Prestongrange Mining Museum

Morrison's Haven, Prestonpans,
East Lothian EH32 9RX

TEL 0131 653 2904
WEBSITE www.prestongrange.org
OPEN Visitor Centre and exhibitions daily,
    beginning Apr to end Oct

PRESTONGRANGE PLAYED AN IMPORTANT
part in the history of the Industrial
Revolution in Scotland. It was the location
for a 16th-century harbour, 17th-century
glass works, 18th- and 19th-century
potteries, and a 19th- and 20th-century coal
mine and brick works. The last brick-making
operations ceased in the 1970s and since
1993 the site has been in the care of East
Lothian Council Museums Service. Many
remnants of these industrial operations
can be seen at the museum, including the
Hoffman Kiln and a Cornish beam engine,
the latter still on its original 1874 site. Also
at the museum are the remains of the former
colliery railway, along with rolling stock and
Andrew Barclay 0-4-0ST 'Prestongrange
No. 6', which has recently been restored to
working order.

Riverside Museum, Glasgow

100 Pointhouse Place,
Glasgow G3 8RS

TEL 0141 287 2720
WEBSITE www.glasgowlife.org.uk/museums
OPEN Daily throughout the year

OPENED IN 2011, THIS modern new museum
alongside the River Clyde was designed by
internationally renowned architect Zaha
Hadid. It includes the collection from the
closed Glasgow Museum of Transport that
was once situated in Kelvin Hall. Railway
exhibits include Caledonian Railway 4-2-2
No. 123, Highland Railway 'Jones Goods'
4-6-0 No. 103 and ex-NBR Class 'D34'
4-4-0 No. 256 'Glen Douglas'. Built by the
North British Locomotive Company of
Glasgow in 1945, a massive Class '15F' 4-8-2
South African steam locomotive, that once
pulled the 'Blue Train' from Cape Town to
Johannesburg, is the star of the ground floor
exhibits. Other exhibits include Glasgow
trams and the Glasgow 'Subway' system.

Royal Deeside Railway

Milton of Crathes, Banchory,
Aberdeenshire AB31 5QH

WEBSITE www.deeside-railway.co.uk
ROUTE Milton of Crathes towards Banchory
LENGTH 1 mile | GAUGE Standard
OPEN Most weekends and selected weekdays,
    Apr to Sep; Santa Specials in Dec (see website)

THE 43¼-MILE BRANCH LINE from Aberdeen
to Ballater opened in stages between 1853
and 1866, although a planned extension
to Braemar was never finished following
pressure from Queen Victoria. Famous for
its royal trains, the line closed in 1966. Since
then, much of the trackbed has become a
footpath and cycleway known as the Deeside
Way. However, the Royal Deeside Railway
Preservation Society has relaid track for
nearly 2 miles from their headquarters at
Milton of Crathes, towards Banchory. Trains
are hauled by one of the railways two Class
'03' diesel shunters, or recently restored
1897-built Andrew Barclay 0-4-0 saddle
tank, 'Bon-Accord'. The railway also has the
original two-car battery electric multiple
unit, known as 'The Sputnik', that ran on
the line in the 1950s and early 1960s. These
historic vehicles are presently hauled by one
of the diesels.

Above GNSR 4-4-0 No. 49 'Gordon Highlander' is on display at the Scottish Railway Exhibition.

Scottish Railway Exhibition

Bo'ness Station, Union Street,
Bo'ness, West Lothian EH51 9AQ

TEL 01506 825855
WEBSITE www.srps.org.uk
OPEN Daily, Apr to Sep and during Bo'ness &
    Kinneil Railway operating days in Oct
STATION Heritage railway station Bo'ness

OPENED IN 1995, THIS large railway museum is situated adjacent to the Bo'ness & Kinneil Railway station (see page 233). By using the Scottish Railway Preservation Society's large collection of rolling stock, the exhibition traces both the practical and social aspects of the development of railways in Scotland. Ex-Great North of Scotland Railway 4-4-0 No. 49 'Gordon Highlander', built in 1920 by the North British Locomotive Company, and Midland Railway compound 4-4-0 No. 1000, are stars of the show.

Strathaven Miniature Railway

George Allan Park, Strathaven,
South Lanarkshire ML10 6EF

ROUTE Two circuits within park
LENGTH 330yds and 110yds | **GAUGES** 2½in,
    3½in, 5in and 7¼in
OPEN Weekend afternoons, Easter to Sep

OPENED IN 1949, THE Strathaven was originally laid to 7¼in gauge and operated steam trains along 110yds of track within George Allan Park. Completely rebuilt by the present club owners, the Strathaven Model Society, the present site now includes four different gauges on two different routes. The dual gauge (5in and 7¼in) ground-level line is 330yds long, while the raised section of triple gauge (2½in, 3½in and 5in) track is 110yds long. On open days, up to 20 different locomotives can be seen operating.

Strathspey Railway

See page 242

Summerlee Museum

Heritage Way, Coatbridge, ML5 1QD

TEL 01236 638460
WEBSITE www.northlanarkshire.gov.uk/summerlee
OPEN Daily throughout the year

REOPENED IN 2008 AND known as the Museum of Scottish Industrial Life, this large museum is set in 22 acres around the site of 19th-century Summerlee Ironworks and alongside the Hornock branch of the

Monklands canal. Industrial railway locos are on display and an electric working tramway (the only one in Scotland) using a restored Lanarkshire tram takes visitors through a sawmill to a reconstructed coal mine and miner's cottages.

Vogrie Park Miniature Railway

Vogrie Country Park, Gorebridge, Midlothian EH23 4NU

WEBSITE www.vpmr.eskvalleymes.org.uk
ROUTE Within grounds of Vogrie Country Park
LENGTH 576yds | **GAUGE** 7¼in
OPEN Sun afternoons, Easter to end Sep

OWNED AND OPERATED BY the Esk Valley Model Engineering Trust, this multi-gauge, ground-level miniature railway carries visitors through Vogrie Country Park – a Victorian parkland estate with sweeping carriage drives, landscaped vistas, a walled garden and 11½ miles of waymarked paths.

Waverley Route Heritage Association

Whitrope Siding, Hawick, Scottish Borders TD9 9TY

WEBSITE www.wrha.org.uk
OPEN See website for details of open days

THE CLOSURE OF THE Waverley Route between Edinburgh and Carlisle in early 1969 is well known and documented. What is less well known is that the Waverley Route Heritage Association has opened a new heritage centre at the site of Whitrope Siding, 11 miles south of Hawick and close to the line's summit, at 1,006ft above sea level. Its long-term aims are to open a

heritage railway southwards to Riccarton Junction. In the meantime, the group are busy reconstructing Whitrope signalbox, erecting signs, benches and tourist information along the 5 miles of trackbed as far as Steele Road, and surveying Whitrope Tunnel for its possible reuse. At Whitrope Siding, a short platform has already been built and ½ mile of track has been laid. A Ruston diesel shunter has recently been loaned from the Rutland Railway Museum (see page 119). The tunnel is fenced off and currently out of bounds to walkers due to a roof collapse.

Wester Pickston Railway

College Road, Methven, Perth PH1 3RX

WEBSITE www.smet.org.uk
ROUTE Within Scottish Model Engineering Trust wooded grounds
LENGTH 1,200yds | **GAUGES** 3½in, 5in and 7¼in
OPEN See website for details of open days

OWNED AND OPERATED BY the Scottish Model Engineering Trust, this miniature railway comprises a dual gauge, ground-level line and a dual gauge elevated line. Visitors are taken on a ride through 7 acres of wooded grounds behind a selection of members' steam and diesel locomotives.

Below Still life: a grounded salt wagon at Whitrope Siding near Hawick.

Strathspey Railway

**Aviemore Station, Dalfaber Road,
Aviemore, Inverness-Shire PH22 1PY**

TEL 01479 810725
WEBSITE www.strathspeyrailway.co.uk
ROUTE Aviemore to Broomhill
LENGTH 8¼ miles | **GAUGE** Standard
OPEN Selected Wed, Thu, weekends and Bank
    Holidays Feb to Oct; Wed to Sun, Jun to Sep;
    daily, Jul and Aug; Santa Express in Dec;
    see website for special events
STATION National rail network station Aviemore

THE FORMER HIGHLAND RAILWAY main
line from Aviemore to Forres was opened by
the Inverness & Perth Junction Railway in
1865 and closed by British Railways in 1965.
A preservation group started track relaying
on the section to Boat of Garten in 1972
and trains started operating in 1978, with
a further extension to Broomhill opening a
few years later. Broomhill station was used
as the location for Glen Bogle in the BBC
series *Monarch of the Glen*. Train services
are operated by a variety of restored steam
and diesel locomotives, including former
Caledonian Railway 0-6-0 No. 828, built
in 1899, BR Class 2MT 2-6-0 No. 46512,
built at Swindon in 1952, and BR Class 31
diesel D5862. The railway has been used
for location filming for several other TV
programmes, including *Dr Finlay's Casebook*
and *Strathblair*. Historic railway rolling stock
is on display at Boat of Garten, where there
is also a museum housing railway artefacts.
Work is progressing on a 3¾-mile extension
northwards from Broomhill to Grantown-
on-Spey (West). The 80ft-span bridge
over the River Dulnain will be the major
engineering feature on this section.

Right In Caledonian Railway blue livery, '812'
Class 0-6-0 No. 828 halts at Garten station.

MAIN-LINE STEAM

Rarely a week goes by without some form of main-line steam special somewhere on Britain's rail network. Here are some highlights from Scotland.

Left Ex-LNER 'K4' Class 2-6-0 No. 61994 'The Great Marquess' pilots 'A4' Class 4-6-2 No. 60009 'Union of South Africa' to Druimuachdar Summit, with the Perth to Inverness leg of the Railway Touring Company's 'Great Britain', on 10 April 2007.

Below Ex-LNER 'K4' Class 2-6-0 No. 61994 'The Great Marquess' heads the Scottish Railway Preservation Society's 'Forth Circle' tour, off the Forth Bridge at North Queensferry on 18 May 2008.

Above Peppercorn 'K1' Class 2-6-0 No. 62005 heads a charter train across Rannoch Moor, midway between Rannoch and Corrour on the West Highland Line, in October 2009.

Below Remote Kyle of Lochalsh is occasionally visited by steam charter trains. Here, ex-LMS Stanier Class '5' 4-6-0 No. 45407 arrives at Kyle station, with the 'North Briton' charter train in 2008.

MAIN-LINE RAILTOURS

Following the end of standard gauge steam on British Railways in August 1968, only Alan Pegler's ex-LNER 4-6-2 'Flying Scotsman', equipped with two tenders, was allowed to make a few outings on the main-line network. A blanket ban was then slapped on such activities until 1971, when preserved GWR 4-6-0 No. 6000 'King George V' sallied forth from the Bulmer's Railway Centre in Hereford to haul trains on the main line once again. Since then, and especially in more recent years, the growth of steam (and more recently heritage diesel) operated excursions on Britain's railways has been phenomenal – in 2011 alone there were over 350 different railtours organised. Catering for a wide range of tastes, routes and destinations, a large and growing number of these railtours operate over many parts of Britain's rail network throughout the year. The list of companies organising railtours is also growing every year.

Branch Line Society

73 Norfolk Park Avenue, Sheffield S2 2RB

TEL 0114 275 2303
WEBSITE www.branchline.org.uk

ESTABLISHED IN 1955, THE Branch Line Society provides a news service, railtours and visits around the UK.

Compass Tours by Rail

46 Hallville Road, Liverpool L18 0HR

TEL 0151 722 1147
WEBSITE www.compasstoursbyrail.co.uk

A FAMILY-RUN ORGANISATION WHICH specialises in the planning of excursion by charter trains often using scenic and interesting routes.

Cruise Saver Travel

2 Albert Road, Bournemouth BH1 1BY

TEL 0800 358 1101
WEBSITE www.cruisesavertravel.co.uk

SPECIALISES IN CHARTERED TRAINS from Edinburgh and Glasgow, calling at various cities en route to connect with cruise liner departures from Southampton Docks.

Pathfinders 2006

Stag House, Gydynap Lane, Inchbrook, Woodchester, Gloucestershire GL5 5EZ

TEL 01453 835414 or 01453 834477
WEBSITE www.pathfindertours.co.uk

ONE OF BRITAIN'S LEADING excursion operators, who organise 30–40 railtours each year along famous and less well known routes to a wide variety of destinations.

Above Ex-LNER Class 'A4' 4-6-2 No. 60019 'Bittern' at Stukeley, north of Huntingdon, on 12 April 2008 with the King's Cross to York leg of the Railway Touring Company's 'North Briton' charter train.

PMR Tours

PO Box 6233, The West Shed, Ripley, Derbyshire DE5 4AD

TEL 01773 743986
WEBSITE www.prclt.co.uk

BASED AT THE MIDLAND RAILWAY – Butterley (see page 113), the Princess Royal Class Locomotive Trust owns two BR Standard Class 4 2-6-4Ts, LMS Princess Coronation Class 4-6-2 No. 6233 'Duchess of Sutherland' and LMS Princess Royal class 4-6-2 No. 46203 'Princess Margaret Rose'. The Trust operates a small number of steam-hauled charter trains each year, currently to raise funds to enable the return of 'Duchess of Sutherland' to the main line.

Railtourer

42 Kingston Road, Willerby, Hull HU10 6UB

TEL 01482 659082
WEBSITE www.railtourer.co.uk

OFFERS A WIDE VARIETY of railtours and short break holidays in the UK and Europe.

Railway Touring Company

14A Tuesday Market Place, King's Lynn, Norfolk PE30 1JN

TEL 01553 661500
WEBSITE www.railwaytouring.net

TRAIN CHARTER COMPANY SPECIALISING in steam railway day trips, tours and long-haul holidays in the UK and overseas. Travelling by steam the length and breadth of Britain, the nine-day flagship 'Great Britain Tour' in April attracts enthusiasts globally.

Steam Dreams

PO Box 169, Albury, Guildford, Surrey GU5 9YS

TEL 01483 209888
WEBSITE www.steamdreams.com

USING CHARTERED MAIN-LINE STEAM locomotives, Steam Dreams organises day trips to destinations in Britain and also the 8-day steam-hauled 'Cathedrals Explorer'.

Spitfire Railtours

PO Box 824, Taunton,
Somerset TA1 9ET

TEL 0870 879 3675
WEBSITE www.spitfirerailtours.co.uk

A FAMILY-RUN COMPANY SPECIALISING
in railtours, using classic diesel and electric
locomotives on a wide range of routes
throughout Britain.

Scottish Railway Preservation Society Railtours

82 Busby Road, Carmunnock,
Glasgow G76 9BJ

TEL 01698 263814 or 01698 457777
 (Mon to Fri evenings)
WEBSITE www.srps.org.uk

FORMED IN 1961, THE Scottish Railway
Preservation Society has been organising
a programme of main-line excursions to
destinations mainly in Scotland, but also
to northern England, since 1970. Trains are
hauled by a variety of preserved steam and
heritage diesel locomotives.

Statesman Rail Ltd

PO Box 83, St Erth, Cornwall TR27 9AD

TEL 0845 310 2458 or 0845 310 2489
WEBSITE www.statesmanrail.com

STATESMAN RAIL ORGANISES A number
of steam- and diesel-hauled railtours
throughout Britain, including the popular
steam-hauled 'Fellsman' over the Settle &
Carlisle line on selected Wednesdays during
the summer months. A number of restored
Pullman carriages offer deluxe rail travel for
the discerning traveller.

Torbay Express Ltd

Stag House, Gydynap Lane, Inchbrook
Gloucestershire GL5 5EZ

TEL 01453 834477
WEBSITE www.torbayexpress.co.uk

TORBAY EXPRESS LTD IS an operator
of steam hauled excursion trains during
the summer months. These include the
'Torbay Express' from Bristol to Paignton
on most Sundays from June to September,
the 'Bath Spa Express' from Poole to
Bristol and the 'Dreaming Spires Express'
from Poole to Oxford, both on selected
Wednesdays from April to December.

UK Railtours

PO Box 350, Welwyn,
Herts AL6 0WG

TEL 01438 715050
WEBSITE www.ukrailtours.com

AIMED AT 'GENERAL INTEREST' travellers,
UK Railtours organise a wide variety of
tours in private excursion trains. They
pledge never to cancel a train through
lack of bookings.

Vintage Trains

670 Warwick Road, Tyseley,
Birmingham B11 2HL

TEL 0121 708 4960
WEBSITE www.vintagetrains.co.uk

USING RESTORED STEAM LOCOMOTIVES,
including those currently residing at
Birmingham Railway Museum (see page 92),
Vintage Trains operate railtours throughout
Britain. Services include a popular
'Shakespeare Express' between Birmingham
and Stratford-upon-Avon on Sundays,
July to mid-September and a Valentine
Express in February.

Venice-Simplon-Orient Express

20 Upper Ground, London SE1 9PF

TEL 0845 077 2222 or 0207 921 4010
WEBSITE www.orient-express.com

THE VSOE ORGANISES LUXURY railtours in Britain using its own restored Pullman and British Railways coaching stock. Tours range from one-day journeys on the 'Northern Belle' to seven days on board the 'Royal Scotsman' (www.royalscotsman.com).

Below Ex-GWR 'King' Class 4-6-0 No. 6024 'King Edward I' leaves Parson's Tunnel near Dawlish with the 'Yuletide Torbay Express' on 6 December 2008.

West Coast Railway Company

Jesson Way, Crag Bank, Carnforth, Lancashire LA5 9UR

TEL 0845 128 4681 or 0844 850 4685
WEBSITE www.westcoastrailways.co.uk

WEST COAST RAILWAYS IS an independent Train Operating Company and has been operating charter trains since 1998. In addition to their well known regular steam trains, such as the 'Scarborough Spa Express', 'The Cambrian' and 'The Jacobite' (see page 236), the company also organises (in conjunction with Railtourer, see page 247) steam- and diesel-hauled day charters and weekend getaways to various destinations in Britain.

RAILWAY WALKS & CYCLEWAYS

By the the First World War, there were 23,440 route miles of railways in Britain. By 2012, this had shrunk to 9,789 route miles. What happened to these lost lines? Although the rot had started to set in prior to the Second World War, rail closures picked up pace in the 1950s when thousands of miles of loss-making branches and cross-country routes were axed by the British Transport Commission's Branch Line Committee. Worse followed after the publication of Dr Beeching's infamous 'Report' in 1963, which closed a further 4,065 route miles. By 1975, Britain's countryside was criss-crossed by thousands of miles of disused railways, their tracks ripped up for scrap, stations sold off to discerning buyers for conversion into private residences and land sold off to farmers and developers. Fortunately, by this time, the railway preservation movement was gathering pace and over the next 25 years succeeded in reopening hundreds of miles of previously closed lines. However, there still remained thousands of miles of disused trackbed, much of which traversed some of Britain's finest landscapes, and the stage was now set for their rebirth as footpaths and cycleways. The first known example of this can be traced back to 1937, when the LMS gave the eight-mile trackbed of the closed Leek & Manifold Valley Light Railway to Staffordshire County Council for use as a footpath and bridleway.

Sustrans

2 Cathedral Square, College Green, Bristol BS1 5DD

TEL 0117 926 8893
WEBSITE www.sustrans.org.uk

FROM ITS EARLY BEGINNINGS in 1984, with the opening of the Bristol to Bath Railway Path, Sustrans has, in partnership with local authorities and landowners, built a 10,000-mile network of routes around Britain. Known collectively as the National Cycle Network, many of these routes incorporate resurfaced railway lines – their fairly level, traffic-free, linear paths passing through some of Britain's most beautiful scenery.

Railway Ramblers

Membership Secretary, 27 Sevenoaks Road, Brockley, London SE4 1RA

TEL 0208 699 5337 (Membership Secretary)
WEBSITE www.railwayramblers.org.uk

IN ADDITION TO SUSTRANS' efforts there are still many other lost railway lines waiting to be discovered – all that is required is a spirit of adventure, a stout pair of walking boots and an Ordnance Survey 1:50,000 Landranger map. For those walkers who like a little organisation to their activities, try joining the Railway Ramblers (whose President is David Shepherd) who organise walks along obscure disused railways.

The following list of railway walks and/or cycleways is by no means exhaustive but does represent a good selection of fairly well known routes. It includes the ever-popular Camel Trail in North Cornwall, and more esoteric examples, such as the Lochaber Narrow Gauge Railway in Scotland, where the intrepid explorer will definitely need good walking boots, waterproof clothes, a map, a compass and a good supply of energising refreshments! Many of these routes are explored in detail in *The Lost Lines of Britain* by Julian Holland (AA Publishing).

Above Closed in 1956, the trackbed of the Yelverton to Princetown railway in Dartmoor is now a superb footpath and cycleway.

WEST COUNTRY & CHANNEL ISLANDS

- Bath to Bristol Railway Path
- Bideford, Westward Ho!
  & Appledore Railway
- Camel Trail – Padstow to Wenfordbridge
- Cornish Mineral Railways – Devoran
  to Portreath
- Dartmoor – Yelverton to Princetown
- Drake's Way – Plymouth to Tavistock
- Jersey Railway Walk – St Helier to
  La Corbiere
- Lee Moor Tramway – Marsh Mills
  to Lee Moor
- Lundy Island Tramway
- Rodwell Trail – Weymouth to Portland
- Somerset & Dorset – Glastonbury
  to Shapwick
- Steep Holme and Flat Holme
  Military Railways
- Strawberry Line – Yatton to Cheddar
- Tarka Trail – Braunton to Barnstaple
  and Meeth
- West Somerset Mineral Railway –
  Watchet to Brendon Hills

SOUTH & SOUTH EAST ENGLAND

- Castleman's Corkscrew – Brockenhurst
  to Hamworthy
- Cole Green Way – Hertford to Welwyn
- Cuckoo Trail – Heathfield to Polegate
- Forest Way – East Grinstead to
  Groombridge
- Meon Valley Railway Path – Knowle
  Junction to West Meon (Alton
  to Fareham)
- Northern Heights Parkland Walk –
  Finsbury Park to Alexandra Palace
- Round the Island Cycleway (IOW) –
  Newport to Cowes; Newport to
  Sandown; Freshwater to Yarmouth
- Rye & Camber Tramway
- Tiddley Dyke – MSWJR Cricklade
  to Marlborough
- Worth Way – Three Bridges to East Grinstead

CENTRAL ENGLAND

- Brampton Way – Northampton
  to Market Harborough
- Churnet Valley – Oakamoor to Denstone
- Derwent Valley Heritage Trail – Bamford
  to Ladybower Dam
- Five Pits Trail – Tibshelf to Grassmoor
- Greenway – Stratford-upon-Avon to
  Long Marston
- High Peak Trail – Dowlow to High
  Peak Junction
- Manifold Way – Waterhouses to Hulme End
- Melbourne Railway – Shackerstone
  to Worthington

- Monsal Trail – Chee Dale to Bakewell
- Peak Forest Tramway Trail – Bugsworth Basin to Bridgeholm Green
- Sett Valley Trail – New Mills to Hayfield
- Severn & Wye Railway – Forest of Dean circular
- Stonehouse to Nailsworth
- Tissington Trail – Ashbourne to Parsley Hay
- Wye Valley – Redbrook to Tintern
- Wyre Forest Line – Tenbury Wells to Woofferton

EASTERN ENGLAND

- Blyth Valley Walk – Halesworth to Southwold
- Flitch Way – Braintree to Dunmow (Bishop's Stortford to Witham)
- Hadleigh Railway Walk
- Marriott's Way – Reepham to Hellesdon
- Middy Railway Path – Brockford to Haughley
- Spa Trail – Woodhall Junction to Horncastle
- Water Rail Way – Washingborough to Woodhall Junction
- Weavers' Way – Melton Constable to Yarmouth

WALES

- Elan Valley Railway – Cwmdauddwr to Craig Coch Dam
- Glyn Valley Tramway – Glynceiriog to Hendre Quarry
- Lôn Eifion – Caernarfon to Bryncir
- Lôn Las Ogwen – Tregarth to Port Penrhyn
- Mawddach Trail – Barmouth to Dolgellau
- Mid-Wales Line – Moat Lane Junction to Three Cocks Junction
- Mold to Denbigh
- Prestatyn to Dyserth
- South Wales Mineral Railway – Briton Ferry to North Rhondda

NORTHERN ENGLAND & ISLE OF MAN

- Battersby to Rosedale Abbey
- Consett & Sunderland Railway Path
- Durham to Sunderland
- Ingleton branch (viaducts)
- Isle of Man Steam Heritage Trail – Douglas to Peel and Lower Foxdale
- Keswick Railway Path – Keswick to Threlkeld
- Kielder Forest Border Railway Trail – Deadwater to Kielder
- Longdendale Trail – Hadfield to Woodhead; Dunford Bridge to Penistone
- Nidd Valley Railway – Pateley Bridge to Gouthwaite Reservoir
- Pennine Way – Alston to Haltwhistle
- Scarborough & Whitby Railway Path
- Tees Valley Railway Path – Middleton-in-Teesdale to Barnard Castle
- York to Selby Railway Path

SCOTLAND

- Ballachulish Branch – Connel Ferry to Ballachulish
- Churchill Barriers – Orkney Islands
- Deeside Way – Aberdeen to Ballater
- Dornoch Branch – The Mound to Dornoch
- Formartine & Buchan Way – Dyce to Peterhead and Fraserburgh
- Leadhills Railway – Elvanfoot to Wanlockhead
- Lochaber Narrow Gauge Railway – Fort William to Loch Treig
- Lochwinnoch Loop – Johnstone to Kilburnie
- Longniddry to Haddington Railway Path
- Montrose to Inverbervie
- Paisley & Clyde Railway Path – Johnstone to Greenock
- Red Kite Trail – New Galloway to Gatehouse of Fleet via Loch Skerrow (Castle Douglas to Challoch Junction)
- Rob Roy Country – Dunblane to Crianlarich via Glen Ogle; Killin Junction to Killin
- The Innocent Railway – St Leonards branch, Edinburgh
- Waverley Route – Whitrope to Riccarton Junction and Steele Road
- West Fife Cycleway – Clackmannan to Dunfermline

LOCATION INDEX

ACKNOWLEDGEMENTS

The author would like to thank the many individuals and organisations who have contributed photographs to this book. Luggage labels used on the endpapers and regional chapter openers are from the author's collection.

t = top; b = bottom; r = right; l = left; m = middle

AA World Travel Library/W Voysey 83; Adrian Allum 40l; Audley End Miniature Railway 130; Barleylands Farm Museum 131; Barton House Railway/John Mason 132; Beale Railway 41; Bentley Miniature Railway 42tr; Black Country Living Museum 93tl; Jack Boskett 101; Peter Bryant 212; David Cole 9; Colour-Rail 3l, 3r, 4, 5, 14, 15, 19, 25, 26l, 30/31b, 32, 34, 36tl, 37t, 37b, 47, 56, 59, 64, 66mr, 70ml, 71tl, 74, 84bl, 88, 89, 92b, 98tr, 100, 111tl, 111br, 112/113t, 114, 115, 116, 117, 124t, 124bl, 125, 126tl, 126b, 127t, 127b, 135, 140tr, 140ml, 152tl, 152b, 153t, 153br, 156, 159, 162tl, 162/163t, 169, 171, 176ml, 178, 180bl, 184b, 185t, 185br, 191, 196tr, 210, 211tr, 217t, 220br, 226tl, 226br, 228tl, 229t, 229b, 230, 234tl, 238, 244tl, 244b, 245t, 247, 249; Constitution Hill Cliff Railway 158; Drusillas Zoo Park 50; East Herts Miniature Railway 51; East Somerset Society of Model & Experimental Engineers 10tl; Eden Valley Railway 195tl; Elsecar Railway 195br; Epping-Ongar Railway 53; Mike Esau 39, 61, 62/63b, 68tl, 68/69t, 69br, 72, 84t, 85t, 146tl, 147br, 166, 228bl; Richard Evans 46; Gainsborough Model Railway Museum/Paul Otter 138tr; Clive Gilpin 23; John Goss 10br, 12/13t, 21tr, 24l, 40br, 42bl, 44/45b, 45br, 55tr, 55mr, 60br, 78, 79, 81, 85b, 160, 173b, 179, 194, 235t; Margaret Haynes 240; Heatherslaw Light Railway 199br; Tom Heavyside 18, 93br, 98mr, 137, 192, 193, 199bl, 204, 206, 209br, 227; Hilcote Valley Railway 110; Julian Holland 8, 16, 17t, 33, 60mr, 99, 108, 148, 176br, 177, 207tr, 241, 251; Ingfield Light Railway 58br; Keith & Dufftown Railway 237; Mike Kite 54; Langford & Beeleigh Railway 138br; Lappa

Valley Railway 17br; Llanberis Lake Railway/ David Jones 165; Llechwedd Slate Caverns 168ml, 168bl; London Transport Museum 66br; Lynton & Barnstaple Cliff Railway 20; Milepost 92½ 7, 12bl, 21b, 26tr, 27, 29, 31mr, 31br, 35tl, 36b, 49, 58tl, 63tr, 73br, 90tr, 90b, 91, 92tr, 95, 96, 97tr, 97b, 102, 103, 104tl, 104/105t, 106, 107tr, 107b, 119, 120, 121b, 122, 128, 134, 136, 139mr, 139br, 142, 143, 157, 161, 164, 167, 170, 173tr, 174tl, 175t, 175b, 180/181t, 181tr, 182, 183, 184b, 187, 188, 189ml, 196bl, 197t, 198ml, 198tr, 200/201b, 201tr, 202b, 203tr, 203b, 205t, 207b, 208, 211b, 214tl, 215br, 217ml, 223bl, 228br, 233tr, 233mr; Mizens Miniature Railway 67; Gavin Morrison 35br, 65, 73t, 121mr, 123, 133, 163br, 172, 174br, 190, 197b, 221br, 234br; Colin Oakley 28br; Old Kiln Light Railway 70br; Pallot Heritage Steam Museum 22bl; www.paradisepark.org.uk 22tr Pentney Park Railway 144br; Perrygrove Railway 118; Malcolm Phillips 144tl; Pinewood Miniature Railway 71br; Hendy Pollock 242/243; Brian Sharpe 24br, 141, 146/147t, 150ml, 151tr, 150/151b, 154, 189b, 214/215t, 219, 224, 236, 245b; Shibden Park Railway 220tr; Sittingbourne & Kemsley Light Railway 76tr, 76b; South Tynedale Railway 223ml; Southport Pier 222; Steam – Museum of the Great Western Railway 28tr; Stephenson Railway Museum/Tyne & Wear Archives & Museums 213; Strumpshaw Hall Steam Museum 149; Swanley New Barn Railway 80; Archie Thom/ Ayrshire Railway Preservation Group 232; Tyne & Wear Archives & Museums 209tl; Vintage Carriage Trust 225; Barbara Ward 57; Wellington Country Park 82